The Politics of Patronage in Africa

Parastatals Privatization & Private Enterprise

The Politics
of Patronage
in Africa

Parastatals
Privatization
& Private Enterprise

Roger Tangri

*Formerly Chair of Sub-Saharan African Studies
at the Foreign Service Institute, Arlington, Virginia*

JAMES CURREY
OXFORD

FOUNTAIN PUBLISHERS
KAMPALA

AFRICA WORLD PRESS
TRENTON

Published under the title
The Politics of Patronage in Africa

James Currey Ltd
73 Botley Road
Oxford OX2 0BS

Africa World Press
PO Box 1892
Trenton, NJ 08607, USA

Published in Uganda and East Africa
under the title
Parastatals, Privatization & Private Enterprise

ISBN 9970-02-171-0 (Fountain Publishers)

Fountain Publishers
PO Box 488
Kampala, Uganda

British Library Cataloguing in Publication Data

Tangri, Roger
The politics of patronage in Africa : parastatals,
privatization & private enterprise
1. Privatization – Political aspects –Africa, Sub-saharan
2. Government business enterprises – Africa, Sub-Saharan
I.Title
338.9'6

ISBN: 978-0-85255-834-8

Typeset in 10/11 pt Plantin
by Saxon Graphics Ltd, Derby
Printed and bound in Great Britain by
Marston Book Services Limited, Oxford

Contents

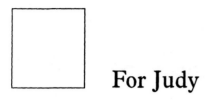 For Judy

Acknowledgements

This book has been a long time in the writing. During this lengthy period, I have incurred many debts of gratitude, and it is a pleasure to acknowledge the help and stimulus I have received from so many people. None of them, of course, is responsible for the contents of this work.

I started work on some of the topics of this book while teaching in the Department of Political Science at the University of Ghana, Legon. My eighteen months there (January 1990 to June 1991) were very happy ones, and I received much intellectual and other support in my work from many Legon academics. For their friendship and academic assistance, I wish to thank Joseph Ayee, Kofi Drah, Florence and Kofi Dolphyne, Kwame Gyeye, E. Gyimah-Boadi, Kwesi Jonah, G.K.A. Ofosu-Amaah, and Sandra Peprah. Outside of Legon, I thank the many business people who shared their experiences with me; and I extend my special gratitude to John Atta-Nyamekye, Nancy and Willy Keteku, and Eric and Christine Kwei. I also thank members of the Achimota Golf Club (and, in particular, E.N. Omaboe) for much enjoyable golfing as well as for many conversations on business and politics in Ghana. Foreign academics who have worked on Ghana's contemporary economic and political life were also very helpful and my thanks go to Jeffrey Herbst and Richard Jeffries for their comments and suggestions.

After Legon, I taught in the Department of Political and Administrative Studies at the National University of Lesotho for three years (August 1991 to July 1994). Once again, I am grateful to many Roma academics for their assistance in my work, and I thank, in particular, Ron Cadribo, Chris Dunton, Larry Frank, Rob Gordon, Khabele Matlosa, Sean Morrow, and Sehoai Santho. Outside Roma, Frank Baffoe, and Joan and Paseka Khabele provided friendship and gave me the benefit of their insights into the state of the private business sector in Lesotho.

After NUL, I was fortunate to spend three very happy years (1994–7) in the Department of Political Science and Public Administration at

Makerere University, Uganda. Members of the department gave me much assistance and guidance. It would be invidious of me to single any out but I would like to express my great appreciation to Foster Byarugaba, Sabiti Makara, Aaron Mukwaya, Akiiki Mujaju, Apolo Nsibambi, Quintas Obong, Juma Okuku, Paul Omach, and Sallie Simba. I am especially indebted to all of the MPA students I taught during those years. I tested out my ideas on them while their reactions contributed greatly to the evolution of arguments of this book. As in Ghana, many businesspeople rendered me much assistance, and I thank particularly K.K. Chapaa, Ephraim Kamuntu, William Kalema, and Hilary Obonyo for many informative discussions as well as socially enjoyable occasions. The Kampala Golf Club provided much enjoyable golfing and many of its members, including returnee Asian business people, gave me much information on matters relevant to my work. Once again, foreign academics with a strong interest in Uganda's contemporary political economy proved most supportive, and I wish to thank my friends Tom Forrest and Nels Kasfir for many helpful comments on earlier drafts of this work.

I want to thank as well the many public servants in Ghana. Lesotho and Uganda who gave me so much assistance. I am unable to mention them by name but my work could not have advanced without the tremendous help I received from dozens of civil servants and parastatal officials. Special thanks are also extended to friends and erstwhile colleagues elsewhere in Africa who over the years provided me with relevant documents and materials and who discussed my work with me at various seminars and conferences. John Daniel (University of Durban-Westville), Mustapha El-Sayyid (American University in Cairo), Ken Good (University of Botswana), Walter Oyugi (University of Nairobi), Christian Peters (Harare), Roger Southall (Rhodes University), and John Rapley (University of the West Indies at Mona) have always been of great help.

In Britain, Bill Tordoff and Ralph Young of the University of Manchester have been ever-supportive of my work and given me much encouragement. They provided me with books and articles and also offered cogent criticism of an early draft of this book. Christopher Clapham also found time to comment on my manuscript and provided useful suggestions.

In the USA, Ernie Wilson invited me to join his colleagues at the Center for International Development and Conflict Management at the University of Maryland at College Park, and provided me with a congenial environment to finalize the manuscript for publication. In Washington, D.C., Peter Lewis at the American University and Liz Hart at USAID also gave comments and suggestions on my chapters as well as lending me theses and other unpublished materials.

Finally, two organizations have been most helpful throughout the years of this study. The Institut für Afrika-Kunde in Hamburg, Germany has a well-equipped and well-run library, and I thank its librarians for their help on many occasions. I also thank Goswin Baumhogger of the institute for providing me with materials on Zimbabwe and for his general support. Secondly, the assistance I have received from the United States Information Service in Ghana, Lesotho, Uganda, and Kenya, especially from its local staff and librarians, is inestimable. I am greatly indebted to them. Most important at USIS, and at USIA in Washington, D.C., I want to thank my wife who has always been unfailing in her support of my work.

Introduction

Economic crisis

With few exceptions, African countries south of the Sahara have been experiencing a serious economic crisis for at least the past two decades. The litany of economic woes in the region has been a long one. Dramatic decreases have occurred in agricultural output, both in food production and in exports of cash crops. Manufacturing production has also gone down, as has industrial capacity utilization. Production falls have led to acute balance-of-payments difficulties; exports have declined while imports (particularly of foodstuffs) have risen. Domestic budget deficits have also become common, as have mounting government borrowings and rising inflation rates. Almost all sub-Saharan countries have been confronted with an endemic financial and debt crisis leading to external indebtedness and high debt-service obligations.

Moreover, economic misfortunes have begotten other problems. Everywhere physical infrastructure has been crumbling and public services have been breaking down. Unemployment has escalated while, at the same time, increasing numbers of skilled professionals have been leaving to seek a better life abroad. Private capital has been disinvesting and substantial amounts of private wealth have been transferred overseas. All these indicators of economic and social trouble highlight the severity of the African crisis,[1] which for most people has been dramatically reflected in the decline in living standards to below pre-independence levels. In response to this serious malaise, African governments have, since the early 1980s, begun introducing economic reform or structural adjustment programmes. Although registering some improvements, these have yet to overcome the region's troubled existence and pave the way to sustained economic and social recovery.

External causes of economic crisis

What have been the causes of sub-Saharan Africa's economic decline? Economic deterioration is, of course, the product of many factors. However, these factors have tended to be presented in two analytically distinct ways: one emphasizing domestic factors, the other stressing external considerations. Although both domestic and external factors are intimately interlinked, scholars have tended to view them as mutually exclusive alternatives.[2]

Those favouring exogenous causes[3] have attributed Africa's economic stagnation to the impact of various adverse features of the international economic environment. For countries highly dependent on the export of primary commodities, the relative decline in world commodity prices as well as in the terms of trade has been perceived as especially damaging for African economies. Additional constraints stemming from the external economy – a major economic recession in the West in the late 1970s resulting in a sharp reduction in demand for Africa's exports as well as precipitating large declines in world commodity prices; and global price shocks such as the oil price rises of 1973 and 1979 (particularly harmful for most African countries reliant on oil imports) – have not only influenced Africa's economic performance negatively but also posed serious limits to the region's prospects for economic growth.[4]

One important shortcoming of the external argument is that it does not enable us to understand why some African countries, confronted with the same difficult international economic environment, have fared better than others. There are differences – at times large ones – between African countries as regards economic performance.[5] These differences can, however, be explained as the outcome of differences in domestic economic management and politics. Many scholars now consider Africa's economic *travails* to be primarily the result of unsound economic policies as well as political factors impinging on implementation. Explanations ascribing Africa's economic ills to external factors have been found wanting in various respects.[6] Those attributing overall economic deterioration in the continent to domestically rooted factors – economic and political actions – have gained greater plausibility.[7]

This is not to disregard the importance of an adverse external environment to Africa's economic plight. Relatively small economies such as those in most African countries, in which high ratios of foreign trade to total economic activity prevail, are vulnerable to the vagaries of the external economy. Periodic declines in world commodity prices during the 1960s and 1970s had negative consequences for African economies.

But adverse developments in international trade only critically affected African countries in the 1980s when they were already in economic decline. Sharp falls in the prices of commodity exports seriously worsened the economic situation of indebted African countries, forcing them to turn to the international financial institutions for assistance. This enhanced the leverage of the International Monetary Fund and the World Bank who, through their wide-ranging structural adjustment programmes, have had profound consequences for African economies and polities.

International factors, therefore, impinge on domestic African affairs in various ways. Changes in international terms of trade can be important but so also is the international leverage exercised by the multilateral financial organizations. The role of multinational companies may also be economically and politically influential. Later in this work, we will consider some of these international links to some extent. But the prime focus of our study will be on domestic causes as having compounded certain external factors in Africa's economic decline.

African governments have done little to minimize or mitigate the deleterious impact of exogenous factors on their economies. Instead, this external impact has been exacerbated by domestic factors. For example, various studies have shown that international firms have had a negative impact on Kenya's political economy. But these studies have also concluded that 'it is ultimately the [domestic] political environment that facilitates MNCs' dominance' over Kenya's economy and society.[8] Domestic economic and political practices are central to any explanation of Africa's economic troubles.

Internal causes of economic crisis: political factors

'Perhaps the greatest misfortune of modern African nations' writes the historian Roland Oliver, 'was that their approach to independence coincided with a period when it was generally believed that the way to a better future lay through more and longer term state planning, with its implementation led by a large and ever-expanding public sector'.[9] The Second World War had seen 'a vast enlargement of the role of the state' in Europe, and, shortly thereafter, a more active, developmental perspective informed colonial policy in Africa. Colonial administrators began to attempt to plan and mobilize the economic resources of their African territories to promote 'colonial development and welfare'. Development plans were formulated, regulatory powers increasingly exercised by colonial officials, and state-owned enterprises set up. Prime among the public enterprises were the official agricultural marketing boards. However, as Oliver observes, 'because they were government enterprises, economic systems were tilted in their favour, at the expense of farmers who formed the main body of private enterprise producers'.[10] State economic involvement during the terminal colonial period was not without its costs.[11] After the attainment of independence, increasingly pervasive public ownership and government regulation would prove even more pernicious for African economies.

Governments in independent Africa have assumed a leading and wide-ranging interventionist role in their economies. This intervention was encouraged by almost all governments after independence following import-substitution policies which required that the state play an active economic role. It also reflected widespread agreement that, in the absence of well-developed indigenous private sectors as well as the presence of substantial foreign economic ones, the state would play a particularly central role in directing development. And state economic involvement has been extensive both in the domestic economy as well as in external economic relations. Domestic financial markets, market prices, interest rates, licences and contracts have been regulated or controlled by governments, as have foreign trade, foreign-exchange markets, and foreign direct investment. Moreover, the state has been heavily involved in the economy as an entrepreneur. Many economic activities have been directly owned and managed by the state. State-run enterprises (parastatals) have operated financial institutions as well as various agricultural, commercial, manufacturing and mineral ventures. In all sub-Saharan countries, the public sector's economic role (and share of GDP) has expanded substantially since independence. Heavily statist systems of economic management have been established throughout the Africa region.[12]

In largely state-run African economies, most of the important economic policy decisions have been made by politicians and government officials. And the way government leaders have made economic decisions and economic allocations has been strongly politicized. The way contracts, licences and foreign exchange have been allocated, as well as the way investment projects and their location decisions have been determined, have all been based, to a marked extent, on political calculations. Political motives such as those of maintaining political control as well as how political concerns can best be promoted have constituted key considerations in the making of economic decisions. Political interventions and manipulations in the economic realm have posed major obstacles to the achievement of development goals; they have underlain economic decline and deterioration on the continent. Economic and administratative factors have also contributed to Africa's macroeconomic problems but it is political ones that are given the greatest attention in this book. Understanding the political dynamics influencing state economic decisions provides an important explanation regarding the poor economic performance of African countries.[13] It is also valuable in understanding the political obstacles that have to be overcome if economic recovery is to be promoted.

Outline of study

These introductory remarks notwithstanding, this book is not concerned directly with the politics of Africa's economic decline and economic recovery. It does concern itself, however, with some aspects of political and economic interaction in contemporary Africa as well as issues of economic stagnation and economic revival.

A principal focus of concern is with Africa's state-owned enterprises. As already mentioned, public enterprises had been established during the colonial period. But their growth assumed major proportions after independence. By the 1980s, the parastatal sector occupied a pivotal position in the economies of all sub-Saharan countries. The following chapter examines, first, the reasons for the expansion of Africa's public enterprise sector. But, secondly, by virtually any measure of performance, the record of government enterprises has been disappointing. They have proved a drain on public finances and have generally been characterized as inefficient and unprofitable. As our discussion shows, the dismal record has not been the result of public ownership as such. Rather, it has been a function of essential political factors impinging upon decision-making. In particular, patronage politics has frequently prevented the effective establishment and operation of state-run enterprises. Chapter Two seeks to examine the purposes and performance of African public enterprise. An understanding of the poor performance of African parastatals is important to an appreciation of the crisis of African development. Poor parastatal performance has become increasingly interlinked with the region's overall economic stagnation.

Chapter Three is concerned with the nature and extent of restructuring of African public enterprise sectors. By the early 1980s, the widespread politicization of economic decision-making and the various deficiencies of state economic management had become viewed as the central causes of economic stagnation and decline in Africa. Within a context of economic adversity, calls began to be made, especially by external agencies, for a reassessment of the economic roles of African governments. With considerable pressure from international financial institutions (the International Monetary Fund and the World Bank) and Western bilateral aid donors, a number of state-sector reforms were advocated and implemented in African countries. Public sector reforms have sought a reduction in the economic role of the state, particularly by privatizing inefficient state-owned enterprises or commercializing the operations of those firms that have remained in state ownership. But state enterprise privatization has been a highly political issue. And, indeed, until very recently, it has been implemented only to a limited extent. As discussed in Chapter Three, political factors have influenced the nature and extent of public enterprise divestiture in Africa. In this respect, our argument corresponds with a 'key finding' of a recent World Bank report on state-owned enterprise 'that political obstacles are the main reason that state enterprise reform has made so little headway in the last decade'.[14] Furthermore, the question of to whom parastatals are divested has become an increasingly important issue as the pace of privatization has picked up in recent years. Many divestiture decisions have been favourable to the politically well-connected, and, as our discussion shows, patronage politics has underlain the actual implementation of privatization.

Private sector development is a second major area of concern of this work. Wide-ranging public sector economic involvement since independence led to a greater reliance on the state over the private sector in economic activities. One consequence was that private economic initiative was largely suppressed. State economic intrusion was not conducive to the growth of a formal private sector strongly committed to domestic investment and production. It was also discouraged politically; governments were unwilling to allow the emergence of vigorous private capitalism although, at times, some politically well-connected local and foreign businesses were permitted and assisted to thrive. In the main, and as discussed in parts of Chapters Four and Five, political and especially patrimonial considerations have caused African governments to be less than encouraging and supportive towards private capital.

The liberalizing tendency in recent economic thinking has also called for a re-evaluation of the relationship between public and private sectors on the continent. Reducing the scope of state ownership and enhancing that of the private sector have been advocated. Under pressure from international donors, African governments have been urged to open up their economies to market forces and rely on private capital. And, as a result, greater encouragement and support for private domestic business as well as foreign investors has been forthcoming. But private local entrepreneurs have continued to feel insufficiently courted and assisted to develop, and although foreign private investment has increased again, its investments are selective and unlikely to expand more broadly. Once again, and as examined in Chapters Four and Five, political factors have been at the fore in influencing the levels and prospects of private (domestic and foreign) investment.

Nevertheless, some growth is taking place in the scale of private capitalism, and, as argued in these chapters, political patronage considerations are prominent in determining which private entrepreneurs are to be the most favoured and supported ones.

Neither privatization nor private enterprise promotion has led to a fundamental revision of public-private enterprise boundaries in African countries. Notwithstanding 'extensive privatization efforts of the past two decades' a recent World Bank report concluded that 'divestiture has yet to change substantially the balance between the state-owned and private sectors...'[15] Achieving a markedly different balance between public and private sector activity has proved to be an especially political process. Nevertheless, as considered in our final chapter, a critical reappraisal of the economic role of the state is under way, and nearly everywhere a gradual process of reorienting state economic functions is occurring. Moreover, international donors have been attempting to strengthen state economic management as well as to promote 'good' state governance in the economic sphere. But progress in these areas as well as in regard to privatization and private sector development has been subject to the political interests of those in state power. Although external agencies have been firmly behind many of the public-private sector changes taking place, it is the calculations of African governments as to how their political concerns can best be served that have decisively shaped public-private enterprise relations, with important consequences for the development and recovery of Africa's ravaged economies.

Patronage politics and Africa's political economy

To provide a setting for the consideration of the politics of public and private enterprise in sub-Saharan Africa, we present a profile of the region's political economy over the past several decades. We discuss some pertinent factors that have shaped contemporary economic and political realities on the continent. We also introduce the notion of the politics of patronage in this section. Patronage politics has not only constituted a pervasive form of governance in Africa but also it has been a principal form of influence on state economic management in the region since independence. First, Africa's contemporary political economy is rooted in its colonial experience.

Present-day African countries were created by European colonialists who often ignored ethnic and cultural factors in determining national boundaries. Colonially demarcated boundaries arbitrarily brought together diverse peoples within a single colonial territory. Under colonialism, ethnic and cultural feelings were stimulated, even sharpened. Administrative areas were often based on ethnic lines. Also, social and economic change was uneven. Some regions produced cash crops and mineral products while others lacked major natural resources. Mission schools proliferated in some areas while others received little exposure to Western-type education. At independence, African countries largely lacked a national identity, partly because colonial policy did much to strengthen ethnic, as opposed to, national consciousness, and partly because the countries were too recent in existence to elicit a sense of common nationhood.[16]

Colonialism did, however, result in some degree of socio-economic differentiation. Western education and economic change were the main factors underlying a limited social stratification. A tiny middle class arose composed mainly of those with Western education (lawyers, doctors, civil servants, teachers) and some accumulation of capital (traders and petty commodity producers). A small labour force also emerged. But these modern capitalist classes – bourgeoisie and proletariat – were embryonic; they were weakly developed. By far the largest group numerically was the peasantry. However, most peasants were drawn only to a partial extent into the evolving market economy. Peasants were predominantly subsistence producers. African countries were primarily rural societies marked by low levels of economic development. As Richard Sandbrook notes, African societies were overwhelmingly peasant societies, not capitalist ones.[17]

During the colonial period, the various social strata pursued group - and interest-based political activity. Workers gradually became conscious of their common interests and engaged in worker organization and worker protest. Peasants – especially the better-off ones – also began organizing themselves to advance their group interests. For instance, they formed marketing co-operatives so that producers could strengthen their position in bargaining with buyers. They also engaged in crop withholding. But prior to the 1940s much of the political activity was organized by the educated elements and the petty bourgeoisie. They formed a variety of associations which petitioned colonial governments for greater representation and influence on decision-making bodies. Concerned primarily with their own class interests, they did little to mobilize the large majorities of rural populations.[18]

Anti-colonial nationalism, however, brought together different classes and strata under the leadership of the educated and petty bourgeois elements. Political leaders preached that with independence the African population as a whole would benefit. The grievances and deprivations of different local groups and classes would only be righted and resolved once political power was attained. Especially from the late 1940s, political leaders succeeded in harnessing diverse discontents and mobilizing large numbers of people to the wider cause of anti-colonialism and national independence. But the extent of unity within African nationalism was limited. Only in a small minority of colonial territories did one political organization dominate the nationalist movement (for example, in Malawi and Tanzania). In much of colonial Africa, a number of parties competed with each other. Most drew their support from particular ethnic groups or regions, as in Nigeria, Uganda and Zaire (Congo-Kinshasa). Parties were invariably built around communal groups and led by communal leaders as well as local notables. These rival parties were held together by considerations of clientelism. Leaders attained support by promising to allocate public resources – schools, hospitals, jobs, licences – to particular localities or groups. Competing parties, based on ethnic and regional groups, and led by the educated and petty bourgeoisie, garnered support on the basis of patron-client networks while at the same time seeking national independence for the African population as a whole.[19]

Anti-colonial movements contributed to the attainment of political independence for most African countries in the late 1950s and early 1960s. New regimes were brought to state power. Indigenous politicians now occupied and controlled the higher echelons of the state. Given the low levels of economic transformation and the limited development of civil society, Africa's new rulers also possessed a relatively autonomous position in policy-making. Senior state personnel – leading politicians and high civil servants – enjoyed considerable discretion in domestic decision-making. Large undiversified and highly dispersed rural populations were unlikely to challenge the political ascendancy of those controlling the state apparatus. State power was to be monopolistic and could not be brought under the social control of a mass of barely literate peasants.

Unlike East Asian state elites of the same period who are perceived as having been strongly oriented towards developmental goals, African post-independence elites appear to have been motivated much more by political and personal concerns than by economic and social development. From the beginning, the new civilian rulers were concerned with the twin objectives of staying in power and building an economic base for themselves. Wanting to hold on to power was not simply a lust for power. Many of the triumphant nationalist leaders saw themselves as unique liberators of their people who deserved unlimited tenure to rule their newly independent countries. But power also brought with it many opportunities for attaining wealth in an African context of extreme scarcity and poverty as well as limited private accumulation. To be in key administrative and political positions was to have access to the major means of acquiring coveted material resources, the more so as states were accorded such a dominant role in the post-independence national economies. Through the state, top office-holders controlled an extensive array of resources and could influence their distribution and accumulation often with an eye to political advantage as well as personal gain. Other avenues to wealth, such as through the private economy, were more restricted, especially as the larger private enterprises were in non-African hands and an indigenous capitalist class was weakly developed. Thus, political office in sub-Saharan Africa assumed major significance. Not surprisingly, political power became the focus of intense struggle. Nearly everywhere, desperate struggles have ensued to attain or maintain state power.[20]

For th[e]... [p]ower, diverse means have been employed to remain in power. [P]rime among them have been intimidation and repression of politica[l opponent]s. Post-independence African governments have commonly resorted [t]o various authoritarian means to hold on to power. Post-[c]... [st]ates have resurrected the many autocratic practices of colo[nialism] and have also tended to be military regimes or civilian one[-party syst]ems in which a single ruler or a small oligarchy possessed al[most unres]tricted power. Given the weakness of civil societies, social f[orces have] been unable to counterbalance state dominance. Centralized [as w]ell as personalized rule prevailed in most African countries. [Recent ye]ars have seen some degree of political liberalization (multi[party ele]ctions, less restricted media, and more assertive legislatures) in [many] sub-Saharan Africa, but personalistic and authoritarian political [practic]es still enable incumbent rulers to impede full political competi[tion as] well as to maintain themselves in power.[21]

[Apar]t from authoritarianism, a vital, non-coercive form of consoli[dating] power has been to rely on patronage. To secure political incum[ben]cy, public benefits have been distributed and opportunities to profit provided along political lines. Thus in their quest for self-preservation, state elites have dispensed government-controlled resources – jobs, licences, contracts, credit – to select political allies as well as mediating access to economic opportunities in favour of close associates so as to enhance their hold over state power. In Africa, ethnic identities have comprised the key bases for building clientelistic coalitions. Political leaders have allocated public resources and amenities to key intermediaries and their ethnic clienteles in ways designed to fashion a following and ensure political support.[22] As a result, most regimes have been identified with specific ethnic and regional interests, but many have also been able to consolidate their hold on state power for long periods by promoting a relatively ethnically balanced distribution of the resources of government.

In order to enhance patronage resources available for distribution, Africa's new rulers 'extended the scope of direct government - involvement in the economy'. They 'expanded the public sector of the economy' and thereby 'multiplied opportunities for patronage and clientelism, and allowed regimes to channel economic resources to targeted social groups'.[23] Politically mediated access to resources and economic opportunities controlled by the state became a key mechanism of consolidating power. To be sure, the resources available to the state have, at times, decreased markedly as, for example, in the cases of Zambia and Zaire (Congo) where copper prices collapsed from the mid-1970s. Moreover, recent economic reform programmes initiated by the international financial institutions have brought about cuts in state spending and reductions in the public benefits that could be exchanged for political support. Nevertheless, African political leaders have continued to use the state and its resources to maintain themselves in power. Patronage politics has been integral to post-colonial efforts to maintain political control in poor, ethnically diverse peasant societies. Yet, although valuable in helping to consolidate ruling coalitions, the dynamics of patronage relations have proved economically highly damaging.

State economic management has taken place in this special environment of governance based largely on patronage networks as well as the virtual absence of scrutiny over public resource allocations. The logic of patrimonialism has shaped the economic actions of top politicians and administrators running largely authoritarian regimes. But, as Sandbrook notes, patrimonialism is 'potentially economically destructive'. In Africa, 'its short-term political rationality of personal and regime survival' has generated 'a variety of economic irrationalities that smother capitalism's expansive dynamics'.[24] Top public-sector positions, especially in the important government economic ministries as well as key parastatals, have often been filled by politically loyal officials. Distribution of public services and economic infrastructure is attributable to a markedly patrimonial administration. The use of government bureaucracies for clientelist purposes also led to the employment of large numbers of public servants who were not only costly to maintain (on average they consumed over one-half of government expenditures) but were often unproductive and ineffective. And political manipulation further produced a highly corrupt state apparatus as senior state personnel and their close associates engaged in much rent-seeking and private appropriation of state resources. In sum, economic resource allocation has served political and personal ends with less than salutary consequences for the growth of Africa's economies.[25]

At the time of independence, African countries possessed the classic characteristics of the phenomenon of underdevelopment. Sub-Saharan Africa was primarily an agricultural and primary products producer. Primary products and raw materials constituted some three-quarters of total exports. The predominance of agriculture (constituting the primary means of employment and income for the majority of the population) exemplified the undiversified nature of African economies. Only a very limited manufacturing development had taken place. African education was also limited. Acute shortages of educated and skilled personnel existed, and everywhere expatriates held the main positions in the civil service and larger economic enterprises. For the new African governments, raising the economic and social standards of their peoples was imperative. The new governments assumed greater economic roles to foster more prosperous economies. Strengthening agriculture and developing an industrial base were viewed by political leaders as essential economic goals to be engaged in by an activist state. Improving the level of social welfare for the mass of the people was another key objective, also to be achieved by expanding public services, particularly in the fields of education and health. A developmental state was to be the panacea for a situation of underdevelopment.

When the colonialists departed from Africa, they left behind economies which were largely in the hands of foreign owners. Western European trading companies dominated the import-export trade, while multinational subsidiaries controlled the extractive industries, manufacturing, construction and plantation sectors as well as the banks, insurance and financial institutions. The commercial sphere was predominantly owned by persons drawn from non-African settler communities (Asians, Europeans, Levantines). African entrepreneurial groups were weakly developed. The indigenization of African economies was a key concern of the new African political leadership. Typical was the statement by the Zambian president, Kenneth Kaunda, that 'Political independence without matching economic independence was meaningless'. Moves towards national economic participation were initiated after independence throughout the continent. Although foreign firms were to retain their dominance in a few sectors, economic nationalism was to be a vital force underlying initiatives to secure greater indigenous ownership and control of the economy.[26]

In pursuing the twin goals of economic nationalism and national socio-economic improvement, African governments did so through a combination of private and state-owned enterprise. Some governments emphasized the increasing role of an indigenous private capitalism, others the expanded role of the state sector. However, irrespective of the private/public path actually followed, senior state personnel intervened in various ways to regulate economic affairs. And, as we have seen, economic decisions were often placed at the service of political and personal ends. This is not to argue that policy-making in the new African countries was attributable solely to the autonomous actions of those who controlled the state apparatus. The latitude of state elites in decision-making was not unfettered. For instance, they have been subjected to pressures from powerful external forces such as those of foreign capital and, more recently, international financial organizations. Nevertheless, government ministers and senior officials have enjoyed a significant degree of relative autonomy in the post-colonial period. They have been able to act in their own interests and have, as a result, exerted a determining influence over the character of public and private enterprise in contemporary Africa. They have also been largely responsible for Africa's economic fortunes taking the perverse form they have since independence.

The allocation of state-controlled resources on the basis of patronage politics had damaging economic consequences. The political forms of government economic intervention led to domestic fiscal deficits and international indebtedness. In response to the growing financial and debt crisis of the early 1980s,[27] African governments began introducing stabilization and structural adjustment programmes usually under the auspices of the IMF and the World Bank. These involved comprehensive reform programmes following a standard package. Because domestic government intervention was blamed for Africa's economic deterioration, the reforms sought to reduce state economic involvement and promote economic liberalization.[28] In particular, emphasis has been placed on the privatization of public enterprises as well as increased private investment. But international donors also have been pushing for a general reassessment of state economic roles and 'good' state economic governance. Changes are taking place in the political economy of African countries impelled by the international financial institutions. But these externally induced reforms have been subject to the political and personal interests of African rulers. Domestic political imperatives are shaping developments in regard to privatization, private sector development, state economic reorientation, and state economic management. If African countries are to achieve economic recovery, then ways have to be found of reducing the impact of the specific nature of politics, namely patrimonial governance, which has proved so detrimental to post-independence African economies.

Outline of the argument

Patron-client ties have constituted the primary means of maintaining power in African countries. In an authoritarian context as well as one in which they have rarely been held accountable for their actions, state elites have used public institutions to dispense an array of public benefits – jobs, credit, contracts, subsidies – to select clients and ethnic constituencies to build political support and consolidate themselves in state power.

Public enterprises have been one of the public institutions operating within this authoritarian and patronage-based political system. Since independence, state-owned enterprises have become of major economic importance throughout sub-Saharan Africa. But everywhere their economic performance has been adversely affected by economic and political factors, most notably patronage politics.

Since the early 1980s, in the midst of a serious economic crisis, international donors have been calling on African governments to privatize their state-owned companies. But because privatization threatens their control of patronage resources, political leaders have been slow in implementing state enterprise divestiture. However, under intense external pressure to sell off their public companies, African leaders have, especially in the 1990s, been engaging in greater privatization. Nevertheless incumbent leaders have not been subject to close control by international donors in this activity, with the result that many divestiture decisions have favoured cronies and supporters of their regimes and thus helped to enhance the political position of those in control of the state.

A strong and independent indigenous private sector has always been seen by those in control of African states as a potential political force capable of providing an alternative government. During the first two post-independence decades, little was done to promote local business-people. But under structural adjustment since the mid-1980s, local private capital development has been pushed strongly by international donors. Once again, however, African state personnel have been in a position to influence the process of providing support for domestic business. Select entrepreneurs have been favoured, usually ones with close connections to those in state power, and the emergence of a crony capitalism is seen as one unlikely to pose a political threat to incumbent regimes.

Foreign firms and resident expatriate economic minorities have also attempted, where possible, to enter into close working relationships with African state rulers. These relationships have generally proved mutually beneficial. In exchange for economic favours, non-African investors have provided opportunities and resources that have helped state leaders remain in power as well as build large private fortunes. Yet the political nature of state-foreign business relations is an important reason why sub-Saharan Africa has failed to attract much foreign direct investment since independence.

Moves to reduce the economic role of the state and therefore access to patronage resources, as in the ubiquitous structural adjustment programmes, have been resisted by African state elites. Yet the reform programmes have been pushed strongly by the international financial institutions and have resulted in a contraction of state patronage.

However, those in control of the state apparatus still retain access to a large fund of public resources; and new opportunities for state patronage have also emerged, as in the privatization programmes of African governments. Moreover, moves by international lenders to improve state economic management through the adoption of 'good' governance measures have also not progressed very far. Patronage politics has persisted within public institutions and has been little touched by governance reforms.

The international financial institutions are the sources of African structural adjustment programmes and the various reforms to reduce the economic role of the state as well as to create more effective state economic management. Although well aware of the importance of patronage politics, they have been unable to do much about minimizing its significance in the running of Africa's public institutions. Patrimonial governance remains prevalent throughout the Africa region with special consequences for its economic and political development.

NOTES

1. For general discussions of Africa's economic crisis, see, for example, John Ravenhill, (ed.), *Africa in Economic Crisis* (London, 1986); Michael Roemer, 'Economic Development in Africa: Performance Since Independence', *Daedalus*, CX1,2 (1982), 125–48; Richard Sandbrook, *The Politics of Africa's Economic Stagnation* (Cambridge, 1985); and the World Bank, *Sub-Saharan Africa. From Crisis to Sustainable Growth* (Washington, DC, 1989).

2. See, for example, Michael F. Lofchie, *The Policy Factor. Agricultural Performance in Kenya and Tanzania* (Boulder, CO, 1989), Chaps.2 and 3.

3. See, for example, Susan George, *A Fate Worse than Debt* (Harmondsworth, 1988) and Morris Szeftel, 'The Crisis in the Third World', in Ray Bush, Gordon Johnston and David Coates, (eds.), *The World Order. Socialist Perspectives* (Cambridge, 1987).

4. See Sandbrook, *op. cit.*, pp.20–29.

5. Michael Lofchie presents one such contrast – at times overdrawn – between Kenya and Tanzania. Botswana's generally favourable economic position since independence also contrasts markedly with that of most sub-Saharan countries. Moreover, other Third World countries have performed better than African ones in spite of the poor world economic climate. The plausibility of exogenous factors as key to understanding Africa's economic crisis is undermined by the fact of Africa's poor economic performance as compared with other Third World regions.

6. For one forceful critique of the paradigm that attributes Africa's economic malaise to factors external to the continent in explaining Ghana's economic demise during the 1970s, see Robert M. Price, 'Neo-Colonialism and Ghana's Economic Decline: A Critical Assessment', *Canadian Journal of African Studies*, 18,1 (1984); 163–93.

7. For good case studies, see Kenneth Good, 'Debt and the One-Party State in

Zambia', *Journal of Modern African Studies*, 27,2 (1989), 297–313; 'Zambia's acute malaise is a consequence chiefly of internal factors derivative of the single-party state and Kenneth Kaunda's personal rule' (pp.297–8); and Richard Jeffries, 'Rawlings and the Political Economy of Underdevelopment in Ghana', *African Affairs*, 81,324 (1982), 307–17.

8. Maria Nzomo, 'External Influence on the Political Economy of Kenya: The Case of MNCs', in Walter O. Oyugi, (ed.), *Politics and Administration in East Africa* (Nairobi, 1992), p.454.

9. Roland Oliver, *The African Experience* (London, 1991), p.241.

10. *ibid.*, For a detailed study of marketing boards, see Gerald K. Helleiner, *Peasant Agriculture, Government and Economic Development in Nigeria* (Homewood, IL, 1966).

11. For a discussion of state economic involvement in colonial Africa, see Crawford Young, 'Africa's Colonial Legacy', in Robert J. Berg and Jennifer Seymour Whitaker, (eds.), *Strategies for African Development* (Berkeley, CA, 1986).

12. For a discussion of the role of states in francophone African economies which is also relevant for other African countries, see Bernard Contamin and Yves-André Faure, 'State Intervention in the Economy', in Anthony Kirk-Greene and Daniel Bach, (eds.), *State and Society in Francophone Africa since Independence* (New York, 1995).

13. For an elaboration of how the politics of personal rule has stunted development, see Sandbrook, *op. cit.*, For an important study of how economic performance has political origins, see Robert H. Bates, *Markets and States in Tropical Africa. The Political Basis of Agricultural Policies* (Berkeley, CA, 1981). For a discussion summarizing various arguments on the politics of African development, see Michael F. Lofchie, 'The New Political Economy of Africa', in David E. Apter and Carl G. Rosberg (eds.), *Political Development and the New Realism in Sub-Saharan Africa* (Charlottesville, VA, 1994).

14. World Bank, *Bureaucrats in Business. The Economics and Politics of Government Ownership* (Washington, DC, 1996), p.xi.

15. *ibid.*, p.32.

16. For a good discussion of matters contained in this paragraph, see Arnold Hughes, 'The Nation-State in Black Africa', in Leonard Tivey, (ed.), *The Nation-State. the Formation of Modern Politics* (Oxford, 1981).

17. Sandbrook, *op. cit.*, p.63.

18. For a more detailed discussion, see Roger Tangri, *Politics in Sub-Saharan Africa* (London, 1985), pp.4–17.

19. *ibid.*, pp.17–23.

20. *ibid.*, pp.28–33. That those in power are so interested in 'eating' is a principal theme explored in great detail by Jean-Francois Bayart, *The State in Africa: The Politics of the Belly* (London, 1993).

21. Writing a few years into Cameroon's democratization process, Piet Konings commented that the 'power of the President is still relatively unlimited; the separation between the state and [ruling] CPDM party is still insufficient; censorship of the press, violation of human rights and military excesses are still commonplace'. See his 'The Post-Colonial State and Economic and Political Reforms in Cameroon', in Alex E. Fernandez Jilberto and Andre Mommen (eds.), *Liberalization in the Developing World* (London, 1996), p.261. Such a comment could also be made of most other sub-Saharan countries in the midst of political liberalization in the 1990s. For a general discussion, see Richard Joseph, 'Africa, 1990–1997: From

Abertura to Closure', *Journal of Democracy*, 9,2 (1998), 3–17. Michael Bratton and Nicolas van de Walle also argue for the first half of the 1990s that 'the most common path of regime transition was liberalization without democratization'. See their *Democratic Experiments in Africa* (Cambridge, 1997), p.119.

22. For more detailed discussions, see Sandbrook, *op. cit.*, pp.90–111 and Christopher Clapham, *Third World Politics. An Introduction* (London, 1985), pp.44–50, 54–60, 77–84. For military governments seeking to stay in power, similar considerations of developing a clientelist political base are essential to ensure political survival. For case studies of African patronage-based politics, see, for example, Thomas M. Callaghy, *The State-Society Struggle. Zaire in Comparative Perspective* (New York, 1984), and Richard Joseph, *Democracy and Prebendal Politics in Nigeria. The Rise and Fall of the Second Republic* (Cambridge, 1987).

23. Catherine Boone, *Merchant Capital and the Roots of Power in Senegal 1930 – 1985* (Cambridge, 1992), pp. 16, 17.

24. Richard Sandbrook, 'Economic Crisis, Structural Adjustment and the State in Sub-Saharan Africa' in Dharam Ghai, (ed.), *The IMF and the South. The Social Impact of Crisis and Adjustment* (London, 1991), p.100. See also, Richard Sandbrook, *The Politics of Africa's Economic Recovery* (Cambridge, 1993), pp.27–34 for a more detailed discussion.

25. For a discussion of the economic weaknesses of patrimonial government, see Robert H. Jackson and Carl G. Rosberg, 'The Political Economy of African Personal Rule', in Apter and Rosberg, *op. cit.*, pp.300–314. This article also has a brief discussion of those few African governments which have placed economic development before political spoils. See also E. A. Brett, 'State Power and Economic Inefficiency: Explaining Political Failure in Africa', *IDS Bulletin*, 17,1 (1986), 22–29, and Claude Ake, 'How Politics Underdevelops Africa' in Adebayo Adedeji et al (eds.), *The Challenge of African Economic Recovery and Development* (London, 1991), pp.316–29 for discussions on the nature of African politics and its impact on African economies.

26. See Adebayo Adedeji, (ed.), *Indigenisation of African Economies* (London, 1981).

27. Although emphasis is placed here on patronage politics, sub-Saharan Africa's economic decline is not attributable solely to domestic political factors. But even scholars emphasizing external factors in the region's 'gradual slide into crisis' are now also coupling their explanations with domestic factors such as 'the increasing bureaucratisation of the economic decision-making process and the organic interconnection of that process with forms of patronage that were becoming increasingly dysfunctional'. See Adebayo Olukoshi,' The Impact of Recent Reform Efforts on the African State', in Kjell Havnevik and Brian Van Arkadie (eds.), *Domination or Dialogue. Experiences and Prospects* (Stockholm, 1996), p.52.

28. For a wide-ranging volume on structural adjustment reform in Africa, see Thomas M. Callaghy and John Ravenhill (eds.), *Hemmed In. Responses to Africa's Economic Decline* (New York, 1993).

The Political Economy
of Africa's Parastatals

Central to any definition of public enterprise are two key components. One is public ownership or, at least, majority government ownership. Thus the public enterprise sector is made up of enterprises in which the state holds a controlling share (or a stake exceeding 50 per cent). The other is the notion of enterprise, implying the production and sale of goods and services. In this work, we focus on enterprises in which governments have a controlling interest and which operate as commercially oriented entities (i.e., they market their goods and/or services to recover costs or to make a profit).

Publicly owned enterprises have been key instruments in the development efforts of most sub-Saharan governments. Some data on them from the mid-1980s show the major role parastatals have played in African economies. The contribution of public enterprises to the gross domestic product (GDP) of African countries ranged from a low of around 10 per cent to a high near 40 per cent, the median being 15 per cent. As a share of total gross domestic investment, parastatals ranged from 10 per cent to over 50 per cent (the median being around 25 per cent). The ratio of public enterprise employment to total formal sector employment also varied (from 10 per cent to over 60 per cent), the median being about 25 per cent. As much as one-third of domestic credit was for state-owned enterprises which were also major borrowers in international credit systems.[1]

Government enterprises have been engaged in virtually every aspect of economic activity including many strategic sectors of African economies. In most African countries, the transport, communications and power sectors are dominated by parastatals. Primary exports – agricultural and mineral – are also usually run by public companies. Financial institutions and commercial and manufacturing ventures are often operated as state-owned concerns. And public corporations are found in the utilities.

African public enterprise has its origins in the colonial period. Public utilities (such as water and electricity) operated as public undertakings, and infrastructural services (such as ports and railways) were organized as state enterprises. Crop marketing boards handled many agricultural exports. There was also a small amount of state participation in the manufacturing sector under the auspices of industrial development corporations. Nevertheless, at independence, the size and scope of the state enterprise sector was limited. State intervention in various socio-economic spheres was more extensive. Colonial administrators initiated development plans and exercised certain regulatory powers (such as wage and price controls). But most of the areas of economic activity were privately owned and operated, and the public enterprise sector was not sizeable or significant.

Growth and performance of public enterprises since independence

Nearly all African countries witnessed a marked enlargement in their parastatal sectors after independence. Over one-half of the public enterprises existing in sub-Saharan Africa in the early 1980s were created in the late 1960s and 1970s. The proliferation of public sector companies was the result of many factors. Reinforcing various economic and developmental factors (such as capturing economies of scale and improving techniques of production as well as implementing the prevailing development strategy of import-substituting industrialization) were a number of socio-political concerns demanding that the state play an active economic role. Generally, statist conceptions of development together with economic nationalism and the need for political patronage led to the extensive growth of state-owned enterprises.

The 1960s was a time when 'statism' was a key feature of development thinking and strategy in the continent. The view that the state should be the prime motor of development was widely shared; ownership and intervention by the state was accepted as the dominant development paradigm. That the state had a central role to play in directing the development process was especially acknowledged in an African context of a weakly developed indigenous private sector as well as substantial foreign economic presence. Various forms of state economic intervention inherited from the colonial period were expanded and generalized in the years after independence, leading, in particular, to the marked expansion of public enterprises undertaking important shares of production and investment in African countries.

Strong feelings of 'economic nationalism' stemmed from the weakness and subordinate status of African private enterprise as well as from the fact that African economies at independence were largely in the hands of foreigners. Public sector enterprise was seen as enabling the state to carry out activities that African private entrepreneurs could not perform and also to reduce the dominance of foreign enterprise. Throughout the continent, political leaders sought to secure greater indigenous ownership of the economy, especially of the activities a country depended on for its foreign-exchange earnings. They also sought to achieve greater local control of the economy, particularly to ensure that economic decisions were consonant with governmental interests. Foreign economic control posed constraints on state personnel exercising decisions affecting the economy; it also made the possibility of foreign owners intervening in domestic politics much more likely. On nationalistic and political grounds, therefore, government leaders desired economic independence. Attaining greater ownership and control of 'the commanding heights of the economy' would enable governments to influence the broad direction of national development.

Various African governments nationalized foreign economic concerns and turned them into state-sector concerns. In Tanzania and Zambia in the late 1960s, majority state participation was undertaken in a number of private, foreign-owned industries; this was intended to give the state a basis for influencing corporate policies on production, pricing and investment. In Nigeria, the federal government acquired controlling shares in the petroleum sector in the 1970s to enhance national control of the economy. In Ghana in the mid-1970s, economic nationalism underlay government acquisition of majority equity in foreign-owned gold mines, banks, insurance, aluminium and timber companies. In the 1980s, the Minerals Marketing Corporation of Zimbabwe was set up to regulate foreign-controlled companies which dominated the mining sector. Also in Zimbabwe, South African-owned companies were nationalized to reduce economic dependence on the apartheid state.

In many countries, new public enterprises were created to accelerate Africanization of the economy. For example, in Kenya state enterprises were established to promote private African business. As a government document put it:

> The scarcity of private domestic savings, management talent, and entrepreneurial experience, especially among Africans, meant that if Kenyanisation was left to natural forces in the private sector, it would proceed very slowly indeed. Government participation could speed up the process[2]

The Agricultural Finance Corporation provided credit and technical assistance to help Africans acquire and develop white settler farms; the Kenya National Trading Corporation helped Africans to enter commerce at the expense of Asian traders; and the National Construction

Corporation helped Africans to enter the construction field which was dominated by large European companies.

State-run enterprises have emerged in all sub-Saharan countries, regardless of ideological differences between governments. In some of them, however, ideological principles have been of particular importance both in the expansion and the extensiveness of a state-owned sector. This has occurred in countries where political leaders have proclaimed an adherence to socialism and the state has been the predominant economic agent. In Ethiopia, Mozambique and Tanzania, for example, private business – foreign as well as local – was placed in the hands of public enterprises, as were various new undertakings. In many countries, however, where socialist ideas were of little political consequence, the growth of a smaller state-owned sector occurred in response to a variety of other problems. State involvement arose where an indigenous private sector hardly existed and public enterprises were created to take over from a foreign-controlled private sector or to promote a weak national private sector.

Another political factor, and at least as important in the growth of government enterprises, centred on political elites seeking to maintain themselves in state power. Everywhere, African governments have been subjected to intense pressures for providing employment and the redistribution of public resources. An extensive public enterprise sector has offered political leaders manifold economic resources and an array of opportunities to meet some of these demands. Moreover, state-owned enterprises could be appropriated to reward followers and thereby obtain their support. Thus jobs could be provided to political loyalists and goods and services dispensed to particular sections of the population in exchange for political support. Carolyn Baylies has remarked upon the importance of Zambia's post-1968 takeovers of foreign firms as enabling the state to strengthen its capacity to dispense goods and services, especially jobs and credit. And, similarly, in the case of Cameroon, Nicolas van de Walle has argued that public enterprises 'proved to be an ideal instrument to distribute state resources in the form of jobs, rents, power, and prestige' enabling President Ahmadou Ahidjo to reward allies and co-opt opponents and thus 'secure his own power base'.[3] State parastatals were evidently beneficial to state officeholders in terms of consolidating power and maintaining political incumbency.

The growth in the number of state-owned enterprises since independence was based on diverse political and economic objectives. A variety of competing objectives makes it difficult to assess the performance of public enterprises. An evaluation of the extent to which state firms fulfilled political objectives is not attempted here. It is impossible to assess the 'political benefits accruing from the erection of impressive-looking factories, the spending of money, the creation of jobs, the avoidance of foreign domination of the economy, and the financing of party activities'.[4] Rather, we focus on economic objectives and argue that economic performance has been impaired by the existence of competing political purposes.

The expansion in the number of public enterprises in the economy meant that the efficiency with which they carried out their work was of critical importance to a country's overall economic performance. How to evaluate the economic operations of the state enterprise sector is a complex matter.[5] One criterion often applied to appraise the record of state enterprises is to consider their financial returns. However, financial indicators may not constitute accurate guides to parastatal performance. This is especially so where public entities are used in pursuit of non-financial objectives, such as when output prices are fixed by government at artificially low rates or where a state-owned firm has to carry out non-commercial goals which cannot be conducted at a profit. Financial profitability is therefore an imperfect form of assessing performance. But it is often taken by international financial institutions as an important measure of determining the efficiency of public enterprises. Many African governments have also made it clear that commercial parastatals must cover their costs and earn profits; and this provides a key reason for judging state-owned companies by their profitability. For instance, successive governments in Ghana, and especially that of President Kwame Nkrumah, were insistent on state concerns making profits as well as generating investible surpluses.[6]

Measured on the basis of financial criteria, the evidence available supports the conclusion that the overall performance of Africa's state-owned sector has been disappointing. Many public companies have shown net losses and in nearly all countries public enterprise deficits are large, and have contributed to spiralling national debt. In a number of Francophone African countries (such as Niger and Togo) net deficits were roughly 4 per cent of GDP in the early 1980s. In Cameroon at the same time subsidization of losses incurred by the parastatal sector amounted to some CFAF150 billion a year, roughly 7 per cent of GDP. Similar results were evident in Anglophone countries. In Ghana in 1982, the total operating deficit of state-owned firms amounted to over 3 per cent of GDP – equivalent to total government spending on education, health and social welfare. In fact, public enterprise sectors in many African countries have been permanent loss-makers. Moreover, African state corporations have contributed very little to government revenues; instead, they have constituted a major burden on domestic budgets. In Ghana between 1979 and 1983, the net flow of budgetary transfers to the parastatal sector amounted on average to about 10 per cent of total government expenditure. In 1989, subsidies to loss-making parastatals added up to 14 per cent of the Zimbabwean budget.[7] Considered in non-financial terms, state-run enterprises have also not been distinguished by adequate results. As regards the provision of goods and services, a below-par performance has been common. Productivity returns in the agricultural and industrial sectors have been manifestly disappointing. In Ethiopia, industrial public enterprises were shown to have low economic efficiency, low economic profitability and negative value added.[8] In much of sub-Saharan Africa, basic utilities do not operate adequately. Electric power supply is often unreliable, while various transport services are haphazard and infrequent. The public provision of goods and services is also unduly costly.

Public agencies involved in various ways in Africa's agricultural sector have generally not performed well; their poor performance has been seen as an important contributor to the continent's economic difficulties and, in particular, the agrarian malaise. Referring to Ghana's state farms as an example of poorly performing public production schemes, Robert Bates concluded that they 'have consumed an enormous portion of the public resources available for agriculture, and they accumulated large debts'.[9] Similarly, in Nigeria, the River Basin Development schemes not only produced little food but never covered operating costs. Moreover, all over Africa, the history of parastatal crop marketing boards – state trading enterprises for agricultural products – has been a flawed one.[10] For example, by the early 1980s, Tanzania's official marketing authorities had accumulated vast debts and were the recipients of over half the total commercial bank loans. In 1987, Kenya's grain marketing parastatal – the National Cereals and Produce Board – had accumulated debt exceeding 5 per cent of the country's GDP.

As regards the multiple development objectives African public sector firms have sought to pursue, such as employment generation, income redistribution,[11] regional equity, appropriate technologies,[12] and export production,[13] results have also been limited.[14]

On various indicators, therefore, the empirical evidence demonstrates that the overall record of Africa's public sector companies has been poor. In a major speech in 1975, Zambian President, Kenneth Kaunda, acknowledged that 'the name Parastatal is now virtually a derogatory term', and that in a country with one of sub-Saharan Africa's largest parastatal sectors.[15] However, not all public enterprises have been failures. The range of parastatal performance varies widely from the very poor to the very good. In Kenya, for example, about one-half of the parastatals performed well for substantial periods of time.[16] But many of these specific parastatals have found it difficult to sustain their good performance since the 1980s.[17] And, more generally, state enterprise records have been ones of low efficiency and low profitability imposing unsustainable burdens on government budgets. Poor parastatal performance has had negative repercussions for African economies.

Parastatal performance: non-political factors

Amongst the various non-political reasons commonly adduced to account for the poor record of parastatals, four receive particular stress: inappropriate pricing policies, poor investment decisions, substantial overstaffing, and chronic management problems.[18]

It is apparent that pricing policies have undermined the financial viability of many state-owned entities. Many state enterprises lack price autonomy. Government control of public enterprise prices for both the materials they buy as well as the products and services they sell, has resulted in major financial difficulties. Price controls have contributed largely to operating losses and made state-run concerns dependent on government subsidies. For example, public transport companies (such as Kenya Railways) have experienced problems in raising fares to match cost increases, and grain marketing boards (such as Kenya's National Cereals and Produce Board) have been required to sell commodities at well below cost. Where governments have paid inadequate subsidies to cover the financial effects of pricing policies, then state-owned firms have incurred large losses.[19]

Investment decisions have been poor for various reasons. Sometimes feasibility studies have been inadequate or not carried out at all. As a result, there are many projects which were not soundly conceived and which should never have been started. Or projects have been initiated without adequate provision being made for financing. Funding limitations have hindered the state concern's ability to implement the project efficiently. Or parastatal projects have been located in the wrong places and this has raised the costs of production. Many factories are located according to considerations of regional equity and balance. But such factors impose large economic hardships on projects. Finally, poor project planning has led to costly technical deficiencies being encountered.[20]

Severe problems of overstaffing have been a contributing element in Africa's public sector malaise. Throughout the continent public enterprises employ people well in excess of requirements. In 1983, the Ghana Cocoa Marketing Board employed over 130,000 people who handled a crop less than half the size dealt with more efficiently by 50,000 employees twenty years earlier.[21] Moreover, enterprise managers are often unable to dismiss or reduce their large workforces. At times, they do not possess discretionary rights to determine the salaries and benefits of their employees, especially at the lower levels. Costly, often unproductive, workforces are a major financial burden on state concerns.

Deficient parastatal performance often derives from managerial shortcomings. Many management positions are in the hands of less-than-qualified persons. The shortage of personnel, especially with accounting skills, has resulted in disarray in financial administration involving various economic costs. Moreover, because governments have readily offset parastatal deficits, the notion of financial constraint has hardly existed in parastatal operations. Many wasteful practices have occurred, including overspending and misuse of resources. Parastatal managements have also been subjected to frequent transfer and turnover so that few managers have remained long enough in their positions to acquire expertise and experience. Of all public enterprises, agricultural marketing boards have experienced the greatest difficulties in their operations, often stemming from poor managerial and organizational factors. Throughout Africa, food stocks have not been stored properly; much grain is ruined through exposure to the elements. Much pilfering of stocks also takes place and embezzlement of funds at buying and selling points is common. But perhaps most importantly, large bureaucratic organizations appear distinctly unsuited to carrying out the diverse and small-scale transactions of agricultural marketing efficiently.

The politics of parastatal performance

Political motives were important in the expansion of Africa's publicly owned enterprise sector. As we argue, they have also influenced the operation of state-owned enterprises decisively.

Africa's political leaders have sought to remain in power. They have also sought to enhance the wealth of those in power. Both of these goals have been pursued through the political dispersal of public resources. The state has been the prime locus of resources and benefits in all sub-Saharan countries. Those in control of the state have used public resources and positions within public service institutions in ways designed to further the twin goals of power retention and material accumulation. A large public enterprise sector has provided abundant opportunities for politicians wanting to achieve these goals. State-owned enterprises have therefore constituted highly valuable mechanisms for political leaders seeking to stay in power as well as wanting to promote their personal wealth.

However, manipulation of the state sector for political and personal purposes has contradicted the norms of parastatal productivity and profitability. Political and personal imperatives have subverted the goal of operating state enterprises efficiently, and have been significant factors in impeding the positive economic performance of parastatals in Africa.[22]

As noted in the previous chapter, state office-holders have occupied a relatively autonomous position in African policymaking. African state elites had considerable discretion in decision-making especially in the first two post-independence decades. Moreover, as African governments have tended, until recently, to be mainly authoritarian, top politicians and government officials have exercised authority over various matters affecting the operations of state institutions, including state-owned enterprises. Ministers, military leaders, and senior civil servants have all intervened in the affairs of public enterprises, usually without having to account for their actions. Such interventions have been concerned with developmental goals or operational efficiency; but they have also served, primarily, political and personal objectives. Tony Killick argued in the case of Ghana that politicians 'declined to give consistent priority to the developmental objective in running the public sector'. Instead, they 'demonstrated a willingness to sacrifice economic benefits for short-term party, constituency and personal advantage'.[23]

Political and personal considerations have been important influences in a variety of parastatal policy matters (investment, tendering, siting, pricing, choice of machinery, employment levels, management appointments, etc.). For example, many decisions have been made to build patron-client linkages of support for those in state power. This has accounted for the politically inspired distribution of contracts and credit, as well as gross overstaffing, inappropriate siting decisions, and unsuitable management selections. With regard to marketing boards engaged in the distribution of farm inputs (fertilizers, seeds, equipment), Bates writes that such public resources 'have been channelled to those whose support is politically useful or economically rewarding to the state'.[24] Political leaders have also made decisions on grounds of enriching themselves personally. Public enterprise tenders for goods and services have commonly been awarded in total disregard of the procedures laid down and without inviting open tenders (as in the case of the Kenya National Trading Corporation in the 1980s and early 1990s). Tenders have often been awarded to 'dubious' companies which have not delivered the required goods and services. Political loyalists have benefited from such awards but so also have government officials and politicians, especially where project costs have been grossly inflated. Those awarding contracts have also extracted handsome kickbacks which have rendered many parastatal projects (for instance,

Kenya's Kisumu Molasses Plant) uneconomical. In sum, pervasive political interventions – guided by the need to build a political following or by the desire for personal economic gain – have been significant in impairing the operations of public enterprises.[25]

Public sector enterprises of all sorts have been subjected to politically and personally motivated interventions. State-owned banks have often been a prime target of such pressures. 'To every regime, the Uganda Commercial Bank (UCB) was a gravy train. New ministers, army officers and parliamentarians would descend upon it and take out huge loans, often with inadequate or non-existent collateral ... These people saw the loans as rewards for bringing the government to power.' Government-owned banks have been obliged to lend often considerable amounts to the politically prominent. Many of these loans have been irrecoverable, and public commercial banks have been made insolvent by such large 'nonperforming' assets. In 1994, UCB was reportedly 'carrying nearly $100 million in bad loans to politicians, soldiers, and other functionaries of the regime and their wives'.[26]

Government control of the agricultural marketing board system also proved an essential mechanism for enhancing state power and personal wealth. As argued in the case of the Senegalese groundnut marketing board, its primary role was neither commercial nor developmental but political. ONCAD (1966 to 1980) served 'as a distributor of political patronage'. Most of the board members were appointed on political grounds, and jobs and resources invariably went to political supporters. ONCAD experienced 'problems of overstaffing, corruption and inefficiency', and political manipulation was well-known to have affected its operations. As elsewhere in Africa, state intervention in the agricultural marketing circuit 'permitted the accumulation of substantial personal fortunes by some of those involved'.[27] Official agricultural marketing boards throughout sub-Saharan Africa, especially those concerned with export crops, provided considerable sums for state elites to use as they wished for personal and political purposes.

In examining the performance of public enterprises, account also has to be taken of the excessive dependence of African economies on foreign economic interests. The dimensions of dependence are various and include reliance on foreign capital, technology and personnel. As the following case study seeks to show, public enterprise management has been influenced significantly by foreign factors as well as domestic ones.

Public Enterprise and Industrial Development

The case of the Industrial Development Corporation of Zambia[28]
In the field of manufacturing industry, the Zambian government began from 1968 to acquire majority shareholdings in a number of mostly resident expatriate manufacturing companies. Public ownership was instituted in order to reduce dependence on foreign private capital. 'State participation', according to an important document of the ruling party, 'is designed to guarantee the control of the economy by the Zambian people [and] the reduction of the impact of foreign influence in shaping national destiny.'[29] It was also envisaged that state enterprise in manufacturing would promote industries which were import-substituting, export-oriented, and employment-generating, relying as far as possible on local resources. Further objectives included the establishment of small-scale industries in the rural areas in order to provide more geographically balanced industrial development. The Industrial Development Corporation of Zambia (INDECO) was assigned the task of achieving these objectives in manufacturing.

Not only was INDECO unable to reduce dependence on foreign capital, but public ownership failed to lead to the emergence of a structure of production in accordance with official party and government objectives. Much manufacturing development initiated by INDECO was judged to have been capital-intensive, urban-based, and directed towards consumer goods requiring the importation of a considerable volume of raw materials and intermediate products.[30] Finally, INDECO undertook projects that were not always profitable; indeed, the level of returns was low and in some years losses were incurred. Why did INDECO's performance not live up to expectations?

In all the takeovers of private companies and the new ventures entered into after 1968, INDECO was obliged to accept a large degree of continued dependence on foreign economic interests. Continuing dependence on foreign administrative and technical management as well as on inflows of foreign capital had an important impact on the pattern of manufacturing development. As in other African countries, many of INDECO's investment decisions as well as the structure of investments (choice of technology, location of plant, etc.) were based on the advice and recommendations of foreign partners.[31]

Zambia's industrialization, based on import-substitution, produced mainly consumer goods. The fact that these products aimed to satisfy the consumption needs of the higher income groups led to adoption of the production techniques of Western industrialized countries. INDECO was obliged to incorporate Western technology in the industries it set up such as a car assembly plant and various grain-mills. Even in cases where alternative technologies were available, factories were installed that were dependent on highly capital-intensive technology from abroad. Zambia Clay Industries, for example, set up two ultra-modern brick factories in 1975 despite the existence of a number of older, labour-intensive operations scattered throughout Zambia. The bias of investment in favour of capital-intensive production may also have ensued because overseas firms derive their highest profits from the supply and maintenance of machinery and equipment as well as the provision of technical services. In other ways as well, foreign companies may have influenced the adoption of capital-intensive techniques. INDECO was dependent for about one-half of its capital on foreign financial sources. The availability of foreign credit for overseas projects favouring the use of foreign equipment was noted by President Kaunda:

> It has been our experience in the past that foreign economic assistance has the tendency to distort our choice of technology for it has been invariably tied to purchase of machinery and equipment, etc. in the respective donor country. This condition has resulted in the importation of machinery and equipment which have generated very little employment for the local people.[32]

A final problem to be noted stemmed from foreign companies, commissioned to provide plant, not carrying out their work properly, with the result that technical deficiencies afflicted INDECO companies. When the German contractors handed over the brick-making factory at Kalalushi to INDECO it was discovered that the machines did not have any spare parts; that the machinery installed was obsolete so that it could not be replaced or repaired; that the machines were unsuited to local types of coal; and that the cost of the machinery was exorbitant. A Japanese company was responsible for commissioning a factory to produce fertilizer for Nitrogen Chemicals. Technical problems, however, consequent upon failures of construction, led to the factory being shut down on various occasions, and to INDECO being paid compensation of nearly one million *Kwacha*. In the case of machinery installed by a Finnish company at Mansa Batteries, a parliamentary committee commented that the machinery was

> installed on an experimental basis since it had never been used elsewhere in the world including its country of origin ... the key problem of machine failure to reach its estimated output arose from the fact that it was a proto-type, i.e., it was the first of its kind to be made and used and its basic design was not intended for continuous operation for long periods.[33]

Taking into consideration the repayment of foreign loans for financing the plant, and the expenses of foreign management, dependence on foreign contractors and managers clearly had its price.

But internal factors also affected INDECO's performance. In the first place, the government's industrial development strategy was not of sufficient precision to provide INDECO with clear guidelines for its activities. Clearly defined and unambiguous criteria for investment and operating decisions were not officially enunciated. The result was that many of INDECO's investments were selected according to *ad hoc* criteria. In the absence of any overall strategy, the assumptions of government and parastatal officials were no different from those of the foreign associate. For both parties, decision-making tended to be dictated primarily by short-term opportunity and local demand considerations (for beer and cigarettes, or cars). By adopting short-term profit criteria, INDECO preferred investments in import-substitution industries producing more or less luxury goods as well as large, capital-intensive projects in the urban centres.

Secondly, INDECO was subject to a series of *ad hoc* political directives on specific operational issues, including type and location of investments. Projects were undertaken on political considerations although, as in the case of Mansa Batteries, the feasibility study concluded that the project based in Mansa would be uneconomic. Moreover, projects such as the Chinese maize mill at Chingola were started without any feasibility study being undertaken; the decision was a purely political one, which led to the already planned and evaluated maize mill in Kitwe being abandoned. Directives were also issued regarding the location of projects. The locations of Livingstone Motor Assemblers, Kapiri Glass Products and Mansa Batteries, all subsidiaries of INDECO, were decided on the basis of providing employment opportunities outside the main urban areas. These and similar projects ran into difficulties for various reasons, partly because, being located in up-country centres, they were situated a long way from the main markets. Multi-million dollar brick factories were set up under official directive in the rural areas at Kalalushi and Nega Nega, but transporting the bricks long distances to the construction sites raised their cost to uneconomic levels, with the result that the construction industry increasingly switched to the use of concrete blocks. Because of declining demand for its products, the brick works at Nega Nega was forced to close down in 1979 and the factory at Kalalushi incurred large losses.

The acute shortage of administrative and managerial expertise was a recurring problem in INDECO. But effective Zambian management was adversely affected by political involvement. The parastatals suffered an extremely high rate of transfer of middle and top management, stemming from conscious political decisions to move managers between state companies, in particular to avert corruption. Inevitably the result was loss of efficiency. Management was also seriously affected by the politically inspired appointments of many less-than-qualified managers. The ensuing mismanagement was accompanied by a growing degree of corruption. State officials increasingly used their positions within INDECO to benefit themselves, and co-operated with politicians and foreign businesspeople to their mutual advantage.[34]

Reform of public enterprises

The operational ineffectiveness of Africa's parastatals has long been recognized. Over the years, reforms of various sorts have been prescribed in an effort to improve Africa's faltering public enterprise sector. During the 1960s and 1970s, state enterprise reform was carried out in an *ad hoc* manner. Reform measures were fragmentary and entailed tinkering with specific internal management and financial issues. Little noticeable improvement in public enterprise operations occurred. The 1980s, however, have seen more comprehensive reform strategies being devised. Persistent and intense financial and economic crises – linked in part to the poor performance of public agencies – have compelled African governments to undertake extensive public sector changes. The financial and debt crises of the early 1980s brutally exposed the seriously deficient state of Africa's parastatal sectors, especially the extent of their chronic deficits (often in Africa the single largest determinant of a country's overall budget deficit) as well as the substantial subventions they received from government. In the mid-1980s, the median contribution of African parastatals to public sector deficits was estimated to be nearly 50 per cent. Also, extensive borrowings by African state enterprises in international credit markets added substantially to the region's external public sector debts. In the mid-1980s, parastatals accounted for almost 20 per cent of the public foreign debt in sub-Saharan countries.

Public enterprise reform emerged as a priority issue. Reforms have comprised the commercialization as well as the divestiture of state enterprises.[35] Divestiture or privatization connotes a number of different processes such as leasing, liquidation and the transfer of ownership and assets from public to private hands. Commercialization entails reform of public enterprises so that their operations are subject to competition and market forces. In this latter case, no alteration in state ownership and control takes place; ownership is still vested in the state.

Despite large proposed programmes of state enterprise divestiture (considered in the following chapter), a sizeable public enterprise sector has remained, at least until very recently. Many public sector firms have been retained in government ownership and not divested to private ownership. This has reflected various concerns among African political leaders, including many of the developmental and socio-political reasons that had inspired the growth of state enterprises in the post-independence period. State enterprise divestiture has been viewed as incompatible with fundamental socio-political objectives such as those of enhancing national autonomy, establishing indigenous capabilities, and providing benefits for lower-income groups.[36] Critics emphasize the adverse economic and social effects of privatization, namely, that it will lead to large worker lay-offs and retrenchment, diverse negative distributional consequences, concentration of ownership among certain favoured domestic groups, and increased foreign ownership and control. Equally important, politicians have been unwilling to allow the privatization of state companies which, in their hands, have been used to build up their support bases.

It was initially in connection with the large number of remaining government enterprises that commercialiazation measures were scheduled. State enterprise reform was also supported by external organizations concerned about the financial and efficiency shortcomings of public companies. Indeed, World Bank thinking in the early 1980s was that commercialization of state-owned parastatals was more feasible than their privatization.[37]

The essence of commercialization reforms has been to expose public enterprises to market forces so as to make them operate as profit-making commercial ventures. Some reforms have pushed price liberalization whereby price controls are lifted and price increases permitted. Others have removed barriers to the entry of private firms so that the latter can compete with state agencies. Further reforms have enhanced the autonomy of state enterprise managers, giving them wider discretion in determining prices, hiring and firing employees, and making investment decisions. Moreover, performance contracts and performance evaluation systems have been introduced.[38]

There is insufficient empirical evidence to evaluate the performance of public enterprises which have undergone more thoroughgoing reforms. But even if the few indications showing positive results are correct,[39] African governments have nonetheless been increasingly pressed to dismantle rather than reform their publicly-owned concerns. In the 1990s, World Bank officials have no longer put much stock on state enterprise reform, arguing that state enterprises have continued to be vulnerable to political interference and weak financial discipline, and also that African state sectors were overextended, with governments carrying out many activities that could be more efficiently undertaken by private agents.[40] Moreover, the World Bank complained that African governments continued to intervene in parastatal decision-making, and many appointments to senior management positions were still made on the basis of political connections. A 1991 report stated directly in regard to public enterprises that the 'Bank has had but limited success in dealing with the patronage and political-appointee problems'.[41] Furthermore, the burden of public enterprises on the public treasury remained large and the available funds continued to be limited. With state enterprise deficits averaging 4 per cent of GDP, privatization was advocated as an important means of reducing public deficits at a time of generally severe fiscal crisis in African countries.

From the late 1980s, there has been strong insistence on the divestiture or privatization of state firms. Within multilateral financial institutions as well as Western aid organizations, it has been contended that divestiture would lead to more efficient and productive economies emerging in the African continent. Improvements in productivity, fiscal performance, and service delivery as well as the attainment of higher returns would be more likely to be better served under private than under state ownership.[42] Part of the reason for this is that commercial profitability would become the main objective of managers who would be judged on their ability to achieve this goal, and partly that under private ownership there would be little or no political influence in the decision-making processes of the firm. Privatization has been especially favoured on the grounds that it would depoliticize economic decisions as well as end the mismanagement and corruption endemic in enterprises controlled by politicians.

A further impetus for state divestiture has again come from Western governments and international financial institutions wanting to create more market-run economies in the African region. Privatization is one part of the wider economic reforms of structural adjustment being pressed on African governments. These wider reforms seek to enhance the scope of the private sector, contending that private enterprise is superior to the state ownership of enterprises in terms of economic performance. Promoting the private sector would be made much easier if the state is not deeply involved in the economy. Privatization presages the shifting of the balance of power between state and private sector in Africa.

NOTES

1. Daniel Swanson and Teffera Wolde-Semait, *Africa's Public Enterprise Sector and Evidence of Reforms* (World Bank Technical Paper, No.95, Washington DC, 1989), pp. 6–8.

2. Quoted in David Himbara, 'The Failed Africanization of Commerce and Industry in Kenya', *World Development*, 22,3 (1994), p.471. See also Barbara Grosh, *Public Enterprise in Kenya. What Works, What Doesn't, and Why?* (Boulder, CO, 1991), pp.15–16.

3. Carolyn L. Baylies, 'The State and Class Formation in Zambia' (The University of Wisconsin-Madison, Ph.D., 1978), pp.615–16; and Nicolas van de Walle, 'The Politics of Public Enterprise Reform in Cameroon', in Barbara Grosh and Rwekaza S. Mukandala, (eds.), *State-Owned Enterprises in Africa* (Boulder, CO, 1994), pp.155–6.

4. Tony Killick, *Development Economics in Action. A Study of Economic Policies in Ghana* (London, 1978), p.248.

5. For a general evaluation of public enterprise performance, see Ramesh Adhikari and Colin Kirkpatrick, 'Public Enterprise in Less Developed Countries: An Empirical Review', in John Heath, (ed.), *Public Enterprise at the Crossroads* (London, 1990). See also J.B. Knight, 'Public Enterprises and Industrialisation in Africa', in Frances Stewart, Sanjaya Lall, and Samuel Wangwe (eds.), *Alternative Development Strategies in Sub-Saharan Africa* (Basingstoke, 1992).

6. See Killick, *op. cit.*, pp.216–18.

7. Swanson and Wolde-Semait, *op. cit.*, Chaps. 3–4; Grosh, *op. cit.*, pp.7–8, 153–5, 164–5; van de Walle, *op. cit.*, p.157; John R. Nellis, 'Public Enterprises in Sub-Saharan Africa' (World Bank Discussion Paper, No.1, Washington, DC, 1986), pp.17–20; Tony Killick, *Policy Economics* (London, 1981), pp.282–7; and Jeffrey Herbst, 'Political Impediments to Economic Rationality: Explaining Zimbabwe's Failure to Reform its Public Sector', *Journal of Modern African Studies*, 27,1 (1989), pp.73–5, 77–8.

8. Adhikari and Kirkpatrick, *op. cit.*, p.37.

9. Robert H. Bates, *Markets and States in Tropical Africa. The Political Basis of Agricultural Policies* (Berkeley, CA, 1981), p.47.

10. See Kwame Arhin, Paul Hesp and Laurens van der Laan (eds.), *Marketing Boards in Tropical Africa* (London, 1985).

11. In Zambia, subsidiaries of the manufacturing parastatal, INDECO, failed to realize the goals of redistributing income. Price controls on refined oils and fats produced by its agro-based enterprises resulted in large industrial users and affluent urban dwellers being heavily subsidized. See Mahmood A. Ayub and Sven O. Hegstad, 'Management of Public Industrial Enterprises', *World Bank Research Observer*, 2,1 (1987), p.91.

12. Perkins showed that in Tanzania public enterprises, as compared with private-owned firms, did not use appropriate, small-scale, labour-intensive techniques in industrial production. See F.C. Perkins, 'Technology Choice, Industrialisation and Development Experience in Tanzania', *Journal of Development Studies*, 19,2 (1983), 213–43.

13. World Bank figures show that the value of exports from state-controlled mining companies, predominantly in the copper sector, increased 36% between 1960 and 1989. In contrast, the value of exports from mining companies under private control increased 350% over the same three decades.

14. Tony Killick, 'The Role of the Public Sector in the Industrialization of African Developing Countries', *Industry and Development*, 7 (1983), 57–87.

15. Cited in Baylies, *op. cit.*, p.923. Speaking in 1994, Julius Nyerere was quoted as saying that 'it was foolish, and I now regret why I nationalised most industries and

other enterprises in Tanzania when I was president'. Nyerere argued that national-ized enterprises have a 'shorter life-span' than those left in the hands of private investors because those in government hands were often mismanaged. See *The New Vision* (Kampala), 24 September 1994, p.1.

16. Grosh, *op. cit.*, pp.21–5. Moreover, the Kenyan public enterprise sector was not a major drag on public finances: in 1991, 'it was only about 1 per cent of total expen-diture'. See World Bank, *Adjustment in Africa. Reforms, Results and the Road Ahead* (Washington, DC, 1994), p.107.

17. For a recent critical assessment of Kenya's public enterprises, see Gurushri Swamy, 'Kenya: Patchy Intermittent Commitment', in Ishrat Husain and Rashid Faruqee, (eds.), *Adjustment in Africa. Lessons from Country Case Studies* (Washington, D.C., 1994), pp.223–5. See also World Bank, *Re-investing in Stabilisation and Growth through Public Sector Adjustment* (Washington, DC, 1992), Chap.4 for a more detailed discussion.

18. See Killick, 'Role of the Public Sector', *op. cit.*, pp.82–5; and Nellis, *op. cit.*, pp.21–4, 30–31. See also Knight, *op. cit.*, pp.324–7. For a detailed discussion of the diverse reasons for the poor performance of Ghanaian public enterprises in the early 1960s, see Killick, *Development Economics, op. cit.*, Chap.9.

19. Pricing policies have also seriously affected the volume of purchases by agricultural marketing authorities. Low producer prices have led to smuggling. Large volumes of cocoa were smuggled from Ghana to the Ivory Coast in the 1970s. In 1980, two-thirds of Senegal's groundnut harvest was sold illegally in The Gambia. Low prices have also diverted crops from official marketing channels into private channels; some 70% of food crops in Tanzania in the early 1980s were sold through unofficial markets.

20. For a more detailed discussion of the diverse ways poor project planning was inim-ical to the performance of state enterprises in Ghana in the early 1960s, see Killick, *Development Economics, op. cit.*, pp.228–34.

21. Crawford Young, *Ideology and Development in Africa* (New Haven, CT, 1982), p.41.

22. The political allocation of public resources to secure personal gain and political sup-port is considered in Richard Sandbrook, *The Politics of Africa's Economic Stagnation* (Cambridge, 1985), pp.90–111. See also Bates, *op. cit.*, p.102. For specific country examples of the politicization of public enterprises, see Herbst, *op. cit.*, pp.77–80; Peter Lewis, 'Development Strategy and State Sector Expansion in Nigeria', in Grosh and Mukandala, *op. cit.*, pp.63–81; and Rwekaza S. Mukandala,'The State and Public Enterprise' in Walter O. Oyugi, (ed.), *Politics and Administration in East Africa* (Nairobi, 1992).

23. Killick, *Development Economics, op. cit.*, p.254.

24. Bates, *op. cit.*, pp. 49–54. Public enterprises also assist politicians, especially minis-ters in charge of them, at election times. In Uganda in 1993, at the time of the Constituent Assembly elections, the managing director of Uganda Railways Corporation gave 40% (or $5000) of the corporation's donations budget to help finance the election campaign of the minister of transport. See *The New Vision*, 19 March 1997, p.32.

25. For examples of public enterprises being used for political purposes, see Sandbrook, *op. cit.*, pp. 126–7, 136–7; and Bates, *op. cit.*, pp.104–5. The 1962 Coker Commission of Inquiry into the Statutory Corporations of Western Nigeria pro-vided one of the earliest and most extensively documented discussions of how

African public enterprises have provided copious patronage opportunities. It examined the relationships between the Action Group and the regional Development and Finance Corporations and reported on the political allocation of jobs, contracts, investments and loans as well as the ensuing bankruptcy of various state enterprises. For an example of a public enterprise being used for purposes of personal enrichment, see Mbatau wa Ngai, 'Stakeholders Must Act on Looting', *Sunday Nation* (Nairobi), 4 August 1996, p.25. He writes about the collapse of the Kenya National Assurance Company in 1996 that the 'causes of the fall of KNAC are well known. For years, a clique of political placemen have colluded with corrupt but politically-correct ambulance-chasing lawyers to siphon millions of shillings out of the company through wildly inflated insurance claims'.

26. Charles Onyango-Obbo, 'Why UCB Became the Sacrificial Lamb', *The East African* (Nairobi), 4 September 1995, p.9. For a similar discussion of the near-bankruptcy of the National Development Bank in Botswana, see Kenneth Good, 'Corruption and Mismanagement in Botswana: a Best-Case Example?', *Journal of Modern African Studies*, 32,3 (1994), 509–12. In Tanzania, the National Bank of Commerce was declared to be 'basically bankrupt or insolvent. Its liabilities exceed its assets. Its accumulated losses by the end of June 1995 reached approximately $251 million.' See *The East African*, 1 January 1996, p.3 for the comments of the Governor of the Central Bank in Tanzania. TNBC's financial distress was due partly to its being used for political patronage purposes but mainly to its having to extend loans to parastatals, especially the crop marketing boards, which did not service them.

27. Nim Caswell, 'Peasants, Peanuts and Politics: State Marketing in Senegal, 1966–80', in Arhin et al, *op. cit.*, pp.79, 112.

28. The Zambian case study was written originally in 1979 and was published in Klaas Woldring, (ed.), *Beyond Political Independence. Zambia's Development Predicament in the 1980s* (Berlin, 1984). A revised version is presented here but the information still relates to the period up to 1979 and no account is taken of subsequent developments.

29. United National Independence Party, *National Policies for the Next Decade 1974–1984* (Lusaka, 1973), p.39.

30. Ann Seidman, 'The Distorted Growth of Import-Substitution Industry: The Zambian Case', *Journal of Modern African Studies*, 12,4 (1974), 601–31.

31. *ibid.*, p.615. See also Issa G. Shivji, 'Capitalism Unlimited: Public Corporations in Partnership with Multinational Corporations', *The African Review*, 3,3 (1973), 359–82.

32. *Third National Development Plan 1979–1983* (Lusaka, 1979), p.v.

33. *Report of the Committee on Parastatal Bodies* (Lusaka, 1979), p.55.

34. See Morris Szeftel, 'Political Graft and the Spoils System in Zambia – the State as a Resource in Itself', *Review of African Political Economy*, 24 (1982), 4–21.

35. See Nellis, *op. cit.*, pp.42–65 for a discussion of reform strategies. See also World Bank, *The Reform of Public Sector Management: Lessons of Experience* (June 1991), Chap.4.

36. See Thandika Mkandawire, 'The Political Economy of Privatisation', in Giovanni Andrea Cornia and Gerald K. Helleiner (eds.), *From Adjustment to Development in Africa* (Basingstoke, 1994). But, in reality, African public enterprises have hardly achieved any of these objectives. Tom Forrest writes that 'the whole history of the public sector in Nigeria suggests that it has not been associated with any enhanced

capacity to pursue national goals and development objectives or with self-reliant patterns of economic development'. See his *Politics and Economics of Development in Nigeria* (Boulder, CO, 1995), p.223.

37. See Don Babai, 'The World Bank and the IMF: Rolling Back the State or Backing its Role?' in Raymond Vernon (ed.), *The Promise of Privatization: A Challenge for U.S. Foreign Policy* (New York, 1988), and Paul Mosley, 'Privatisation, Policy-Based Lending and World Bank Behaviour', in Paul Cook and Colin Kirkpatrick (eds.), *Privatisation in Less Developed Countries* (Hemel Hempstead, 1988).

38. See World Bank, *World Development Report 1983* (Washington DC, 1983), Chap.8 for an early general discussion on improving state-owned enterprise efficiency.

39. See World Bank, *Reform of Public Sector, op. cit.*, for positive assessments. For a contrary view, see Sunita Kikeri, John Nellis, and Mary Shirley, *Privatization. The Lessons of Experience* (World Bank, Washington, DC, 1992), pp. 16–20.

40. See John Nellis and Sunita Kikeri, 'Public Enterprise Reform: Privatization and the World Bank', *World Development*, 17,5 (1989) for this argument put forward by two World Bank officers. They state (p.663): 'more reforms have failed than succeeded. Persistently, governments have established and then violated quasi-contractual commitments to grant greater autonomy to PE management... Repeatedly, governments have allowed PEs to make expensive investments of dubious or clearly poor quality.' Also, they state that governments 'cannot resist the temptation to interfere' in the affairs of public enterprises (p.663) and that there is a tendency 'to overstate the capabilities of governments to reform PEs' (p.664).

41. World Bank, *Reform of Public Sector, op. cit.*, p.46. In Uganda in 1997, there was much evidence of harmful political interventions in the affairs of public enterprises. Apart from 'the direct political appointees' as chairmen of state companies, the directors of Uganda's security organs 'use their powers to plant cronies and relatives in key [parastatal] positions'. Political appointees 'use their positions to misappropriate company revenues with impunity well aware of the political protection of the appointing authority'. 'Ministers, too, have regularly preyed on parastatals under them to make contributions for their foreign trips or fundraisings in their constituencies.' See the editorial in *The Monitor*, 21 May 1997, p.3.

42. Nellis and Kikeri, *op. cit.*, pp.663–4.

The Politics
of Africa's Privatization

The deteriorating performance of public enterprises and the growing burdens of public sector subventions and subsidies aroused much concern with regard to the state sector's role in African economies. In the early 1980s at a time of scarcer public resources as well as generally adverse economic circumstances, the relatively dismal performance of parastatals led to calls not only for state enterprise reform but also for state enterprise divestiture. But public sector firms could not easily be divested. For Africa's political leaders in particular, state parastatals have served as valuable patronage mechanisms which could not readily be given up. However, pressure from international donors led by the International Monetary Fund and the World Bank pushed powerfully for divestment. Increasingly from the late 1980s, the availability of external funds was made contingent on African compliance with donor-driven economic reform programmes of which state divestiture was an integral part. Given their troubled economic conditions and their acute dependence on foreign financial flows to revitalize their economies, African governments officially accepted privatization so as not to forfeit the international support crucial for their domestic economic and political survival.[1]

Most sub-Saharan African countries have, indeed, proposed quite large programmes of privatization. But the actual number of state-owned enterprises divested has been modest, at least until very recently. Only a limited number of transfers to private ownership has taken place. Explanations of the halting steps towards state divestiture have identified various economic constraints. One is the lack of public resources to pay the outstanding liabilities of the divested firms, including sometimes costly severance packages for laid-off workers. Another is the manifest difficulty in determining the valuation of public assets for sale. (In 1998 the privatization of Zambia's two biggest copper mines ran into trouble because the offer from the Kafue consortium – a group of foreign mining companies – was well below the government's expectations. The Zambian President accused the consortium of wanting to buy the mines at 'give-away' prices. 'We shall not do this', he declared.) There have also been difficulties in finding buyers with the requisite capital to acquire the larger state concerns, given the limited development of an indigenous private sector. And there have been problems of assessing the prospects for economic returns from the enterprises privatized which will be subject to greater economic competition. Moreover, the poor financial and material condition of state-run enterprises (as well as the poor location of some of them) has affected the willingness of buyers to invest in them when more profitable forms of investment are readily available.

Evidently, these economic problems pose serious obstacles to privatization. But, as with explanations of poor state parastatal performance, limited divestment of state enterprises also has to be accounted for by non-economic factors. We need to draw on political as well as economic factors to achieve a fuller understanding of the slow pace of privatization.[2] Many of these political factors are a mirror image of the political concerns that led to the creation of so many public enterprises in the years after independence.

The political constraints to privatization up to the early 1990s

Privatization in Africa has been a highly controversial and politically contentious issue.[3] As the head of Uganda's Public Enterprise Reform and Divestiture Programme (PERDP) put it: 'there are many problems but the mother of them all is that PERDP is a delicate economic activity that is extremely politically sensitive'.[4] Governments have been attentive to the various political constraints and have been cautious in prosecuting divestiture policies. In Kenya in 1992, for example, where there were some 300 parastatals, the government was planning to divest them only gradually, at around 10 enterprises a year. Ghana, with over 200 state enterprises, was privatizing at the same time at a rate of barely 20 a year.

The political impediments to privatization begin within the publicly-owned enterprises themselves. Where enterprise officials have been concerned about their positions and perquisites, divestiture programmes may face bureaucratic resistance from state sector managers.[5] Public sector labour unions have also organized against state divestiture particularly on the grounds that it would result in large job losses. Under pressure from labour unions, and in situations where alternative employment prospects are dim, governments have been reluctant to proceed with privatization for fear of the political consequences arising from the mass shedding of labour. This is what happened in Nigeria following the campaign launched by the Nigerian Labour Congress in the mid-1980s. Strong pressure from trade unions led to little progress being made in the government's privatization programme for a number of years.

Political leaders are also sensitive to privatizing public entities which have served as important vehicles of state patronage. Privatization of parastatals poses a threat to the patronage opportunities of those in power whose capacity to consolidate their position may be undermined. As Uganda's privatization co-ordinator stated: 'over the years politicians have used public enterprises as centres of patronage to reward or appease relatives, friends, political supporters or as sources of profit in one way or another'.[6] The need to retain control over patronage resources deriving from such politically indispensable concerns as state-owned enterprises becomes even more essential at a time when structural adjustment programmes are eliminating opportunities for patronage in other economic and political arenas. Moreover, top officials and politicians have not wanted to lose the financial perquisites and benefits deriving from their privileged access to patronage and spoils. As a government-owned newspaper in Uganda stated in an editorial, state firms are 'cash cows which can be milked by the ruling class' and 'the elite did not want the state to surrender its control over ... parastatals because it would lose the easy pickings it had enjoyed since independence'.[7] For various reasons, therefore, state elites have preferred to retain a large public enterprise sector, devising instead ways of improving its efficiency and effectiveness.[8]

Ideological factors have presented further obstacles to privatization. Private capitalism may be ideologically unacceptable to socialistically inclined political leaders. President Robert Mugabe of Zimbabwe has on many occasions vowed to maintain state economic control as the only way to mitigate capitalism's 'venomous head', deriving from its tendency towards profiteering and speculation. 'This we must guard against', he warned, arguing for a continuation of 'socialism' in key economic sectors.[9] Similarly in Tanzania, where even though the closing years of President Julius Nyerere's nearly two decades of socialist rule had been marked by severe economic hardship, President Ali Hassan Mwinyi's successor government was reluctant to abandon key elements of socialism, retaining an abiding conviction that the state rather than private enterprise was the only way to build a more just, humane and egalitarian society. Tanzania's political leadership continued to exhibit ideological preferences opposed to private ownership of the means of production as well as the new market reforms, including reform of the parastatal sector.

Finally, the possibility of important publicly-owned assets being purchased by foreigners often arouses vocal nationalist sentiments;

divestiture of state companies to foreign private owners may be viewed as inimical to the national interest. In Zambia, opposition politicians have accused the government, through its privatization policies, of 'selling the country to the South Africans' as well as to resident expatriates; such criticisms served to slow down the divestiture process. In Zimbabwe, local business organizations have called upon the government to take 'full cognisance of the historical economic disparities' of the country in its privatization programme. The President of the Indigenous Business Development Centre declared that it 'would not accept any form of privatisation ... which is done outside the context of a deliberate programme for the indigenisation of the economy'.[10] In Kenya, the prospect of foreign as well as certain local ethnic groups being the principal beneficiaries also stalled that country's privatization programme because it was perceived as augmenting the economic power of Asian and Kikuyu businessmen. 'Though the government agreed to the principle of privatisation a whole decade ago', wrote the editor of the *Weekly Review*, 'no parastatal has been privatised to this day. The reason is that the only people with the wealth to buy up the privatised parastatals are Asian Kenyans and the people of central province.'[11] Privatizing public enterprises to foreign investors may not only jeopardize popular support for the government in power; fears are also expressed that it may enhance foreign and resident expatriate economic and political control of African countries.

If political factors constitute serious constraints to privatization, on the other hand, few political supports for privatization exist. As in other regions of the world, state enterprise divestiture in Africa is 'not likely in the medium term to improve income distribution, to create many new jobs, or to appeal to a broad range of functional interests in society'.[12] Apart from a few economists and technocrats within government and some business entrepreneurs, privatization has not achieved much popular backing, at least in its early stages. Some governments have made conscious efforts to create political and social constituencies supportive of divestment. Pita Agbese has argued that the Nigerian Government relied on abstract appeals to national interest as well as moral precepts to base its case for privatization. It was contended that state-owned enterprises were corrupt, had benefited only a small number of Nigerians, had failed to improve the material conditions of the majority of the population, and had diverted essential resources from the more needy sectors of the economy. Public ownership of enterprises could not be morally justified. By reducing the role of government in the economy, these moral vices would be eradicated. Corruption would be minimized and a more equitable and efficient distribution of societal wealth established. But moral arguments were unable to elicit a wider constituency for privatization. They had to be accompanied by repressive measures against trade unionists and other critics of privatization.[13]

In Nigeria as elsewhere in sub-Saharan Africa, the pace of privatization was slow at the outset. State divestiture was implemented in a hesitant fashion. Where divestiture occurred, the state assets disposed of were small and low-value firms, a number of which were previously under private ownership,[14] and where fewer jobs would be lost than in larger public enterprises with far fewer political risks. Moreover, more prevalent than asset transfers were leasing and management contract arrangements as well as liqidations of insolvent enterprises. Because the latter have often been far less politically contentious than outright sales (especially to foreign owners), African governments have preferred them. Closures and liqidations have constituted the most common form of privatization, as in Guinea where 70 per cent of the divestitures in the late 1980s involved the liquidation of non-viable retail outlets.[15]

The early 1990s saw more vigorous pressure from international lending agencies on African governments to prosecute privatization in a more resolute fashion. International lenders sought a redefinition of the role of the public enterprise sector as a whole, advocating that state enterprise involvement be limited to a small number of strategic state firms. African rulers were subjected to a growing barrage of criticism regarding their state-owned companies. Parastatal performance was said to have been rarely in the public interest. Their economic record had been universally poor, and their socio-political purposes had also been far from achieved. Publicly-owned concerns had been misused for the political and personal interests of state elites. As a Kenyan journalist put it, privatization in his country 'will plug a notorious loophole for the plunder of public funds and relieve taxpayers from shoring up money-guzzling parastatals'.[16] Moreover, public enterprise reform efforts had proved less than successful in improving performance. In particular, political considerations had impeded effective implementation of commercial reforms. In the view of the external financial institutions, such has been the extent of the failure and political manipulation of the public enterprise sector that its scale and scope should be drastically cut back.[17]

With international financial institutions at the forefront, there has been increasingly forceful pressure on Africa's political leaders to reduce public economic operations, and especially to diminish the overall involvement of the state-controlled enterprises. The leverage exercised by powerful lending agencies increased as external sources of finance declined and the domestic funds for modernizing and running state firms became so limited. Some two-thirds of the IMF and World Bank structural adjustment lending to African governments in 1989 to

1991 involved parastatal reform, and a high proportion was concerned with the privatization of public companies.[18] Partly as a result of such financial leverage, most government leaders began asserting commitments to reduce the size and scope of their public enterprise sectors.

In fact, most governments publicly affirmed their commitment to more state enterprise divestiture as well as embarking on quite extensive privatization programmes. Even those led by long-time proponents of state-led development and economic nationalism, such as Zimbabwe's Robert Mugabe, attempted to dispose of some of their state-run enterprises. Some governments have proclaimed a desire to privatize virtually all their state-owned firms. President Frederick Chiluba is reported to have said 'we will privatize everything in Zambia'. Intense donor pressure doubtless induced Africa's leaders to agree to privatization. But there were also a variety of mainly pragmatic reasons, among them the growing awareness of the intolerable fiscal burdens that the operating deficits of poorly performing public enterprises imposed on public finances at a time of severe economic crisis and financial austerity, as well as that privatization was an important means of reducing public deficits. For example, because Tanzania's state enterprise sector was 'indebted to the tune almost of Tsh. one trillion and making huge losses,' for President Mwinyi 'the decision to reform and privatize parastatal enterprises is an economic imperative'.[19]

More and more leaders openly acknowledged as well that state parastatals had had a negative impact on African economies. Africa's economic difficulties were seen as due to an excessive state enterprise presence which had failed to perform adequately. Many politicians and bureaucrats no longer favoured the idea of numerous government-owned organizations selling goods and services to the public. As the Zambian Finance Minister put it: 'Our experience conclusively shows that the state is incapable of managing commercial activities and that bureaucrats cannot run business enterprises'.[20] Moreover, some form of state divestiture was accepted as a more efficient way of providing goods and services. 'Eventually', argued Ugandan President Yoweri Museveni, 'by selling off public enterprises we shall gain from the new jobs created, increased production and more taxes when they are revived'.[21] Public opinion was also moving gradually in favour of privatization. In Zambia, as a result of the old state-owned system there 'were no goods in the shops, and you would wait five hours for a bus. So the political outrage that could create a climate for privatisation was there.'[22] In many African countries, urban public sentiment had expressed some disapproval not only of the economic shortcomings of state firms but also of their use by politicians for political and personal purposes. Survey research in urban Uganda showed the public increasingly viewing state enterprise as inefficient and its divestiture as necessary and beneficial to the economy.[23]

To be sure, privatization remained contentious and presented political difficulties for the authorities. Sharp differences still prevailed within political leaderships. Uganda's Finance Minister, J. Mayanja-Nkanji, has said on numerous occasions that 'many in the cabinet and parliament were opposed to privatization' which 'made it difficult for Government to proceed', and 'that it would take time for everyone to be brought on board to support the process'.[24] But ownership by the state was no longer so widely perceived as essential to the economic transformation of African countries as it was in the 1960s and 1970s. A domestic lobby in favour of privatization was gradually building up. Nearly everywhere plans for quite extensive privatization were being proposed while divestiture was also beginning to be actively pursued. It was becoming apparent that the existence of a large and wide-ranging state enterprise system was under siege.

The number of state-owned enterprises opening up to private sector participation was increasing. Many public firms, including some major ones, were being approved for sale. Important public concerns which governments originally intended to retain in state ownership were being offered for divestment. The number of publicly-owned enterprises deemed to be of strategic importance, and thus remaining under state control, was declining. In Guinea, for example, public enterprises in banking, insurance, water, power, and telecommunications saw their management being privatized as well as some ownership. Even state enterprises which had served as valuable vehicles of political patronage were being put forward for privatization. For example, the preparation of the Uganda Commercial Bank for sale was seen 'as a test of the government's commitment to privatisation'.

> By putting on the market the one institution from which the political class has fattened, the government will demonstrate that it is willing to cut its own pocket. If it had backed away from a UCB sell-off, the privatisation programme would have stalled and the credibility of past sales of state companies would have suffered. If a big institution like UCB goes, the sale of other companies becomes insignificant and the case for keeping any of the big corporations which have not yet been privatised collapses.[25]

Throughout sub-Saharan Africa, moves were under way to reduce the size and scope of state ownership.[26]

But although some progress in asset divestiture was recorded, state sector divestment was not extensive in most countries. Actual state divestiture transactions remained small in comparison to the number of parastatals in existence. Between 1988 and 1993, Africa saw only a modest number of divestitures which 'left the continent with fewer privatizations than any developing region'. By mid-1993, the total value of the state firms sold in Nigeria amounted to less than 2 per cent of the government's portfolio.[27] Similarly in Zambia where within eighteen months of the start of the five-year privatization plan in 1993, only a dozen of around 150 parastatal companies had been privatized. In Uganda, in spite of President Museveni's full support for the sale of loss-making state companies – an attitude characterized by his stating: 'I'd rather sell off all these enterprises to foreigners than keep them in the hands of thieving state bureaucrats' – the country's interim parliament directed the government to suspend the sale of public enterprises in early 1993. Although the privatization process restarted later in the year, by early 1995 less than a sixth of Uganda's state firms had been sold off. By late 1994, less than one-fifth of Africa's state firms were estimated to have been sold off, leased or liquidated.

The size of the public enterprise sector and its share in several economic areas (manufacturing, transport, banking, tourism) had only been partially reduced.[28] State portfolios continued to comprise many public companies. In 1991, the World Bank complained of the large number of non-strategic state concerns – particularly commercial and industrial ones in potentially competitive markets – which the Ghanaian Government wanted to retain in the public sector. In 1994, it voiced similar concern regarding the Ugandan Government's plans to retain control of, or remain actively involved in, many important commercial industries. Moreover, governments continued to invest in public companies, even occasionally setting up new ones. In Uganda, the establishment of the National Enterprise Corporation (the trading arm of the military), as well as the creation of the Uganda Air Cargo Ltd., in 1994 ran contrary to government commitments to disengage from commercially oriented enterprises. Large subsidies continued to be paid to state companies which were assured of ongoing government support. In Ghana, the budgetary burden of the public enterprise sector caused serious worry; in 1991, the World Bank found particularly alarming the level of indirect government transfers to state-owned firms. In Uganda as well, a large public enterprise sector prevailed despite strong political commitment to privatization. It seriously burdened public finances. Direct and indirect subsidies to state enterprises in 1994 were estimated at $180 million, nearly three times the government's contribution to the development budget.[29] Also in Ghana and Uganda and elsewhere in Africa, governments continued to intervene in the pricing, procurement, marketing and employment decisions of parastatals. Only a few of them had lived up to their commitments to cut back the state enterprise sector drastically as well as permit those public companies remaining in government ownership to operate more autonomously.

While African governments were divesting themselves of some of their public enterprises, they were also establishing many new statutory authorities. The 1990s saw some of the following authorities being set up in Uganda: Uganda Revenue Authority, Uganda Investment Authority, Uganda Coffee Development Authority, National Environment Management Authority, Uganda Drugs Authority, Uganda Wild Life Authority, and the Capital Markets Authority. Similar organizations pro-liferated in other African countries. Little critical research has been car-ried out on such institutions, and particularly their relationship to the privatization process. But the following comments on the Ugandan authorities are worth quoting at length:

> they are incompatible with the spirit of privatisation whose goal is to scale down the scope of government, especially in the control and management of the economy. The[ir] performance hardly suggests that they will be more efficient, cost effective, less bureaucratic and more 'public spirited' than the corporations of old. On the contrary, the new institutions seem to be afflicted by the same ills of corruption, political patronage, overmanning, red tape and lack of accountability which eventually led to the demise of the old corporations.[30]

By the mid-1990s, privatization had not led to a substantial reduction in the size of the state enterprise sector or a drastic revision of the bal-ance between states and markets in Africa. Most governments pro-ceeded cautiously as regards state divestiture. At the pace at which privatization was taking place, it would be many years before a markedly different balance between private and public sector activity in the economies of sub-Saharan countries would be achieved. Moreover, the fact that most of the parastatals being privatized were small (in terms of assets and employment) and that many of them were loss-makers rather than profitable ones, meant that, despite some rethinking on the economic role of the state, privatization had so far hardly altered fundamentally governmental attitudes towards the role of state-owned enterprises in the economy. Rarely had gov-ernments divested their holdings in 'strategic' enterprises, such as important transport parastatals, mining corporations, public utilities, and official marketing boards. State monopolies (such as in telecom-munication services and water) and oligopolies (as in banking) also remained.

The process of privatization in Ghana under the Provisional National Defence Council (PNDC) would appear to conform to this picture. Very limited public divestiture was, in fact, implemented. Was this another example of an African country where implementation lagged behind stated declarations of intent to engage in divestiture? The following case study examines this particular question up to the time the PNDC was dissolved in January 1993.

The politics of state enterprise divestiture in Ghana up to the early 1990s[31]

Accepting Public Divestiture

When elements within the military overthrew the civilian government of Ghana on 31 December 1981, they inherited an economy in severe crisis.[32] By any conceivable yardstick, Ghana's economy verged on disaster. The new PNDC Government committed itself to a process of economic reform. In April 1983, it launched one of the most far-reaching structural adjustment programmes undertaken anywhere in Africa.[33] Under this Economic Recovery Programme (ERP), so-called, the government adopted profound policy reforms designed to bring about a turnaround of the country's devastated economy. Public enterprise reform and divestiture constituted an integral part of these reforms.

Espousal of the need for public enterprise reform and divestiture was based on the poor performance of the state-owned sector. Public enterprises had incurred large deficits; their total operating deficit in 1982 amounted to over 3 per cent of GDP. They had also become a significant drain on the government's budget. During the early part of the 1980s, support for them ranged from 10 per cent of government expenditure in 1982 to 8 per cent in 1986.[34] And the sector was a burden on government in various other ways, such as requiring indirect support on tax and loan arrears.

Multilateral institutions were at the forefront in encouraging the PNDC Government to accept rationalization of the parastatal sector as part of the wider reforms incorporated in its programme of structural adjustment. Promptings from the International Monetary Fund and the World Bank were influential in Ghana's decision to reform or divest itself of poorly performing state enterprises. In 1987 the World Bank and the PNDC concluded a development credit agreement on public enterprise reform, including state divestiture.

But this agreement also reflected recognition within the PNDC that a large portfolio of state enterprises had severely burdened the state's administrative and financial resources, and that, given the generally negative performance of parastatals, a re-evaluation of state involvement in them was necessary. The 'perpetual losses' of state companies 'drain investible public resources', and impose a serious drain on the government's budget. To 'check this enormous drain', the government contemplated divesting itself of especially loss-making state companies.[35] It was also aware that if it retained such a large portfolio of state enterprises it would require massive resources for their recapitalization and rehabilitation into viable entities. In 'the face of the many other competing demands', most notably in the provision of health facilities, education, roads, water, electricity, and security, the government would have 'to resort to additional large-scale borrowing' which was untenable.[36] It was partly because of the anticipated budgetary and economic benefits that could be achieved, and partly because a comprehensive programme of macroeconomic reform recommended by the international development agencies was already being implemented, that the PNDC accepted the necessity of reform of the public enterprise sector.

If arguments such as these were paramount in moving the government to accept public divestment, for those technocratic elements within the State Enterprises Commission (the state agency entrusted with the monitoring of public enterprises), state divestiture heralded the attainment of wider economic objectives. 'Governments in all countries have proven themselves incapable of generating sustained real growth and permanently improved living standards...' On the other hand, 'the zeal and zest of private ownership is the route to sustained economic growth'. But in Ghana 'the state sector is crowding out the private sector'. Divestment was, therefore, also viewed as motivating the promotion and development of the private sector and thereby 'generating overall efficiency in, and growth of, an economy'.[37]

The question of state divestiture was intimately linked with the issue of the role and scope of the state-owned sector. At the highest levels of the government, discussion took place regarding the size and role of parastatals in the Ghanaian economy. Since independence, primary emphasis for economic development had been placed on the state, not the private sector. But now, and particularly at the behest of the World Bank, the PNDC Government began to consider a shift in the balance between the public and private sectors. The sheer weight of evidence demonstrating that public enterprise had performed poorly pointed to the need for its role to be reappraised. At the same time, some advocation of the virtues of private enterprise found a response within the government.[38] In re-examining the boundary between the two sectors, the PNDC decided, in early 1988, to reduce the scope of the public sector to a core of eighteen key state enterprises. These core enterprises – mainly in the mining, energy, transportation, and utilities sectors as well as in wholesale and retail trade and cocoa marketing – would be subjected to measures to improve their efficiency. On the other hand, the large bulk of non-strategic public enterprises – mainly in manufacturing industry – would be available for divestiture and privatization.

Reducing the size and scope of the state-owned sector has presented a major barrier to privatization elsewhere in Africa. It has often been seen as being against the political interests of political leaders. Divestiture of public enterprises would undermine the government's ability to use them as an instrument of patronage and employment creation. In the case of Ghana, as we shall see, political considerations also affected the actual course of the divestiture. But in deciding to commit itself to a policy of divestiture, the PNDC Government appeared willing to confront vested interests with a stake in continued government ownership. Given the fact that the PNDC was a relatively new regime as well as one with a military basis, it was perhaps in a better position to make a break with the past regarding the dominant role of the state enterprise sector than would have been the case with a more longstanding and constitutionally elected government. But perhaps the prime reason for the PNDC accepting divestiture was that its political survival was clearly contingent upon implementing the reforms advocated by the external agencies. Only thus would it stave off its external creditors as well as acquire the foreign infusions of financial support so essential to enable it to manage the country's chronic economic crisis.

In 1988 an official announcement was made on the first batch of 32 state enterprises from which the government intended to withdraw. These were essentially loss-making public concerns. Indeed, liquidations of at least a dozen state enterprises were expected.[39] Clearly, at that stage, the PNDC Government wanted to proceed cautiously. It was reluctant to divest profitable public companies, although some profitable ones were included after the government recognized that this 'could have benefits', such as providing 'some momentum to the programme'.[40] Its thinking on which enterprises were available for outright sale was that they should be non-strategic ones that had 'proven to be consistently unprofitable and unable to pay dividends to government, and where it would over-stretch the capacity of Government to use its own resources or mobilise external resources to bring the SOE back to life'.[41]

Which state enterprises were to be in the first list to be divested was the result of nearly a year of intermittent discussions, involving government leaders, state enterprise officials, and the World Bank. Protracted negotiations also ensued regarding the scope of further divestiture. The debate partly revolved around ideological differences (supporters of state economic intervention versus proponents of the free-market) and partly around the political difficulties of selling state assets to foreigners as well as laying off workers. Eventually, in July 1989, a further 46 public enterprises were declared available for divestiture. This list was not made public – perhaps because a consensus within the PNDC could not be reached – but the Divestiture Implementation Committee (DIC) was informed that it could proceed to prepare companies on that list for divestiture. The list contained many profitable state concerns, including some which the government had earlier deemed strategic. In early 1990, PNDC leaders publicly announced that all but 22 state enterprises were being offered for divestiture. As regards the strategic enterprises, these were concentrated essentially in natural resources and the public utilities but they were also involved in the vitally important cocoa industry. The 1990 announcement may have been made to demonstrate official commitment to implementing divestiture at a time when the government was seeking greater private investment, as well as to deflect mounting World Bank disquiet at the lack of progress in the divestiture programme. What is apparent, however, is that, although it had been accepted much earlier within the PNDC, it was only now that the government made explicit that it was not concerned to maintain a large state-owned sector.

In 1988, the first year in which the divestiture programme was actually begun, no state-owned enterprises were divested. By the end of 1989, a few public concerns had been recommended for divestiture by the DIC but approval was still being awaited from the PNDC. In 1990, however, some progress began to be recorded: just over 20 public enterprises were actually closed down or divested. Of these about one-half entailed liquidation of non-viable state firms, another 8 very small concerns were sold, and the remaining few were leased or became joint venture arrangements. Let us consider, first, why only a limited divestiture took place.

Political Impediments to State Divestiture
The sheer technical, informational, and organizational difficulties have been cited as major barriers to progress in Ghana's divestiture programme. Divestment is technically one of the most difficult of all structural adjustment measures. Diverse skills are needed, and Ghana found it difficult to acquire the requisite high-level technical personnel. The paucity of data available on state enterprises, as well as the problems of identifying and valuing assets and liabilities, militated against the speedy implementation of the divestiture programme. The legal procedures to liquidate public companies also turned out to be unduly lengthy. And the use of a foreign consultant firm proved unsatisfactory, the contract with Price Waterhouse being cancelled.

In the view of many Ghanaian officials, however, the prime obstacle to divestment was political.[42] Politics influenced what state firms were to be divested, and to whom, as well as on what terms. And the politics itself was influenced by previous attempts at state enterprise divestiture.

Divestiture was not something new in Ghana. Memories of divestment under the National Liberation Council (NLC) in the late 1960s weighed heavily on the programme of the late 1980s. What happened under the NLC created such a political furore that the PNDC Government was anxious to avoid provoking a similar situation. Criticism of the NLC privatizations revolved around their being detrimental to the interests of the state. In 1967 and 1968, for example, there was a public outcry regarding the sale of the State Pharmaceutical Company to a private American firm, and the sale offer had to be withdrawn. Public opposition focused on the terms of the agreement, 'it being alleged that the government had sold the factory too cheaply'. In addition, 'the fact that the sale represented a transfer of assets from Ghanaian to foreign ownership ... gave heat to the controversy'.[43] Not only did such criticisms hinder the efforts of the NLC to reduce state participation in the economy, but they also resonated in the PNDC's divestiture programme, strongly affecting its implementation.

To which private-sector groups state enterprises should be divested remained a politically contentious issue. Selling publicly-owned assets into foreign ownership was especially sensitive politically; at times, it became politically untenable. In listing the criteria that should be adopted in determining which state enterprises should be privatized, a senior official argued that 'ideal candidates should possess' a 'minimum need for majority foreign ownership to minimise political impact'.[44] For many Ghanaians, public enterprises were a symbol of national sovereignty. Their divestiture to foreign buyers was perceived in nationalist idioms as selling 'our patrimony' and 'our heritage' to outsiders.[45] Such nationalist feelings notwithstanding, the PNDC Government invited foreign investors to participate in its divestiture programme. But in rationalizing the need to seek foreign capital, the PNDC member in charge of divestiture declared that this was 'a disgrace to the nation'. He continued: in requesting foreign participation to run state-owned companies, 'we have let down our forefathers who fought for independence'.[46]

For reasons connected with attracting greater foreign private investment, the PNDC accepted that foreigners could acquire certain state parastatals. But, concerned not to arouse nationalist sentiments, the government was hesitant about divesting public firms to foreign capital. The desire to avoid nationalist opposition may have influenced the choice of state enterprises marked for divestiture in the first list of 1988. Most were clearly moribund, and it appears that the political climate at that time was conducive to the sale of only such loss-making propositions. Moreover, in order not to forfeit public support, the government favoured a form of privatization to foreigners that primarily involved joint ventures and leasing arrangements. Various official statements advocated divestiture to foreign investors 'in partnership with Government or the local private sector'. In this way, the PNDC could acquire the means to resuscitate a state enterprise whilst retaining ownership of it. Leasing and joint venture arrangements were politically more acceptable than outright sales, and were resorted to in nearly all divestitures to foreigners in the manufacturing (glass, paper conversion) and service (hotels) sectors.

Privatization in Ghana also faced opposition from the trade unions. Partly this was on ideological grounds. A notice in the Trade Union Congress Hall read: 'Public service – it's yours; Private service – it's theirs. Join the fight to put public needs before private greed.' But it was the fear of large-scale lay-offs of workers that constituted the main impediment to the PNDC divestiture programme just as it did in the earlier NLC one. Organized labour expressed severe anxiety about divestment being accompanied by mass job losses. A member of the Ghana Trade Union Congress stated, 'It is well known that all African governments are the largest employers of the labour force. The right of the people to work will be curtailed if the public enterprises are privatized.'[47] The government shared these fears and wanted to prevent an increase in the already high levels of unemployment in the country. In the few divestitures that took place, it was clear that the enterprises affected were small in terms of numbers employed. The initial list of 32 enterprises offered for sale had a total of about 12,000 employees, out of a total of 480,000 in the parastatal sector. As for the large-scale public employers such as the State Fishing Corporation, the Food Production Corporation, and most state companies in the mining sector, these were not divested, partly because of the political consequences that would arise from the mass shedding of labour in the state-owned sector.

It came as a major shock to the government to learn that its divestiture programme, designed to achieve budgetary benefits, had the potential of becoming a substantial fiscal burden. Not only had Ghana's state-owned enterprises been subject to gross overstaffing in the past, but collective bargaining agreements were concluded in the 1970s which granted employees relatively generous pension and termination provisions. Retirement benefit obligations to existing public enterprise employees were estimated in 1988 to be over 100 billion *cedis*, an amount approaching Ghana's annual revenue collection. In 1988 and 1989, it was estimated that at least 40,000 employees would leave the parastatal sector and that their total end-of-service benefits would be between 16 and 18 billion *cedis* (or between US$71 and $79 million). Given their weak financial position (for some, liabilities exceeded the value of their assets), state enterprises were unable to meet these costs. Nor did the government have the budgetary resources to finance such liabilities. The inability to pay for these terminal benefits brought divestiture to a virtual standstill. Predictably, the trade unions called for the collective agreements to be honoured. At times suggestions were made whereby government shares in public companies would be sold to workers in exchange for payment of end-of-service benefits. But nothing came of this. In October 1990, the government asked all public enterprises to consider renegotiating terminal benefits to levels they could afford to pay. Unless the government could modify the agreements, its privatization programme would remain captive to these massive liabilities.[48]

During the first two years of its divestiture programme, disagreements within the PNDC hampered the government in carrying out its stated divestiture intentions. Differences between the more populist and nationalist elements and those of a more technocratic and pragmatic bent prevented decisions being arrived at as to which state enterprises should be divested. Because of the absence of agreement, the 1989 divestiture list was never made public. Moreover, some within the government advocated that greater opportunity be offered to workers in state companies and the general public to acquire shares, whilst others pointed to the takeover of government concerns by militant workers in 1982 as standing proof of the failure of worker ownership and management. Such differences, however, became tempered. A growing sense of past policies having failed obliged many within the government to question earlier commitments to socialism and economic nationalism and also to be more willing to adopt market-based economic reforms such as state divestiture. In 1990 the political leadership presented greater unanimity of purpose over divestiture, with differences only on matters of detail such as whether to pay terminal benefits in part or in full.

During the NLC period, rumours of state-owned businesses being 'disposed of cheaply behind closed doors to favoured cronies' were rampant.[49] The PNDC Government studiously avoided being accused of selling public firms to relatives and political loyalists. But a number of less than fully transparent transactions generated some controversy regarding the government's impartiality. Most of the limited number of divestitures that occurred took the form of private placements. In the absence of a capital market in Ghana until late 1990, private offerings were the primary form of divestiture. A number of these were surrounded with rumour and suspicion. As elsewhere in Africa, and as considered in the following section, political considerations very likely influenced the disposal of assets of state companies, some of which which were typically placed into the hands of political associates as well as politically acceptable foreigners.

Ghana found that its state-owned enterprise sector was a major burden on its public finances. There was also an awareness that the public sector was grossly inefficient. Both budgetary and efficiency considerations as well as promptings from the international financial institutions made the PNDC Government see the desirability of privatization and led it to accept a reversal of earlier state policies of widespread public ownership. Although the scale of privatization was a matter of continuing debate, the PNDC proposed divestiture in many areas of state economic activity. But implementation lagged behind stated intentions, and although the divestiture programme was no longer stalled (as it was in 1989), it was moving ahead only slowly. In 1991, when this research was conducted, ways of prevailing over existing political obstructions were required if declarations of intent were to be matched by successful implementation. Three years later, reports from Ghana indicated that privatization continued to be limited – only one-fifth of state-owned enterprises had been divested – in spite of the incessant pressure exerted by the World Bank for greater state enterprise divestiture.[50]

Progress and politicization of privatization in the 1990s

Ugandan, Kenyan, Ghanaian and other African illustrations
Ghana's experience with privatization could be replicated elsewhere on the continent. The evidence from most African countries shows that privatization has been a slow and faltering process. At times, governments have even contemplated restructuring rather than divesting their public sector enterprises. But actual commercialization has been limited and confined to the few strategic parastatals which have remained under state ownership and control. The large majority of state-owned companies have been scheduled for some form of privatization, although actual disposal of them has remained modest.

Privatization has continued to provoke a potent mixture of fears and concerns. Progress in privatization has been constrained by fear of the loss of patronage opportunities deriving especially from the large state enterprise monopolies. Top state personnel have been concerned about losing their latitude to use public undertakings to consolidate themselves in power. But they have also not wanted to forfeit the financial and other benefits arising from their privileged access to state enterprises. As a World Bank report on Ghana put it: reducing 'the privileges granted to public enterprises would hurt the powerful political appointees who control a huge amount of public resources'.[51]

Considerable concern has also been expressed about the acquisition of parastatal assets by foreigners, especially by Asians in East Africa. The Kenyan Minister for Commerce and Industry called for the privatization programme to be suspended if it was established that indigenous Kenyans were unable to buy the firms being sold.[52] In December 1995, the new Tanzanian Government – under pressure about public firms being sold off to Asians and other foreigners – was reported to have halted privatization until a more acceptable way could be found to implement it.[53] Many governments have also feared the consequences of the sale of large-scale state enterprises in a context of already high levels of unemployment. Opposition to labour retrenchment has been sufficiently worrying to limit divestitures to minor public enterprises in terms of assets. Nearly three years after Uganda embarked on privatization in 1992, its small number of divestitures accounted for less than 5 per cent of total employment in the parastatal sector. To be sure, the political and social obstacles to privatization have begun to be addressed. In Uganda, various government leaders have been arguing that privatization is likely to lead eventually to increased rather than diminished job opportunities as well as improved wages and benefits for workers. Moreover, some emphasis has been placed on official regulatory mechanisms safeguarding the interests of consumers and the general public. But everywhere fears and concerns have made implementation of privatization a gradual and limited process confined mainly to small-scale enterprises.

Yet evidence is becoming available of a growing momentum towards privatization. Both the scope and pace of divestiture are on the increase. For example, significant reductions in government holdings have started or are planned in Kenya. 'We were very slow at the beginning but the pace is now faster', reported the head of Kenya's privatization programme.[54] Similarly, the Ghanaian privatization programme gathered speed in early 1994 when the NDC Government (the elected version of the PNDC) announced its intention to divest from several of the country's large, profitable firms. Indeed, most sub-Saharan governments have proclaimed their intentions to divest from an ever-increasing number of public enterprises, including the transfer of larger strategic companies to the private sector. Some governments have proposed the extension of privatization to the mining sector. In Ghana, the government's shareholding in Ashanti Goldfields – the country's largest goldmine – has been reduced substantially through international flotation. In Zambia, the government is planning the sale of shares in the large state-owned Zambia Consolidated Copper Mines, the cornerstone of the economy. Other countries have begun considering the sale of shares in monopoly public utilities. Côte d'Ivoire has been involved in the partial sale of the national electricity utility, while Uganda is negotiating the privatization of the Posts and Telecommunications Corporation. Privatization of state-owned agricultural boards is also under preparation in many countries. Liberalization of food crops and to a lesser extent agricultural export marketing has taken place in Tanzania: the grain marketing parastatal, the National Milling Corporation, has seen its marketed supply of grain plummet from 90 to a mere 2 per cent. And, finally, as in Uganda, divestiture of the large, state-owned commercial banks has begun to be implemented.

Not all countries are speeding towards privatization. Political leaders in Ethiopia and Zimbabwe, for example, are insistent that specific sectors need to remain in state hands in the national interest. But the move to transfer government businesses to the private sector is gathering momentum. The leverage exerted by external agencies, especially the World Bank, is an important determinant of the growing privatization drive. International donors have expressed much concern about African divestiture programmes not meeting their targets for privatization. 'If current conditions prevailed', commented a confidential World Bank report on Uganda's divestiture programme in early 1995, 'less than half of the public enterprise sector would be divested by 1999 and the burden of sustaining many loss-making parastatals would jeopardise continued economic growth.' African governments have come under renewed external pressure to accelerate and deepen their divestiture programmes. In early 1995, President Museveni accepted World Bank recommendations and committed his government explicitly to privatizing 85 per cent of Uganda's public enterprise sector by the end of 1997. Similarly, the Ghanaian Government had come under strong donor pressure in 1993 to effect farther and faster divestiture.

International lending institutions are not only intensifying their pressure but are also providing increasing financial and technical assistance to African governments to enhance progress in their privatization programmes. In Ghana and Uganda, for example, diverse divestiture methods have been adopted to broaden the equity base and thus give privatization greater interest among the local population. Public offerings to small investors of more profitable concerns have been introduced and arrangements for employee participation have also been initiated, both to mobilize popular support. It is hoped that such methods of sale will deflect fears of foreigners being the chief beneficiaries of privatization. Uganda has also seen the launching of a public education programme in 1996 to popularize privatization. By emphasizing the many benefits of privatization, – 'Apart from tax revenue Ugandans have benefitted from the new investments by getting employment opportunities for better pay, the new owners have brought in investment and new technology and home made products on the market have increased, diversified and become cheaper'[55] – the publicity campaign hopes to mobilize its wider public acceptance.

But domestic economic and political factors have also been of importance. Partly state elites have begun recognizing the serious economic failings of state-owned enterprises, particularly the extent of their chronic deficits (often the single largest component of a country's overall budget deficit). Partly also there has been the awareness that chronically loss-making parastatals cannot be permitted to persist at a time of serious public deficits. And partly too there have been serious constraints on the financial resources available to operate and modernize state-owned enterprises.

As important has been the fact that the political obstacles to privatization have been much weaker than expected. To be sure, selling public assets to foreigners continues to arouse much criticism, at times stridently nationalist. But, otherwise, the constituency for retaining government economic entities is of limited political influence. Aside from a few intellectuals and political activists advocating state ownership and control primarily for ideological reasons, popular support for poorly performing parastatals has been hardly evident. Moreover, although opposition from public sector employees and trade unions has arisen, quite forcefully, for instance in Cameroon,[56] worker resistance to privatization has been remarkable by its generally minimal occurrence. To be sure, worker opposition has erupted in many countries including Ghana where, especially in 1993, the Trade Union Congress attempted to block privatization and also demanded a halt to the retrenchment of public-sector employees. But generally worker agitation has been limited (perhaps because so many public firms have been moribund and their privatization has not entailed many job losses), and African governments have been able to carry out their divestitures without provoking much labour unrest. Where organized labour has mounted a challenge, governments have, through a combination of compensation or severance packages and some coercion, been able to soften or defuse it.[57] There is also some evidence of popular disillusionment with the functioning of state-owned enterprises, not just in sectors such as telephones and electricity which affect the interests of the better-off, but also in crop marketing, bus transport and retail trade which concern the majority of the population. Popular discontent has provided some political backing for governments to dispose of ineffectual state firms, although there is much unbudging hostility to these companies falling into non-indigenous hands. In a context where political constraints, although important, are not insuperable, and in a situation where external institutions are providing much-needed support to help ease the costs of economic adjustment, political leaders have begun grasping the opportunities emerging to engage in privatization.

Perhaps as significant in the calculations of politicians, however, has been the extent to which privatization has endangered the stability of their regimes. Where state elites have been able to direct and manage closely the privatization process and, in particular, ensure that privatisation transactions maintain rather than undermine political support for themselves, then governments have been less unwilling to undertake public sector divestiture programmes. Those in control of the state have used their positions to determine the sale of public enterprises in a manner that has helped them to consolidate their own power. Small groups of state personnel have managed and concluded privatization decisions, hardly consulting with interests and individuals outside of the state. And senior politicians have had the final say as regards divestiture decisions. Public information on divestiture has invariably been limited and selective. Nearly everywhere privatization has been a far from open and transparent process. Pointing particularly to Kenya, the *East African* referred to 'the murky nature of the procedures whereby some state enterprises have gone into private hands'. But it also added that country after country in Africa had failed 'to get rid of parastatal organisations cleanly, quickly, openly and, with luck, profitably'.[58] In Kenya, the assets of many public companies have not been valued, and their sale not advertised publicly. In his annual report for 1994/95, Kenya's Controller and Auditor-General echoed these criticisms. He declared that the records kept on the sale of parastatals did not include information on the sale process – tendering, valuation and criteria for selecting buyers. No information was provided regarding the sale or disposal of 52 of the 61 state enterprises divested.

Allegations of discriminatory and non-transparent transactions favouring those with political connections have become pervasive. A British magazine suggested that some of Kenya's parastatals were sold 'at below market rates to influential public figures through private negotiations while higher bids from purely commercial sources were rejected'.[59] The Kenyan divestiture programme 'is geared to favour the current political elite'.[60] In Nigeria in the late 1980s, military officers under the military regime are alleged to have acquired the majority of the shares in four-fifths of the 100 state-owned firms that were privatized.[61] In Côte d'Ivoire, Guinea, and Zaire (Congo-Kinshasa), there was much evidence of public assets being dispensed to supporters and allies of political leaders.[62] In Senegal public enterprises were privatized to the relatives and clients of the political elite.[63] In Congo-Brazzaville a trade union leader reportedly remarked: 'Really and truly the people who are lining up to buy the companies up for sale are none other than members of the government'.[64] And in Uganda a journalist with the government-owned daily newspaper commented that 'in almost each case, buyers are firms that are connected to people in high places'.[65] The logic of patrimonialism has continued to shape the privatization decisions of state personnel. Publicly-owned companies have been used for political patronage purposes, and similar considerations have doubtless influenced the disposal of public enterprise assets in the privatizations that have taken place.

At times, special favours have been granted by governments to privatized companies. Elliot Berg shows that in Guinea certain buyers obtained 'generous sweeteners' before purchasing state firms. For example, 'lengthy payoff periods and high inflation rates (around 30 percent in some years) made real costs to buyers low. . . [also] high levels of protection were freely granted as were duty-free imports of equipment and intermediate inputs. Monopoly rights were granted ... Some enterprises were exempted from sales tax.' All this was on the top of 'extremely low selling prices' of public companies. In Berg's view, the Guinean case was not 'typical of African experience', although 'one or another of its aspects can be seen in other countries of the region'.[66] However, such 'sweeteners' were likely to be disbursed to favoured clients of the government, the more so as public information regarding divestiture transactions (in particular the valuation of public enterprise assets as well as the bids received and criteria used for the selection of buyers) has invariably been so limited. Indeed, African governments have often sheltered their privatization deals from any public scrutiny, possibly to ward off political opposition to particular agreements. Berg himself concludes that 'cronyism and corruption have sometimes marked the [privatisation] process'.[67]

The World Bank and international donors generally are becoming gradually aware of the politicization of privatization in African countries. But, in their desire to promote more rapid and greater privatization, discriminatory and non-transparent transactions have elicited little critical comment. In Uganda, for instance, IMF and World Bank comments on the divestiture programme in 1994 and 1995 focused on the slow pace of privatization as well as the very high level of direct and indirect subsidies to the parastatal sector. Yet opposition politicians both in Uganda and elsewhere had begun to advertise the political biases accompanying cases of privatization as well as other negative effects of the divestiture process. In Uganda, an independent newspaper expressed the view that 'there is public outrage at the secretive manner in which the exercise is handled' and criticized the privatization process for not protecting or promoting the interests of Ugandans.[68] An opposition MP, the chairman of the legislative parastatal accounts committee, declared that 'this lack of transparency is likely to result in a political backlash'.[69] He warned that 'New owners may find themselves in problems when there is pressure to either re-nationalise or renegotiate the terms under which the public enterprises have been handled'.[70] Such statements that privatization decisions would be reviewed have been made in other African countries as well. They are highly unwelcome to incumbent leaders anxious to retain the support of international financial institutions.

Criticism of the ways privatization has been carried out has begun to be increasingly voiced in a number of countries. In 1997 parliamentarians raised diverse complaints regarding Uganda's privatization process. Some criticized Uganda Consolidated Properties Limited for being divested at a cost far below its real value. One MP declared: 'This privatisation thing is beginning to stink'. He claimed 'We are divesting property below its real value, that's robbery'. A journalist reported that 'Members also seemed irked by the fact that the privatised properties were landing in the hands of specific individuals', including the relatives of top state elites.[71] In early 1997, the government sold its shares in the Uganda Grain Milling Corporation to Caleb International Ltd in which Salim Saleh, President Yoweri Museveni's brother, had a controlling interest. The government-owned daily newspaper commented that 'the fear of Movement [ruling political organization] supporters dominating the economy was the main reason behind public disquiet'.[72] In an article on the partial sale of UGMC, a correspondent in an independent privately-owned daily referred to it as fostering 'suspicions of a fishy deal' as well as confirming 'the now rampant view that the privatisation exercise is vulnerable to manipulation and exploitation'.[73] The successful buyers 'bought the companies after winning the bids through political connections or raising money because they can pull strings with the government'.[74] Ugandan MPs have also been critical of those who bought state companies without in fact, paying for them in full, especially if they are politically well-connected. For example, the government-owned daily reported that Sam Engola's M/S Showa Trade had bought Lira Hotel in 1995 but by early 1997 it had paid only UShs50 million out of a total sale price of UShs350 million. Engola was said to be closely linked politically with President Museveni, who himself was shown to have directed the Ministry of Finance to extend to Engola a half million dollar loan out of the divestiture fund.[75] As a letter to *The Monitor* asked: 'Who is this [privatization] exercise intended to benefit if the proceeds of sale are shamelessly being doled out to political cronies?'.[76]

Recent criticism in Uganda – which can also be generalized to other African countries – has focused on privatization being primarily to the benefit of the powerful and privileged. First, 'privatisation is a cute name given to robbery of public assets by selected foreign businessmen and political cronies of NRM leaders'. Not much has been done, as was proclaimed, 'to explore ways in which small Ugandan investors could buy into the companies', with the result that privatization 'has only created a tiny wealthy class'. Secondly, 'privatisation funds have been badly spent ... a lot of money was lent to already rich firms and regime cronies and not invested [as was publicly stated] in social areas benefiting the mass of people'.[77] Privatization funds in Uganda and elsewhere have been used at the discretion of government leaders, frequently in favour of their political supporters.

'Happily, the privatisation and restructuring train is moving', writes a leading Kenyan journalist. 'Unfortunately, too often, it is being mistaken for a gravy train.'[78] Privatization remains an essentially top-down process controlled by incumbent leaders. Despite the public criticism and controversy it has engendered, governments have not encouraged public debate and participation. In Uganda, 'debates and discussions which should have taken place before the exercise, take place at the end when deals have been sealed'.[79] Divestiture decisions have also remained largely outside the domain of public scrutiny. Legislatures have exercised little supervision over privatization activities and rarely has legislative approval been required of decisions taken by the government.[80] Criticism of privatization has been confined to occasional remarks by opposition politicians, trade unionists, journalists, and church organizations. Mass domestic opposition is nowhere in sight as government leaders continue to determine who gets what in their public sector divestiture programmes. By dominating the privatization process, high-ranking politicians and senior bureaucrats have been centrally placed to ensure that the pace and scope of privatization as well as specific divestiture transactions have been congruent with their political and personal interests.

NOTES

1. For arguments that privatization in Africa has been impelled by primarily external factors, see Jeffrey Herbst, 'The Politics of Privatisation in Africa', in Ezra N. Suleiman and John Waterbury (eds.), *The Political Economy of Public Sector Reform and Privatization* (Boulder, CO, 1990), pp.246–7, and Ralph A. Young, 'Privatisation in Africa', *Review of African Political Economy*, 51 (1991), pp.50–52, 54–6.

2. See Elliot Berg and Mary M. Shirley, *Divestiture in Developing Countries*, World Bank Discussion Paper, No.11, (Washington, DC, 1987), pp.6–10; Paul Cook and Martin Minogue, 'Waiting for Privatisation in Developing Countries: Towards the Integration of Economic and Non-economic Explanations', *Public Administration and Development*, 10,4 (1990), pp.391–4; and Nicolas Van de Walle, 'Privatization in Developing Countries: A Review', *World Development*, 17,5 (1989), pp.608–10.

3. For a discussion of the politics of privatization, see Henry Bienen and John Waterbury, 'The Political Economy of Privatization in Developing Countries', *World Development*, 17,5 (1989), 623–30, and Luigi Manzetti, 'The Political Economy of Privatization through Divestiture in Lesser Developed Economies', *Comparative Politics*, 25,4 (1993), 429–53. A more recent discussion by the World Bank is contained in *Bureaucrats in Business. The Economics and Politics of Government Ownership* (Washington, DC, 1995), Chap.4.

4. Robert K. Rutaagi, 'Public Enterprise Reforms and Privatisation; The Ugandan Experience' (paper presented at a workshop on 'Assessment of the Impact of Public Sector Management Reforms in Africa' at UNECA, Addis Ababa, December 1994), p.6. In January 1995, Rutaagi was removed as head of Uganda's privatization programme, mainly because it was progressing too slowly.

5. Only limited evidence exists of parastatal managers actually resisting reforms once the decision to privatize has been made. More common, however, appears to be the 'cannibalization and looting' of public enterprises before privatization. For example, 'With the Uganda Commercial Bank due for privatisation, going by the loans which are being given out, the managers and the politicians look like they are stripping it before it is privatised ... UCB assets are being disposed of in ways which are less than satisfactory ... the big people are taking care of themselves', *The Monitor*, (Kampala), editorial 27 November 1995, p.3. In discussing the management of Uganda Railways Corporation 'selling the staff houses to themselves', the *Monitor* commented that this was another case of 'a parastatal being cannibalised first before selling it'. See the editorial of 9 February 1996, p.3. In Zaire (Congo-Kinshasa), with the 'liberalisation' of the mining industry by the governor of Shaba Province in 1991, which ended the state-owned Gecamines's exclusive right to trade copper and cobalt, 'Gecamine's employees cannibalised the installations, sending lorries of equipment and concentrate to South Africa to be sold. In one notorious incident, 30 Km of high-voltage cable supplying the plants with electricity were simply cut and transported across the border'. See Michela Wrong, 'Foreign Investors Eye Kasombo Mine', *The Financial Times* (London), 26 March 1997.

6. Rutaagi, *op. cit.*, p.11. As noted by a legislative committee on Uganda's parastatal accounts in 1993, 'these institutions [parastatals] were, for a very long time, used as conduits for dishing favours to political allies'. See NRC Committee *Report on Parastatal Accounts*, Vol.1 (Entebbe, 1993), p.1.

7. *The New Vision* (Kampala), 26 January 1996, p.4.

8. Frances Stewart, Sanjaya Lall, and Samuel Wangwe (eds.), *Alternative Development Strategies in SubSaharan Africa* (Basingstoke, 1992), pp.24–5. In the 'new' South Africa, early statements by the Minister of Public Enterprises emphasized that privatization could lead to share ownership being transferred to 'an exclusive group' without granting the nation as a whole the opportunity to benefit from the process. See *Business Day* (Johannesburg), 15 June 1994, p.1. Moreover, other government ministers argued that parastatal companies had a special role to play as suitable conduits for the implementation of affirmative action initiatives.

9. See *The Star* (Johannesburg), 31 December 1993, p.5.

10. Southern Africa Foundation for Economic Research, 'The Privatisation Process in Zimbabwe' (Harare, 1992), p.9. In May 1996, President Mugabe announced that his government would privatize dozens of state-owned companies at a 'calculated slow pace' to ensure the process advanced black economic empowerment. A National Investment Trust would be set up to help black buyers of state firms. Also in Côte d'Ivoire, much criticism was levelled at the privatization programme in the National Assembly. The government was accused of abandoning 'national sovereignty and national security' for having sold gas, petroleum and electricity corporations to foreigners. See *African Business* (London), March 1993, p.17.

11. *The Weekly Review* (Nairobi), 25 January 1991.

12. John Waterbury, *Exposed to Innumerable Delusions. Public Enterprise and State Power in Egypt, India, Mexico and Turkey* (Cambridge, 1993), p.137.

13. Pita O. Agbese, 'Moral Economy and the Expansion of the Privatisation Constituency in Nigeria', *Journal of Commonwealth and Comparative Politics*, 30,3 (1992), 335–57.

14. The Mozambican Government sold off 150 mainly small state-owned companies in 1993 which had fallen into government ownership after being abandoned by foreign

settlers fleeing the country at independence in 1975. In Nigeria, the bulk of the 140 public enterprises divested between 1987 and 1992 were small-scale and economically peripheral ones.

15. Sunita Kikeri, John Nellis, and Mary Shirley, *Privatisation. The Lessons of Experience* (World Bank, Washington, DC, 1992), p.24.

16. *The East African* (Nairobi), 5 February 1996, p.1.

17. John Nellis and Sunita Kikeri, 'Public Enterprise Reform: Privatization and the World Bank', *World Development*, 17,5 (1989), 659–72.

18. As noted at the end of Chapter Two, up to the late 1980s, the World Bank concentrated largely on the reform of public enterprises, but since then it has emphasized much more the divestment of such organizations.

19. The United Republic of Tanzania, *Parastatal Privatisation and Reform* (Dar es Salaam, 1993), p.i.

20. *Southern Africa Business Intelligence* (London), 22 September 1995, p.6.

21. Remarks at a press conference in Kampala in February 1996.

22. Valentine Chitalu of the Zambia Privatisation Agency quoted in Donald G. McNeil, Jr., 'For Sale: Zambia's Rich Copper Mines, All of Them', *The New York Times* (New York), 11 August 1996.

23. *The Market Place* (Kampala), 1 December 1995, p.1.

24. As reported at the Consultative Group for Uganda meeting in Paris, May 1993.

25. Charles Onyango-Obbo, 'Why UCB Became the Sacrificial Lamb', *The East African*, 4 September 1995, p.9. UCB was privatized in early 1998.

26. Although in Africa there has been 'a greater reluctance by governments in the region to sell off large state monopolies' yet divestiture 'in such important sectors as electric and water utilities, transportation and telecommunications, as well as major firms in the financial and industrial sectors' has begun to take place. World Bank, *Bureaucrats in Business*, *op. cit.*,p.2.

27. World Bank, *Bureaucrats in Business*, *op. cit.*, p.27. *The Economist* (London), 21 August 1993, 'A Survey of Nigeria', p.9. In Kenya, out of an initial stock of 207 non-strategic parastatals in the late 1980s, 169 remained to be divested by early 1995. For a further discussion of the slow progress in privatizing public enterprises, see World Bank, *Adjustment in Africa. Reforms, Results, and the Road Ahead* (Washington, DC, 1994), pp.103–6.

28. 'Divestiture and declining investment have yet to reduce significantly the size of the SOE sector in Africa'. See World Bank, *Bureaucrats in Business*, *op. cit.*, p.31. Moreover, only a few African countries such as Benin, Mali and Togo 'have divested as many as half their enterprises ... Even for these countries the entities divested were very small in terms of assets.' See The World Bank, *A Continent in Transition: Africa in the mid-1990s* (Washington, DC, 1995), p.53.

29. *The New Vision*, 25 September 1995, p.1. In 1995 government subsidies to Uganda's state enterprises had declined to $145 million. See *The New Vision*, 14 February 1997. In Ghana, 'non-performing debts and unpaid corporate taxes of public enterprises amount to about 3 percent of GDP'. See World Bank, *Continent in Transition*, *op. cit.*, p.51.

30. Justus Mugaju, 'From Corporation to Authority', *The Market Place*, 10 January 1997, 6–7.

31. The Ghanaian case-study was first published in *African Affairs*, 90, (1991), 523–36. A slightly revised version, including some up-dating of data, is presented here.

32. For discussions on Ghana's economic decline, see Richard Jeffries, 'Rawlings and the Political Economy of Underdevelopment in Ghana', *African Affairs*, 81,324 (1982), 307–17; Robert M. Price, 'Neo-Colonialism and Ghana's Economic Decline: A Critical Assessment', *Canadian Journal of African Studies*, 18,1 (1984), 163–93; Donald Rothchild and E. Gyimah-Boadi, 'Ghana's Economic Decline and Development Strategies', in John Ravenhill (ed.), *Africa in Economic Crisis* (London, 1986); and Gareth Austin, 'National Poverty and the 'Vampire State' in Ghana: A Review Article', *Journal of International Development*, 8,4 (1996), 553–73.

33. Ghana's structural adjustment programmes are the subject of much academic writing. For one stimulating comparative discussion, see Thomas M. Callaghy, 'Lost Between State and Market: The Politics of Economic Adjustment in Ghana, Zambia, and Nigeria', in Joan M. Nelson (ed.), *Economic Crisis and Policy Choice. The Politics of Economic Adjustment in the Developing Countries* (Princeton, NJ, 1990). See also Jeffrey Herbst, *The Politics of Reform in Ghana, 1982–91* (Berkeley, CA, 1993), and J. Clark Leith and Michael F. Lofchie, 'The Political Economy of Structural Adjustment in Ghana', in Robert H. Bates and Anne O. Krueger (eds.), *Political and Economic Interactions in Economic Policy Reform* (Oxford, 1993).

34. William Adda, 'Privatisation in Ghana', in V.V. Ramanadham (ed.), *Privatisation in Developing Countries* (London, 1989), p.306.

35. Quotations from Republic of Ghana, *National Programme for Economic Development (Revised)* (Accra, 1987), p.25.

36. Quotations from 'Divestiture of Selected State Owned Enterprises in Ghana. Invitation to Interested Investors' (issued by the Divestiture Implementation Committee of the Government of Ghana, 1988).

37. Memorandum to the PNDC by PNDC Secretary and Chairman of the Divestiture Implementation Committee dated 30 May 1989, p.2.

38. Adda, *op. cit.*, p.311.

39. See *Financial Times*, 11 July 1989, *Survey on Ghana*, p.3.

40. Adda, *op. cit.*, pp.312, 313.

41. 'Government Policy Statement on the State Enterprise Sector' (unpublished, n.d., but ca 1986), pp.9–10.

42. For further discussions on the politics of state divestiture in Ghana, see E. Gyimah-Boadi, 'State Enterprise Divestiture: Recent Ghanaian Experiences', in Donald Rothchild (ed.), *Ghana: The Political Economy of Recovery* (Boulder, CO, 1991), Colleen Lowe Morna, 'Ghana. The Privatization Drive', *Africa Report*, 33 (1988), 60–62; Fred E.M. Tanoh, Structural Adjustment in Africa. Ghana's Experience in the 1980s (University of Manchester, Ph.D thesis, 1992), Chap.7; and Eboe Hutchful, 'Ghana 1983–94', in Poul Engberg-Pedersen et al. (eds.), *Limits of Adjustment in Africa* (Oxford, 1996).

43. Tony Killick, *Development Economics in Action. A Study of Economic Policies in Ghana* (London, 1978), p.313.

44. W.A. Adda, 'Memorandum on State-Owned Enterprise Rationalisation Programme', (mimeo, 1987).

45. The decision of the Ghanaian Government to sell shares in the Ashanti Goldfields Corporation aroused much controversy in 1993. Critics accused the government of selling the 'family silver' to foreigners. See Ajoa Yeboah-Afari, 'Gold Sale Controversy,' *West Africa* (London), 6–12 December 1993, p.2205.

46. Cited in *West Africa*, 2–8 April 1990, pp.555–6.

47. P.B. Arthiabah, 'Public Enterprises and Privatisation in Africa. A Ghanaian Trade Union View-Point' (Paper delivered at a workshop on Public Enterprises and Privatization in Africa, Accra, May 1988).

48. For further details, see Kikeri et al., *op. cit.*, p.61. In 1992 the government agreed to pay accrued end-of-service benefits which were estimated at 4.5% of GDP. Payment was planned over an unspecified period.

49. *People's Daily Graphic* (Accra), Editorial, 2 June 1988 cited in Ben Ephson, 'Ghana's Divestiture', *West Africa*, 27 June 1988, p.1152.

50. E. Gyimah-Boadi, 'The Political Economy of PE Reforms in Ghana' (report prepared for the World Bank, 20 January 1994). 'Ghana's divestiture programme progressed slowly, with only 54 of 300 nonfinancial public enterprises fully divested by 1993 ... Bank staff attribute the slow pace of privatization ... mainly to insufficient political support'. See Robert P. Armstrong, *Ghana Country Assistance Review. A Study in Development Effectiveness* (The World Bank, Washington DC, 1996), p.99.

51. A 1993 World Bank report on Ghana cited in Eboe Hutchful, 'Why Regimes Adjust: The World Bank Ponders Its 'Star Pupil'', *Canadian Journal of African Studies*, 29,2 (1995), p.306.

52. *The Daily Nation* (Nairobi), 21 September 1994, p.32.

53. See Gemini News, 'Past Leaders Haunt Present Policies', February 1996.

54. Quoted in Manoah Esipisu, Privatisation progressing well – Mitine', *The Daily Nation*, 28 May 1996. In 1996 the government expected to divest some 40 of the 207 companies that remained in its ownership. However, it was also claimed that the Kenyan Government had been accelerating privatization over a 3-year period and had divested from 136 out of the 207 public companies listed for sale in 1993. For a discussion of the 'marked increase in privatization activity in SSA since 1992' see Paul Bennell, 'Privatization in Sub-Saharan Africa: Progress and Prospects during the 1990s', *World Development*, 25,11 (1997), 1785–1803.

55. Address by President Y.K. Museveni on the occasion of launching the public education programme on privatization on 11 February 1996. The government's popularization programme includes a play which ridicules the involvement of the state in business.

56. 'Cameroun's Privatization Nightmare', *New African* (London), January 1995, p.25.

57. See World Bank, *Bureaucrats in Business, op. cit.*, pp.190–203 for a discussion of governments suppressing dissent, defusing opposition, and compensating laid-off workers, which helps to account for the limited degree of worker resistance to privatization.

58 *The East African*, 12–18 December 1994, p.8.

59. 'Kenya. A Very Private Affair', *Africa Confidential* (London), 20 May 1994, p.6.

60. 'Kenya. The New Capitalism and its Cronies', *Africa Confidential*, 2 December 1994, p.4.

61. Agbese, *op. cit.*, p.351. Dr Peter Lewis has confirmed to me that his research into Nigeria's privatization programme has shown that it was subject to a good deal of insider trading and private placement of assets.

62. See Thomas M. Callaghy and Ernest J. Wilson III, 'Africa: Policy, Reality or Ritual?' in Raymond Vernon (ed.), *The Promise of Privatization: a Challenge for U.S. Policy* (New York, 1988). pp.206–7. In Ethiopia, as well, many government-owned industries have been sold in the last few years to leading members of the ruling EPRDF.

63. Simon Commander et al., 'Senegal 1979–88', in Simon Commander (ed.), *Structural Adjustment and Agriculture. Theory and Practice in Africa and Latin America* (London, 1989).

64. Mr Medard Ondzongo of the Posts and Telecommunications Workers Federation quoted in Reuter Agency article entitled 'Congo Vows to Privatise Six State Firms', 19 February 1996.
65. Ofwono Opondo, 'Nepotism in High Places is Alarming', *The New Vision*, 9 April 1997, p.18.
66. Elliot Berg, 'Privatization in Sub-Saharan Africa: Results, Prospects, and New Approaches' (Paper prepared for the World Bank, February 1994), p.9. For further discussion on Guinea as well as Mali in regard to some of their privatization features, see World Bank, *Bureaucrats in Business*, *op. cit.*, p.244.
67. Berg, *op. cit.*, p.13. There is much evidence of special favours being conferred on privatized companies by East African governments as well. In Uganda, some public enterprises, such as the one dealing with ground handling services at Entebbe International Airport, have not been divested into competitive markets.
68. *The Monitor*, 31 May 1995, p.3.
69. Yona Kanyomozi, 'Privatised Companies: Are they Safe from Future Govts?', *The Monitor*, 31 May 1995, p.9.
70. Quoted in *The Monitor*, 2 June 1995, p.24.
71. For this, see Robert Mukasa, 'MPs call ministers over Saleh Karim's UCPL bids', *The Monitor*, 5 March 1997, p.2. Public criticism of public companies being sold allegedly at prices below their real value has been voiced regularly in Uganda. Such criticism emerged in 1995 after a fish-canning plant and two international hotels were sold. Two years later, politicians and journalists once more charged that transparent procedures for valuation and competitive bidding were lacking and that the government was divesting from state assets at giveaway prices mainly to foreigners or to its own political supporters. Protests over the sale of UCPL may have influenced the government's decision to reject all of the bids made on the ground that they were too low.
72. See *The New Vision*, 9 January 1997, p.28. Similarly in Zambia, 'public anger has been triggered by the belief that only ministers and their close business colleagues have gained from privatisation'. See *Africa Confidential*, 14 February 1997, p.6. It is also alleged that Zambian cabinet ministers have been acquiring state-owned enterprises without having the funds to purchase them.
73. See Jim Mugungwa, 'We Need Some Answers ...', *The Monitor*, 1 January 1997, p.3.
74. Charles Onyango-Obbo, 'Where Ugandans See Only Theft', *The Monitor*, 28 May 1997, p.14.
75. See Ofwono-Opondo, 'Engola gets 500m/- Loan from Museveni', *The New Vision*, 5 March 1997, pp.1–2. The Ministry of Finance apparently refused approval of the loan.
76. See letter published in *The Monitor*, 31 March 1997, p.4. Moreover, the two Ugandan manufacturing companies that did secure loans from the divestiture account amounting to $1.7 million in 1995 had not repaid any of the money they owed as the three-year time period of their loan expired. See A. Mutumba-Lule, 'MPs Oppose Lending of Divestiture Funds to Industrialists', *The East African*, 4 May 1998, p.7.
77. See Note 74 above. The Ghanaian authorities also proclaim that the 'proceeds from the sale of enterprises can be used to improve, among other things, infrastructure, health services and education'.
78. Mbatau wa Ngai, 'Theatre of the Absurd Thwarts Civil Society', *Sunday Nation* (Nairobi), 15 September 1996, p.7.

79. Leading article in *The Monitor*, 30 July 1997, p.3. It also stated that 'the divestiture programme has suffered from the failure of a conceited government and the WB/IMF to carry it out as a consensus exercise'.

80. African legislative assemblies have generally played peripheral roles in the privatization process which has tended to be dominated by government executives. But in Uganda, in view of the rising public concern regarding divestiture transactions, the legislature has begun to assert its right to be consulted and to participate in hitherto largely executive-determined privatization decisions. In August 1998 it passed a resolution suspending the privatization process pending investigation into allegations of corruption in the divestiture exercise. A few months later, the report of the parliamentary select committee called for the sacking of four government ministers and prosecution of other major players (including Salim Saleh, President Museveni's brother) for alleged corruption in the privatization process. The report said privatization had been manipulated by nepotism and 'politically powerful families'. See 'Privatization Report Says Nepotism Rife,' *The New Vision*, 9 December 1998, p.1. This view was echoed in an anti-corruption report completed for the World Bank at the same time which concluded that privatization in Uganda was flawed and 'widely criticized for non-transparency, insider-dealing, conflict of interest and corruption'. See James Tumusiime, 'Thieving in govt annoys World Bank', *The Monitor*, 16 December 1998. Also worth noting is the growing importance of the media in providing information on Uganda's privatization process as well as the growing cooperation between journalists and legislators in their investigations of Uganda's divestiture deals.

The Politics
of Private African Capital

If the expansion of state-owned enterprises in post-colonial Africa was based in part on enhancing a country's economic independence, so also the development of local private capital was seen as increasing indigenous economic participation. Most sub-Saharan governments at independence evinced some interest in promoting private sector expansion.[1] But the extent of the development of African private enterprise in the decades since independence has varied quite markedly.

In a small number of countries, private economic concerns (mainly foreign-owned) were nationalized, rather than indigenized,[2] leading to the enlargement of the state sector. In fact, in most African countries there evolved a substantial public enterprise sector accounting for over one-half of the national income. However, African private enterprise was given some support as well. Some governments fostered it strongly, while the majority gave more limited state assistance to domestic entrepreneurs. At the same time, almost everywhere in the Africa region, officials and politicians used their positions to advance their own private business interests.

This chapter first details the above-mentioned developments in Africa's private enterprise sector. It finds that in the first few post-independence decades the political environment was generally not conducive to the growth of a strong local private entrepreneurial class. Secondly, the chapter examines attempts by African governments in recent years to promote a more vigorous private sector. Since the mid-1980s, greater support has been forthcoming for private domestic business, although our conclusion is that indigenous capital has, politically, still not felt sufficiently encouraged to develop. Nevertheless, a small number of larger capitalists is emerging, and, as has frequently been the case since independence, these have been closely connected to those in state power.

State and private enterprise:
The early post-independence decades

Governments have historically been indispensable for the genesis and development of local capital. In nineteenth-century Western Europe, governments saw a strong local capitalist class as a primary precondition for the attainment of higher levels of economic development. They provided substantial support for local business, including financial assistance, tariff protection and preferential taxation rates in addition to investing vast sums of public capital in infrastructure. In East Asia since the 1950s, the state has also played a vital role in providing infrastructure and establishing a set of incentives to promote the development of the private sector.[3] In other regions of the world as well, state support has been significant in enhancing the economic importance of local private business. In sub-Saharan Africa, however, the actual reverse has largely been the case, at least up to very recently.

For most of the colonial period, the emergence of African entrepreneurs was held back.[4] Particularly in Eastern and Southern Africa, numerous restrictions – legal, financial, and bureaucratic – were imposed on Africans by colonial authorities averse to indigenous entrepreneurial endeavour. Even in West Africa, where colonial restrictions were less onerous, African enterprise received little help or protection. Colonial policy and practice openly favoured foreign economic interests and especially the large international firms which benefited from various forms of state subsidy and protection. Other non-African minorities such as Asian, European and Levantine residents were also given some support. At independence, the important economic sectors were predominantly in the hands of foreign and non-African interests.

However, in areas where foreign and non-African capital was not interested commercially, small-scale indigenous enterprise grew and, at times, particularly in West Africa, flourished in cash-crop production, transport, market trading, and many craft activities.[5] Moreover, in the post-1945 period, many of the earlier restrictions imposed on the emergence of indigenous entrepreneurs were eased and eventually removed throughout colonial Africa. Some colonial governments even attempted to promote certain kinds of African enterprise in the years before independence. Nevertheless, local African enterprises were found mainly at the lower end of the commercial hierarchy, organized around individual or family proprietorship, and concentrated chiefly in trade and distribution, although small numbers had become established in contracting, transport, cash-crop farming and small-scale manufacturing.

The years shortly before and after independence saw demands from local capital for government assistance to facilitate private sector growth, particularly that of indigenous business. Local capital wanted state support of various kinds, including preferential access to contracts and credit as well as good business training programmes. There were also demands that foreign and non-African enterprises be prohibited from operating in certain sectors. Throughout the continent, local business groups were concerned about foreign economic control as well as about their own role in African economies. They called for various measures to assist indigenous entrepreneurial development and also to reduce expatriate domination in certain spheres of economic activity.[6] Indigenous business groups, however, had very little hold over state power. African capital had been relatively unimportant in the struggles for independence and was only occasionally a key component in the new postcolonial political leadership. Moreover, the economic power of African business groups was limited; the economic base from which they could advance their interests was weak. Thus the adoption of policies favourable to domestic business depended on the needs and interests of those in control of the state. Given the considerable degree of administrative discretion enjoyed by the new African governments, it was the ideological, personal and political concerns of those who controlled the state apparatus that influenced the extent of development of a local private sector. Government responses to the demands of private capital depended on their 'ideological preferences', their 'development images', and their 'perceptions concerning their own best opportunities for personal advancement' as well as remaining in state power. Up to very recently, political leaders 'have remained largely unresponsive if not hostile to the needs of local capital'.[7]

Hostility to the development of indigenous commercial endeavour was particularly evident in those few countries (such as Ethiopia, Mozambique and Tanzania) where the ideological orientations of the political leaders tended towards socialism and significant state-led economic involvement.[8] A policy of state takeovers of private economic concerns was followed, leading to the enlargement of the state enterprise sector and the stifling of the fledgling private sector. Economic firms in the public domain were strongly favoured, whereas private companies were severely restricted. Private concerns were often debarred from engaging in economic areas where government enterprises were active. The easier access of public enterprises to government credit also made it difficult for private enterprises to enter credit markets, and constituted a serious impediment to private sector expansion. Moreover, as in Ghana in the early 1960s, the import licensing system 'worked in favour of the Ghana National Trading Corporation, which received generous allowances mainly at the expense of the small Ghanaian traders'.[9] And there is ample evidence from Zambia in the

1970s of state parastatals 'outcompeting and thereby thwarting the growth of indigenous capital' in various sectors, mainly through their privileged access to subsidized credit, import licences and tax benefits.[10]

In contrast, in a second group of countries, governments sought actively to nurture a domestic capitalist class by providing various forms of material assistance to private entrepreneurs. This was, again, a small number of countries but in all of them concessionary loans, preferential taxation rates, and protective tariffs were commonly provided to local entrepreneurs. In Kenya, for example, domestic firms were able to enter into successful competition with foreign companies in certain sectors (such as the soap and shoe industries) as a result of the state providing valuable support in the form of various subsidies and loans. Domestic business also benefited from the expansion of state activities. African contractors, suppliers and distributors prospered through special favours from the government including purchase contracts for government ministries. Moreover, indigenization policies were adopted, prohibiting foreigners from engaging in certain economic activities. The 1972 and 1977 Nigerian Enterprises Promotion Decrees reserved many areas exclusively for Nigerians, and somewhat similar indigenization laws were introduced in Kenya, Malawi, Senegal and elsewhere. Nigeria's indigenization decrees enabled indigenous business persons to entrench themselves not only in commerce but also to acquire important niches in manufacturing, construction and services.

Much of this assistance and preferential treatment was provided to favoured clients of the government. Licences, contracts, credit and foreign exchange were channelled to businesspeople who were the relatives or political associates of influential state personnel. Richard Sandbrook writes in regard to indigenization laws that 'political insiders and their partners [were] the principal beneficiaries'.[11] And, indeed, the evidence available shows that a small number of well-placed individuals acquired a disproportionate share of benefits from indigenization.[12] In regard to Kenya's black capitalists, David Himbara states that they emerged 'after independence mainly from the senior ranks of the civil service, the top echelons of state corporations, and politically connected circles.'[13]

Again in connection with Kenya, Himbara argues that 'the groups in control of the state sought to consolidate themselves by empowering a supportive African business class from within their own ethnic ranks'.[14] The discretionary and preferential allocation of state support and benefits was motivated by considerations of political survival. Catherine Boone shows, in the case of Senegal in the 1970s, how the government used its control over the import licence system to 'selectively insert' businessmen into the import trade to 'coopt restive elements of the local private sector into patronage networks linked to the regime' and thus 'defuse challenges to the regime'.[15] And in most sub-Saharan countries, state protection and patronage were distributed to specific domestic entrepreneurs in ways designed to build bases of social support for state personnel to help enable them to remain in power. Material assistance and commercial opportunities were politically inspired and accorded with the patrimonial logic on which African governments are founded.

Out of this minority of countries in which governments actively supported domestic capitalists, in a tiny number of them, such as Botswana, Côte d'Ivoire, and Kenya, the state was crucial to the rise of a class of large capitalists in commerce and industry. It was in these few countries that there took place an increase in the scale of local, African capital which, although remaining mainly commercial in orientation, also moved into large-scale manufacturing. Why these countries saw the emergence of a class of wealthy African capitalists is to be accounted for by local capitalists achieving a strong hold on the state apparatus. Local private capital had more and greater weight within the ruling coalitions of these countries than elsewhere in Africa. The state was thus the leading edge of indigenous capital. In Côte d'Ivoire, for instance, a group of wealthy planters organized the Parti Democratique de Côte d'Ivoire (PDCI) that led the country to independence. The PDCI captured the post-colonial state. This 'bourgeois party filled the state with its people: of the nineteen ministers in the country's first cabinet, nine – almost half the total – came from the country's leading capitalist families'.[16] The state remained in the hands of local capitalists who used it 'to promote the growth and development both of capitalism in general and of Ivoirian capital in particular'.[17] Private Ivoirian capital was cultivated and 'prospered, surpassing the accomplishments of both foreign and state capital'.[18] With the direct assistance of the state, Ivoirian capitalists moved from a strictly agricultural to an urban bourgeoisie and, in the course of the 1960s and 1970s, began asserting themselves in the industrial sector. The original planter capitalists were joined by new entrants into the Ivoirian capitalist class, few of whom had agrarian roots: 'it was state employees, past and present, who were the backbone of this new class of capitalists'.[19] Just as Ivoirian capital utilized state power to further its own objectives, in particular the promotion of indigenous capitalism, so also in Botswana and Kenya, it is argued, policies were enacted at the behest of local capitalists who controlled the post-colonial state apparatus.[20]

However, apart from Ivoirian capitalists who have sustained a remarkable growth both in numbers and in wealth, African entrepreneurial groups in this second group of countries rarely developed into a large and powerful class of entrepreneurs. Partly this is because there was a considerable degree of public sector ownership and economic control which, at times, competed with domestic private business (for example, in retail trade and bus services). In Nigeria, controversy arose periodically over the proper balance between the public and private sectors in national economies,[21] a controversy rarely resolved through joint-venture participation between state and local capital. A largely state-managed economy was seen as essential for enabling those in control of the state to maintain themselves in power. Expansive private enterprises would deprive regimes of the ability to mobilize economic opportunities and resources for political purposes. Thus, there were limits to the extent to which business was encouraged to expand and engage in economic competition with the state. Policies were pursued that controlled and constrained large business, allowing it to develop only if it was in the hands of favoured clients of the state elites and also did not usurp too many of the economic prerogatives of the top state personnel.

Moreover, in view of its strong reliance for its accumulation on political patronage and the state, domestic capital possessed a dependent status which would make it vulnerable to any changes either in state policy or in state power. A turn of political fortunes with the advent of a new ruling group could mean, as happened in Kenya, a redirection of the flow of patronage to a new set of clients.[22] In Kenya, Himbara refers to 'the near extinction of the Kikuyu business elite after their loss of the state in the post-Kenyatta phase'.[23] Indigenous capital has encountered major difficulties in surviving the fall of its political patrons, with serious consequences for the long-term sustainability of its business enterprises. Kenyan capitalists who had been described as strong and expanding in the 1970s – they exemplified the emergence of an African national bourgeoisie[24] – were twenty years later viewed as 'numerically and strategically inconsequential'.[25] Only perhaps in Côte d'Ivoire, where the two state presidents since independence have come from the same Baulé ethnic group as well as the same political party, has a larger and more productive domestic entrepreneurial group been developed.

In a third and majority group of countries, Paul Kennedy argues that 'for the most part governments have been markedly ambivalent in their attitude towards African enterprise'. Indeed, he concludes, they have been more 'harmful than helpful'.[26] The restrictive nature of government policies towards the indigenous private sector is a marked feature of most African countries since independence. Governments have offered only limited support and latitude to African private enterprise. For example, the Zambian Government adopted an equivocal stance towards local private capital, sometimes encouraging it, other times constraining, even threatening, its continued operation. In 1968, President Kaunda made it clear that indigenous private business would only be permitted to operate small- and medium-scale enterprises. 'When a Zambian enterprise developed and reached a certain point we would have to make it a public company and when it grew even further the state would have to take it over.'[27]

Nearly all African governments, including many of those in our second group that actively nurtured private business, viewed the prospect of a powerful, indigenous capitalist group with some concern. A strong, autonomous, capitalist stratum 'could represent an independent force in the political or economic arenas'.[28] Its strength could be used to undermine the regime in power. Little scope was therefore provided for the emergence of large, local entrepreneurial groups. The opportunities for local private accumulation were carefully regulated by the state. Only a few wealthy entrepreneurs emerged and these were invariably politically well-placed individuals loyal to the regime in power. The few indigenous business groups of some economic stature which arose, usually through clientelistic relations with those in control of the state, remained dependent on the patronage of those in state power, not being permitted to become an autonomous force in the political sphere. Nor did their economic fortunes usually outlive the fall of their patrons from power. In many of these countries also, foreign economic minorities were tolerated and even preserved as they could be more easily controlled and would never become serious political rivals of those in power. For example, the first Milton Obote government in Uganda is said to have 'preferred an Asian to an African petty bourgeoisie. The latter was a political threat; the former was not.' Foreign business could also be used – successfully in many cases – to undermine those indigenous entrepreneurs tied to the political opposition.[29]

Quite often public enterprises proved valuable instruments for thwarting the economic expansion of business entrepreneurs, particularly those who might be serious opponents of the regime in power. Throughout sub-Saharan Africa, the state marginalized, or allowed only limited competition from, local private companies in activities in which public enterprises predominated. In many key sectors the scope for private sector competition with parastatals was severely restricted. In the export crop sector, for instance, public firms typically possessed exclusive statutory rights to purchase and market all production. In Senegal, state controls over groundnut collection and purchase served to constrain severely private accumulation by local traders. In other sectors as well, most notably commerce, government concerns had a *de facto* monopoly based on privileged access to financial assistance and government guarantees, or through the operation of the import licensing system. State intervention in domestic commerce in Senegal not only narrowed the opportunities available to local *commerçants* but also enabled government officials to grant commercial licences to the politically favoured. As recorded by Boone, 'Licenses were granted to *bons militants* of the [ruling] UPS'.[30] Thus a large public economic sector was also important for enabling state personnel to mobilize and distribute patronage resources. It resulted in formal domestic private capital being concentrated in small-sized commercial enterprises, with the few bigger and wealthier entrepreneurs emerging generally under state aegis. Indeed, virtually everywhere in sub-Saharan Africa, the formal private sector, composed of small-scale enterprises, was dwarfed by the large public sector firms.

Finally, in all African countries, senior state personnel themselves utilized the state to promote their own accumulation. Everywhere, leading politicians and officials used their privileged access to state resources to accumulate personal wealth as well as to further private capital accumulation through entry into private business. Prominent politicians and senior officials as well as military rulers garnered considerable personal wealth while in office, which they used to enter into private entrepreneurial endeavours, using their official positions to advance their business interests in trade, distribution, commercial agriculture, construction and real estate. Carolyn Baylies shows, in the case of Zambia, that at least one-third of the owners of large-scale businesses were drawn 'directly from high level positions within the state apparatus. Some indeed combined ownership with continued occupation of top level positions within the party, civil service, and parastatals.' 'It was the state itself', argues Baylies, that served 'as a reservoir of recruitment into the indigenous bourgeoisie'.[31]

Capital owned by state personnel constituted a relatively important portion of overall African private capital ownership. Senior state personnel benefitted disproportionately from government preferential treatment and available business opportunities. However, very few of their business concerns appear to have become large-scale industrial and commercial operations, and they were heavily dependent on political influence as well as access to state benefits (rather than market competitiveness) for the advancement of their enterprises, which often did not survive the downfall of their regimes.

State and private sector development under structural adjustment

The depth of Africa's economic crisis since the late 1970s and the continued poor performance of state-owned enterprises have provided the context in which ideas about the need to develop a viable private sector in local economies could be strongly emphasized. In line with the prevailing thinking in Western countries, multilateral financial institutions as well as bilateral agencies have been at the forefront in urging the increased transfer of economic responsibilities from the public to the private sector. Private markets are said to be superior to governments in delivering goods and services, and government provision should be replaced by market provision. Private enterprise, international donors have contended, could make a vital contribution to the region's economic recovery as well as being the engine of economic growth.[32] Strong advocates of challenging the public/private enterprise balance have also been found among indigenous business groups. Private sector associations have pushed for a liberalization of African economies, a dismantling of public enterprises, and increased government assistance to enable indigenous entrepreneurs to prosper. And within African governments themselves some recognition has emerged – as exemplified in the ubiquitous structural adjustment programme – for a change in the economic role of the state. For example, in Tanzania, President Julius Nyerere's blueprint for socialism, the 'Arusha Declaration' of 1967 which led to state takeovers of private property and a proliferation of state-owned enterprises, was in 1990 replaced with the 'Zanzibar Declaration' in which the ruling party resolved to pursue pro-private capitalist policies. Even ex-President Nyerere is now supporting ongoing reforms aimed at transforming Tanzania's state-led economy into a more market-oriented one.

To promote private African enterprise, governments have been considering ways of creating a more auspicious national economic climate. 'The most crucial limiting factor', write Marsden and Belot in regard to promoting Africa's private sector, 'is not entrepreneurship but weaknesses in the physical and policy environment which inhibit effective investment.'[33] In order to establish a more favourable and secure investment milieu, governments have begun to 'remove debilitating restraints on entrepreneurial activity'.[34] In particular, state controls over prices, interest rates, foreign-exchange allocations and so on have been removed as a result of the adoption of structural adjustment programmes. Moreover, various measures have been employed to help indigenous entrepreneurs. Financial institutions in Zimbabwe have been required to direct at least 30 per cent of their lending to local businesspeople. In the late 1980s in Nigeria, legislation was passed directing bank loans to agricultural enterprises and small and medium-sized businesses. In many countries, purchases of goods and services by the government have begun to be contracted much more to domestic businesses. Under its new indigenization policy, the Zimbabwean Government is proposing that certain areas of procurement be set aside for participation only by indigenous-owned enterprises. Moreover, governments have been seeking to reduce corporate tax levels to make business activity more attractive. Also, donor-financed import support programmes have channelled foreign exchange to private sector manufacturers, transporters, building constructors and traders.

But a more favourable macroeconomic environment has not proved sufficiently attractive to promote private sector growth. Private investment and domestic savings – important barometers of private business confidence – have hardly increased as a percentage of GDP since the late 1980s. Private investment has remained very low, comprising a mere 5 per cent of GDP. Sub-Saharan Africa is the only region in the world where public investment still exceeds private investment. A recent World Bank study describes the low level of domestic private investment as the most 'daunting challenge for African countries'.[35] Much has to be done to improve the environment for business development if the desired levels of private investment of around 20 per cent of GDP are to be attained. As in previous decades, it has been political and economic conditions that have proved insufficiently conducive to private sector advance in Africa.

Various economic constraints have impeded private enterprise from emerging as the engine of economic growth. The implementation of trade liberalization as one of the main economic reforms in African structural adjustment programmes has been widely seen as having affected private sector expansion, indeed, to have thwarted the growth of the local private sector. With the removal of, or reductions in, trade restrictions and protection, African markets have been exposed to a flood of foreign exports. Competition from foreign manufacturers has undermined the fortunes of many domestic businesses. Many local manufacturing firms have experienced severe financial distress and have had to close down. The Zambia Association of Manufacturers has organized 'Save Our Industry' meetings about the plight of local manufacturers. The executive director of the Federation of Kenya Employers warned in May 1994 that Kenya risked being turned into an 'industrial cemetery' as a result of the country being saturated with cheaper industrial imports. Some degree of tariff protection has been demanded (as was the case historically in Western Europe and East Asia) to enable the local private sector to compete with more established producers. A few government leaders have given pledges that they would protect efficient local industries threatened by increased competition from imports. And certain politically well-connected local manufacturers have been granted protection in a number of countries. In Uganda imports of beer, soft drinks, and cigarettes have been made prohibitively expensive, not only to protect local producers from foreign competition but also to ensure that the high levels of tax revenues the state receives from such flourishing local firms is not undermined. But generally little has been done to temper the effects of trade liberalization reforms which have made it difficult for certain indigenous businesses to survive, let alone to flourish.[36]

Privatization has also failed to provide the stimulus to a more vibrant private sector by providing insufficient investment opportunities. The weakness of indigenous entrepreneurial groups has posed difficulties in local citizens acquiring state enterprise assets. Little state financing, as well as other measures, has been made available to enable domestic private groups to purchase and run government concerns, especially in areas such as commerce, distribution, and transport in which indigenous entrepreneurs already have some presence. But more generally as well, the cost of credit and access to finance has proved a leading economic constraint to the private sector. Another serious obstacle is the inadequacies of local infrastructural facilities. The quality of roads, access to industrial sites, the availability of regular and reliable power supplies as well as telecommunication services are critical problems in most African countries.

But in much of sub-Saharan Africa, it is the political climate that has not proved as adequate to capital accumulation as might be desired. Political conditions appropriate for private sector development have included political stability, an adequate legal framework and secure property rights, and competent public administration (including a fair and transparent decision-making system and efficient and helpful civil servants). Two World Bank officials noted, in the case of Kenya, that 'the lack of transparent policies and the general perception of capricious governance discouraged potential investors ...'[37] And elsewhere in Africa, bureaucratic obstruction, arbitrary decision-making, and a weak and unreliable judicial system have hardly been conducive to attracting investors.

Equally important has been state personnel being able to accept and tolerate potentially powerful entrepreneurial groups. As we shall see in our case study of Ghana, state personnel have continued to hold perceptions of local business as corrupt and bent on quick returns as well as supporting the political opposition. In June 1993, the Ghanaian President urged people not to buy products from some local businessmen as they were allegedly using their profits to finance the opposition political parties.[38] Such perceptions have undermined confidence among entrepreneurs, and only limited domestic private investment has occurred.[39] Michael Lofchie alludes as well to the question of policy credibility. In ex-socialist countries such as Tanzania, 'where private entrepreneurs have been subjected to decades of harassment and official political disparagement', policy changes by themselves 'may not suffice to provide assurance that those who engage in business activity are no longer personally or economically at risk'.[40] Indeed, in many African countries there is much disapproval of government support being provided for a tiny minority of rich businesspeople in conditions of widespread poverty and economic hardship. Private sector response has also been inhibited by political biases against certain ethnic groups. In Kenya 'the government has sought to deny important benefits such as credit, trade protection, and import licenses to Kikuyu-owned businesses in order to provide business opportunity to non-Kikuyu'.[41] In much of the Africa region, only private entrepreneurs enjoying close connections with those in state power feel sufficiently confident to engage in business investment.

Furthermore, unlike governments in East Asia which did much to nurture and support private sector enterprises in diverse ways (credit, subsidies, information),[42] African regimes have done little to provide various forms of assistance – institutional, technical, infrastructure, microeconomic – which are vital for fostering the conditions for vigorous entrepreneurial activity. In Uganda, indigenous business has pressed government in vain to permit payments by installment so that public enterprise assets could be purchased by Ugandans rather than foreigners.[43] In fact, compared to the rhetoric, very little has been done officially in many areas of entrepreneurial promotion including providing fiscal investment incentives, concessional credits, preferred access to government contracts, attractive tax conditions, export subsidies, and so on. In Tanzania, businessmen argue that 'there are no programmes to support' the private sector. Rather than providing credit 'private banks are speculating in Treasury bills instead of assisting economic actors'.[44] When coupled with the limited effectiveness of the state apparatus in providing public goods and services (such as reliable infrastructure and competent judicial and tax systems), it is clear that governments in Africa have a long way to go before they can be seen to be promoting and supporting indigenous business.

Nearly everywhere in sub-Saharan Africa, there are hardly any forums for consultation between business and government as there were in countries like Japan where liaison agencies were set up in the Ministry of International Trade and Industry to bring together public and private participants to discuss and negotiate government policies. In East Asia the state also strengthened business associations which over time made important contributions to policy debates. In Africa, however, state-private sector interactions have been typically individualized. Until recently, an extensive array of bureaucratic controls, licences and approvals prevailed in most countries. Governments exercised considerable discretion in the application of rules and regulations. Invariably, politically well-connected entrepreneurs were the major beneficiaries of state discretion. It was their businesses that benefitted from tax concessions, subsidies and tariff protection. An indigenous business did not grow outside the state. African capitalism was a political or crony capitalism.[45]

Africa's local private sector has been heavily dependent on the patronage of the state. Not surprisingly, it has hardly been represented in top economic decision-making circles. Business leaders have been consulted only in a limited way about economic matters including the structural adjustment reforms introduced since the mid-1980s. Occasionally, a few well-connected entrepreneurs have enjoyed some involvement in government economic decisions, and there are sometimes effective lobbying organizations such as the Confederation of Zimbabwe Industries and the Commercial Farmers Union in Zimbabwe (these latter bodies being run largely by non-African resident capital). But even in Zimbabwe, where more consultation has occurred than elsewhere, industry leaders are heard complaining that they were only partly involved in the formulation of the two economic reform programmes of 1990 and 1996.

In general, powerful and independent business associations have not been permitted, and governments have often controlled them by creating organizations whose leading members have had close ties to those in state power. Business groups have even been sponsored by the state which also provided much of their funding as well as influencing the selection of their leaders. And governments have not been averse to banning those private sector organizations they disliked or found they were unable to tame.[46] Business associations have not been given much access to economic decision-making, and, more commonly, individual businessmen have been obliged to court the government for favours through personal contacts in the state and other informal channels.

In recent years, as a result of the growing political liberalization in African countries, business has become more outspoken as regards its weak negotiating position. The chairman of the Tanzania Chamber of Commerce, Industries and Agriculture stated that the private sector was unable to influence government economic decisions and pressed for greater presence in policy discussions.

> We would like to see the government sitting with the private sector and charting strategies for development. We would like to be fully involved in government institutions dealing with financial and economic policies. This is not happening. Governments in the West and the Far East have close working relationships with the private sector and their economies are growing fast ... The Tanzania government's support to the business community leaves much to be desired.[47]

Similarly in Uganda, private business has complained about fiscal and monetary policy being 'initiated without consultation with the concerned parties'.[48] The case of Uganda where the Uganda Manufacturers Association protested against various provisions of the 1993 budget and decried the absence of mechanisms for consultation and communication between government and the private sector,[49] could be multiplied throughout the Africa region.

Finally, the limited extent of the dismantling of state-owned enterprises has meant a continuing state presence in African economies. The retention of many strategic parastatals in government ownership, including inefficiently run public infrastructural enterprises,[50] has constituted a major disincentive to potential investors. Governments have demonstrated a reluctance to transfer activities to private enterprise. Instead, they have often continued to invest in parastatals as well as paying large financial and budgetary subsidies to public companies. In Ghana in 1995, the non-performing assets and unpaid taxes of state enterprises amounted to about 3 per cent of GDP. Large budgetary resources to public enterprises have raised the cost of credit and crowded out private investors.[51] At times, only limited competition from private firms in activities in which public sector concerns predominate has been permitted. Private investment has been held back by various regulatory barriers. Few African governments have been willing to recognize the private sector as an equal if not leading partner in economic development, or have wanted to create a genuinely mixed economy with a reduced role for government, especially in commercial, non-strategic areas.

Government-business relations in Ghana[52]

The emergence of a consensus that the performance of the public sector in Ghana had been poor, and that there were limits as to what it could achieve in terms of economic growth, led the Provisional National Defence Council (PNDC) (which ruled Ghana between 1982 and 1992) to implement various policy reforms. As the Governor of the Bank of Ghana argued in 1984: 'Given the dismal performance of the public sector, there is need for greater reliance on private investment in the Government's efforts to resuscitate the economy'.[53] At the same time, the PNDC began to reassess the economic role of the public sector. According to a document prepared by the National Commission for Democracy, 'changed national policies' in Ghana included 'the reduction of the state's role in the economic life of the nation through shifting of more responsibility to the private sector'.[54]

In order to promote national recovery and reverse years of decline, the PNDC launched its far-reaching Economic Recovery Programme

(ERP) in 1983, including market-based reforms intended to enhance the development of the private sector and thereby contribute 'to the achievement of the Government's economic goals'.[55] Writing in 1988, P.V. Obeng stated: 'An important assumption underlying the macro-economic framework for 1988–91 is that the share of the private sector in Gross Domestic Investment (GDI) will exceed that of the public sector by 1991'. According to this senior member of the PNDC, only if private investment increased as projected (i.e. from around one-third to just over one-half of GDI) would the targeted growth in Gross Domestic Product (GDP) be realized, as well as other goals of the programme. The 'success' of the ERP 'will consequently be determined by the extent to which the private sector responds to the challenge to improve investment and productive activity'.[56]

In the words of one financial correspondent, the ERP represented a 'shift'. 'Basically, the public sector is to move away from economic dominance towards greater support for private sector development instead.'[57] Certainly, the plan was for more reliance to be placed on private initiatives to pursue development objectives, while a reorientation of activities in the public sector would entail 'the divestiture of some and the improvement in efficiency of the remaining state-owned enterprises',[58] as well as a general reduction of the pervasive state intervention in Ghana's economic life. However, at the time this case study was completed in mid-1991, the changes had been far less than expected.

For the goals of the ERP to be achieved, the share of investment in GDP had to rise from 12.3 per cent in 1988 to about 19 per cent in 1992, and much of this increase had to be in the private sector.[59] But despite an improved macroeconomic environment, private investment in the formal sector only rose from 2.9 per cent of GDP in 1983 to 4.1 per cent in 1988, as against a corresponding increase in public investment during the same five-year period from less than 1 to more than 10 per cent.[60] Moreover, state-owned enterprises remained a prominent feature in the life of the nation, because only limited divestiture took place, and the government continued to make significant interventions in the economy.

Most African governments have agreed to implement major policy changes via the introduction of structural adjustment programmes. But economic reforms cannot be considered in a political vacuum, and public/private sector relations are shaped by a host of domestic political factors. Hence the need to examine the politics of private investment and the politics of the economic role of the state in Ghana under the PNDC. In exploring the supply responses of private investors, it will be argued that these were conditioned by political factors, and that the state's changing developmental role was the product of internal constraints and conflicts.

Studies of structural adjustment programmes, especially those prepared/sponsored by the World Bank and the IMF on the public and private sectors, often emphasize the economic conditions appropriate for development. The present case study maintains that it is also necessary to examine domestic political conditions for a more complete assessment of the possibilities of promoting economic change.

Business attitudes towards the PNDC Government

The market-based reforms introduced under the ERP notwithstanding, the PNDC was not perceived by Ghanaian business as being a strong and unequivocal supporter of the private sector. Actions taken in mid-1979, when Flight-Lieutenant Jerry Rawlings first came briefly to power, remained deeply etched on the memories of local entrepreneurs. A number of mainly small, private manufacturing firms were confiscated at that time on the grounds that their owners had engaged in various financial or economic malpractices, although suspicions remained that political motives were paramount. The anti-capitalist rhetoric that accompanied the so-called 'Second Coming' of Rawlings in December 1981, and which persisted for much of the following year, was also not forgotten.

Business people continued to bemoan the stigma attached to private profit and entrepreneurship by various PNDC leaders, and objected to being publicly reviled as exploiters. At a rare meeting between private-sector delegates and government officials held in December 1989, one area of concern identified by the former was

> the need for officials at the highest echelons of the government machinery to acknowledge the efforts of the private sector through their pronouncements and actions, and to give due recognition of the role being played by the private sector in Ghana's economic recovery efforts ... [private entrepreneurs] observed with great concern that the harassment of investors by organs of the revolution/security agencies has not changed much.[61]

A leading executive could still claim in 1990, after more than eight years of PNDC rule, that 'the morality of private motive is not as acceptable to government as it should be'.[62]

The revolutionary judicial, investigative, and mobilizational organs, established by the PNDC early in 1982, subjected businessmen, amongst others, to questions, searches, arrests, and punishment. At times, industrial disputes precipitated 'interventions by revolutionary organs', obviously to the displeasure of many in the private sector who felt that in such situations 'it should be possible for the interested parties to seek redress under the provisions of the industrial law for settling disputes'.[63]

The fact, however, that 'harassment' had still not ended by the end of the decade 'obviously has a negative impact on the attractive investment image-building which the government is undertaking'.[64]

In 1991, when the research for the present case study was carried out, private capital still had misgivings about PNDC leaders, not least because of the perception that they wasted no time before acting politically and vindictively against important entrepreneurs with close connections to previous regimes, notably C.A. Appenteng.[65] A number of other prominent businessmen were brought before the National Public Tribunal (established by the PNDC outside the normal judicial system) and charged with committing acts intended to sabotage the economy; they included B.A. Mensah of International Tobacco (Ghana) Ltd, and Kwame Safo-Ado of Imperial Chemical Laboratory Ltd.[66] Inevitably, criticisms were aired not only about businesses being confiscated or closed down arbitrarily, but also that the due process of law was not 'resorted to in addressing economic crimes by investors'.[67] Moreover, entrepreneurs – both Ghanaian and resident foreigners – were detained for extended periods without formal charges being preferred, and some had to pay out large sums of money before being released. Not surprisingly, business representatives continued to urge that those incarcerated for alleged commercial illegalities should be brought before impartial courts for formal trial, and that, otherwise, such state actions would continue to create uncertainty regarding the security of investment and property rights.

The confidence of entrepreneurs and their willingness to invest were affected negatively in various other ways. In the 1960s and 1970s, the private sector had had to operate within a publicly regulated environment characterized by extensive state controls. This government-determined framework generated market distortions and inefficiencies which reduced private investment to insignificant levels by 1983. With the coming of the ERP, policy reforms were premised on the establishment of a more market-oriented economy. Deregulation took place in foreign-exchange transactions, trade and pricing, and administrative controls were substantially eased. But the existing rules and regulations as regards employment of the workforce, administration of taxation, approval of investment, procedures for imports and exports, etc., provided private capital with continuing evidence of strong state intervention in the business sector. Most attempts to control imports and to determine prices (including, for example, soap, beer, and petroleum products) were viewed as unpropitious for new investment, especially since informal and unpredictable enforcements affected the viability of many businesses. They also created uncertainty among entrepreneurs regarding the government's pricing policy, as well as its overall attempts to deregulate the economy.

Private investment was further affected adversely by some of the policy reforms implemented under the ERP. Changes in the exchange rate proved to be particularly detrimental to a number of local firms. Massive devaluations of the *cedi* – from approximately 2.75 to the dollar in 1983 to over 450 in 1992 – created a severe liquidity crisis, as well as rendering it difficult for importers to find so much 'up-front' local currency to purchase foreign exchange. The problem was compounded by attempts to achieve positive rates of interest in an inflationary environment. In the late 1980s and early 1990s, what indigenous business could be viable when borrowing at rates of over 30 per cent? In addition, an exceptionally tight credit policy did not favour long-term investment at a time when the need for working capital increased sharply, due to the price rises of imported inputs in *cedis*. As the Association of Ghana Industries (AGI) complained in 1989, 'many establishments are currently starved of cash resources and face, in consequence, the real prospect of closure'.[68]

For some import-substituting manufacturing firms (garments, leather-processing, cosmetics, plastics), the situation was exacerbated by the competition from imported goods under the liberalized system of trade. A number of them closed down, and declining production in others led to mounting protectionist pressures on the government. The AGI called 'for realistic measures at least in the medium term to protect local industries from the ravages of an open, uncontrolled and unfair competition from cheap imports'.[69]

The generally negative reaction of the PNDC to the plight of indigenous enterprises brought it into sharp conflict with sections of the business community. The regime was not perceived as sufficiently supportive of the economic interests of domestic capital, let alone helping those hurt by the operational consequences of the ERP policy reforms. Indeed, it was viewed as destroying Ghanaian capital by not assisting local concerns to stand up to the rigours of international competition. In 1990, the AGI acknowledged that 'a significant change in attitude towards the problems facing industry today has taken place', but felt that the government had been unduly slow to respond to the financial distress suffered by many companies.[70]

In all the years of economic reform since 1983, the private sector felt inadequately consulted. Only occasional discussions took place between spokesmen of the business community and the key public officials concerned with fiscal and monetary policies, including the Secretary/Minister for Finance and Economic Planning and the Governor of the Bank of Ghana. Business representation on the advisory councils and boards of government ministries and state-owned enterprises was virtually non-existent. Indeed, institutional mechanisms for promoting communication between the various sectors of the economy were either largely absent or moribund. Business groups wishing to press their views on the central authorities were hard put to find any regular channels of access. The highly bureaucratic nature of the on-going programme of state enterprise divestiture reinforced business in its view that the regime intended playing the major, even dominant, role in economic decision-making. To be sure, there were informal contacts as individual entrepreneurs exploited ties with PNDC leaders to obtain favours. But, generally, the owners and/or managers of business felt that they were not respected, and that they were not part of the decision-making process.

Government attitudes towards private business

Ambiguity and equivocation were marked features of the attitudes of PNDC leaders towards local entrepreneurs. Public affirmations of support for their key role in the economy were far fewer and more grudging than statements emphasizing the dishonest and exploitative nature of the private sector. In Ebo Tawiah's opening address to the 'First Dialogue between Government Members and the Private Business Community in Ghana' in February 1990, this leading PNDC member focused on various 'improprieties', including recent financial irregularities in the timber industry (in 1989, nine companies had been closed down, their assets seized, and their directors imprisoned), which had resulted in the loss of a great deal of revenue for the state. Continuing, he argued: 'These observations usually stand to make the government waver in its confidence in the Ghanaian business community', and he called upon the private sector 'to institute a code of ethics among its members'. At the same meeting, Kwesi Botchwey, the Secretary for Finance and Economic Planning, alluded to the 'corrupt business culture' prevailing in Ghana under previous regimes, when firms engaged in 'influence-peddling', profiteering, and corruption. Similar concerns about 'crookery in business' were voiced frequently by the Chairman of the PNDC.[71] In public remarks about supporting local enterprises, government leaders pointedly declared that such assistance was intended solely for 'well-intentioned businessmen and investors'.[72]

Initially, the PNDC's economic thinking revolved around increased state intervention, central economic planning, and the urgent need for the assets of the privileged few to be redistributed.[73] A residue of this early statism and populism remained throughout the years of PNDC rule. According to Tawiah, government still saw wealth as something undesirable, especially in a society where the mass of the people are very poor and 'deprived sections of the community' need to be protected from exploitative capital. 'Business must improve its concerns for labour' and 'management should not lead too affluent a life-style in an environment of hardship' were sentiments widely held and articulated within the higher echelons of the PNDC. As explained by Botchwey, when introducing a super sales tax from 50 to 500 per cent on such items as mineral water and alcoholic liquors in January 1990, 'The Government continues to view with concern the amount of resources being devoted to luxury consumption ... because they deprive the majority of Ghanaians of their fair share of national resources'.[74]

Within two years of coming to power and advocating radical economic policies, PNDC leaders were speaking of reducing the participation of the state and encouraging the growth of the private sector. At a meeting of the Consultative Group for Ghana in Paris in 1984, it was reported that the 'Government recognizes that the private sector has a distinct role to play in successfully implementing the ERP'.[75] Such a statement had been absent when the country's economic programme had been presented to donors the previous year. Obviously the sheer weight of evidence that statist policies had been unsuccessful had prompted some economic rethinking within the PNDC. The direction of this reassessment was also strongly shaped by the policy advice emanating from the World Bank and other external donor agencies, which emphasized the necessity for enhancing private economic activity. 'Admittedly', as was explained to the Consultative Group by Ghana's representatives in 1984, 'a credibility gap exists vis-à-vis the private sector but we intend to fully restore mutual confidence.'[76] Thereafter, World Bank studies began identifying ways of generating a supportive business climate, and, indeed, the PNDC followed closely such proposals for improving the atmosphere for private investment in the country.

PNDC leaders did accept the need to promote the private sector by reducing state intervention in the economy. With World Bank prompting, a number of policy changes reduced the previous constraints exercised by a variety of individuals and institutions. The administrative discretion of public officials was significantly curbed under the ERP. Moreover, the government's state-owned enterprise divestiture programme – launched with World Bank encouragemrnt in 1987 – promised a reduction in the state's role in economic production and trading activity, as well as an enlarged scope in these areas for private capital. In addition, through financial assistance from the World Bank and various bilateral sources, funds were obtained to support business concerns. Actions to develop capital markets were also taken, including the opening of a stock exchange in 1990.

In a 1984 report, the World Bank had pointed to the harm that the People's and Workers' Defence Committees were causing to the PNDC's efforts towards economic recovery.[77] Activists had not only harassed business managers, but also initiated several worker takeovers of firms, including some owned by foreigners. After these PNDC organizations had been reconstituted as Committees for the Defence of the Revolution, with a revised mandate to help raise productivity and not to interfere in management, the World Bank reported with satisfaction in November 1984: 'The need to improve private sector confidence has been clearly recognized, and there has been a steady reduction in the number and frequency of arbitrary actions that might affect the private sector.'[78]

A consultative committee was established in March 1988 to enable entrepreneurs to meet with officials drawn from state ministries and government organizations whose activities affected the private sector. In February 1990, the importance of improving working relationships between the government and the business community was further recognized by the inauguration of a bi-annual dialogue to provide opportunities for more effective interchange of ideas and information.

The promotion of the private sector: political considerations
Although the PNDC adopted various macroeconomic policies which improved the business climate in Ghana from 1983, its recovery programme was threatened by inadequate private investment.[79] This increased, it is true, from 5.7 per cent of GDP in 1989 to over 8 per cent in 1990,[80] albeit mainly attributable to foreign investment in gold mining. From 1990, further reforms were advocated by the World Bank to create a more favourable business environment and thereby enhance investor confidence. Their key recommendations involved improvements in the financial sector, in taxation and investment incentives, and in the legal and regulatory framework. Some mention was made in World Bank documents of the need to reform state-owned enterprises (via commercialization and/or divestiture), as well as to improve dialogue with the private sector. However, given that a more propitious business environment needed to be promoted through various economic reforms, it was not to be forgotten that entrepreneurs were also sensitive to the prevailing political climate.

If the private sector was to play a greater role in Ghana's economic recovery it had to become an integral part of the relevant decision-making process. In the formulation of the ERP, the extent of consultation with representatives of the business community was minimal, and remained so in the various phases of structural adjustment. To be sure, mechanisms were introduced to promote more active communication, but these had still not become institutionalized. By mid-1991, only one of the scheduled bi-annual dialogues had taken place, and the work of the consultative committee, after a spate of meetings, was suddenly brought to an abrupt end. The business community had no direct voice in the leadership of the PNDC, was not adequately represented on important boards and committees, and did not feel 'respected' let alone 'courted'.

The continuing ambivalence of the government stemmed from the populist and socialist views of many of its leaders, especially as they found it difficult to speak out on behalf of the poor and disadvantaged while being perceived as trying to cultivate those regarded as 'capitalists'. It proved almost impossible to reconcile the rhetoric of the 'Revolution' with respect for the profit motive, quite apart from fears that a viable private sector could create a new centre of power, or underwrite the emergence of an alternative political force, or even finance another *coup d'état*. A regime as unsure of its own support as the PNDC was bound to regard such an eventuality as a dangerous threat.

The PNDC's economic thinking evolved from radicalism to liberalism, not least because the survival of the regime seemed to depend on the adoption of a reform programme designed to gain essential financial backing from the IMF, the World Bank and other external donors. Similar practical calculations led Ghana's political leaders to believe that the private sector had an invaluable contribution to make in the country's economic recovery. The concluding of a credit agreement with the World Bank in April 1991 to promote private investment attested to the seriousness of the PNDC's decision to create a more secure and friendlier climate for business. The following month, in its report to the Consultative Group for Ghana, the government stated that 'private sector investment promotion will be accorded the highest priority'.[81] This new supportive attitude as well as the various economic measures were welcomed by indigenous capital, but they proved insufficient to lead to greater private investment. Many of Ghana's particular political impediments continued to inhibit the desired investor response.

The PNDC was not constitutionally elected. It was unaccountable to the people. Decision-making was a restricted affair and few people outside the higher echelons of the central administration were consulted. As business people frequently complained: 'There is government by decree'. Public debate on the ERP was hardly permitted, the press was by no means free, and opportunities to question key decisions were virtually non-existent. Information about the operations and transactions of departments/ministries/parastatals was rarely disseminated or made public. Nor could the judicial system be relied upon to protect personal and property rights. Arbitrary actions against businessmen, including investigations, detentions, and confiscations, were not subject to the due process of the law. In sum, the authoritarian and arbitrary character of PNDC rule was not consonant with the kind of 'governance for development' advocated by the World Bank. In terms of accountability, transparency, openness, predictability, and the rule of law, the regime was far from providing the political environment now widely deemed to be indispensable for a dynamic economy.[82]

Domestic private business called for the rectification of various constraints which had limited private investment, including (i) the excessively suspicious attitude on the part of some PNDC leaders towards private capital; (ii) the failure of the regime to consult adequately with representatives of the private sector; and (iii) the justifiable fears among entrepreneurs regarding the security of their investments. As explained by I.E. Yamson, president of the Ghana Employers' Association, 'The promotion of private enterprise would presuppose Government acceptance of the principle of participatory development in ... policy formulation particularly if these policies will affect the success of the private sector'. For private investors, their supply response would be affected by the extent of opportunities made available for consultation and participation, as well as the creation of an 'enabling environment which will make private investment safe and profitable'.[83]

The PNDC evinced its willingness to permit business associations to become more actively involved in the processes of decision-making. A Private Sector Advisory Group was established in 1991 to promote regular channels of information and communication between private sector groups and the Ghanaian Government. As a result of such meetings, it was reported that various laws criticized by business were repealed. How effective this and similar institutions would be in furthering greater dialogue between government and business remained to be seen. One World Bank economist voiced his pessimism, arguing that 'convincing signs of a new approach and a new partnership with private businesses have not been forthcoming from the government'.[84]

Finally, the president of the Ghana Employers' Association also expressed 'concern at the slow pace of the divestiture programme', and lamented 'the continued over-involvement of the state in the economy' whereby 'state-owned industries still remain a predominant part of Ghana's economy'.[85] Although public enterprises were privatized, unless the political obstacles to state divestiture were removed, there would be only limited progress in this direction, with discouraging consequences for the private sector. Two World Bank economists expressed their concern: 'Lack of clarity in the limits to public sector activity in Ghana remains a major impediment to private sector confidence and investment response'.[86]

Continuing political constraints to private sector development

Ugandan, Zimbabwean, Ghanaian, Nigerian & other African illustrations
As in the case of privatization, so with regard to private sector development, pressures for its promotion have intensified in the past few years. International donors have mounted a major campaign for a greater private sector role in Africa. Not only has the state been held responsible for Africa's poor economic performance but also, it is contended, economic recovery and economic growth will arise from the dynamism of private business enterprise.[87] The World Bank has pushed strongly for the transfer of assets and control of state firms to private ownership as well as for sustained encouragement and assistance to private domestic entrepreneurs. Private sector groups have also pressed vigorously for economic liberalization, especially the privatization of publicly-owned enterprises, and called for larger state support to enable indigenous entrepreneurs to prosper. Moreover, most African governments have affirmed their desire for enhanced private enterprise development. As Ugandan President Yoweri Museveni puts it, his 'government recognizes the vital role that private investment plays in economic development', and it will accordingly provide 'the proper environment for their profitable activities'. Nearly everywhere some effort is being made to stimulate local private investment. Economic reforms, generally in the form of structural adjustment programmes approved by the IMF and the World Bank, have improved the business milieu, as a result of which new businesses have been started, particularly in agriculture and services. Yet sub-Saharan Africa remains a region characterized by 'the low level and poor revival of private investment'.[88]

Until recently, and as considered earlier in this chapter, few governments have created a conducive environment for business development to attain the desired levels of private investment. Such an environment requires a sound and supportive state bureaucracy which is not much in evidence. Corrupt officials pervade government offices at all levels and raise the costs of doing business. Incompetent bureaucrats, including many suspicious of private entrepreneurs, inhibit new private investment. Property rights continue to be inadequately guaranteed and an impartial and predictable legal system is still found wanting. Private enterprise also complains loudly about the inadequacies of local infrastructural facilities for its business needs. Moreover, private manufacturing firms express serious anxiety about the authorities doing little or nothing to control rampant smuggling which is destroying the domestic markets for their products. They also 'scream murder' about being confronted by too much competition, arising mainly from reductions in trade restrictions and protection and which is undermining their businesses. Governments have also only partly reduced the dominant position of the state in their economies. The presence of public enterprises in many economic sectors has constituted a barrier to the entry of private firms. As a result hardly anywhere has a major revitalization of local private capital occurred, and private investment responses have remained disappointing.[89]

A political climate of co-operative private sector-government interactions has been especially lacking. Government consultation with private sector representatives has been limited. However, as a result of the demands of the international financial institutions, governments have undertaken to allow greater private sector participation in economic policy decisions. In Ghana, where relations between the PNDC and local business were marked by suspicion and hostility, the World Bank helped to establish the Private Sector Advisory Group in 1991. Also with World Bank support, the Private Sector Foundation was set up in Uganda in 1995 as an umbrella organization bringing together private sector organizations. Both the PSAG (as well as the subsequent Private Enterprise Foundation) and the PSF have presented to the incumbent authorities the concerns of their members on fiscal and tax measures, business licensing, tariff protection, and access to industrial land.

African governments are realizing that consultation with the private sector is a strategy worth pursuing. They need business support for various reasons, and particularly because entrepreneurs can generate the revenues to pay for diverse state obligations as well as creating much needed jobs. Ghana's President Rawlings is now showing a much more conciliatory attitude towards the business community which, writes a correspondent, 'he has traditionally regarded with suspicion'. 'We will do everything possible to help you to help us', he pledged at his 1997 presidential inauguration, thereby demonstrating his clear understanding of the need to assist private business to function profitably if the country was to attract increasing private investment to generate the resources (revenues, employment) needed for the regime to retain its political popularity.[90] On the other hand, opportunities for consultation and policy dialogue can reduce business complaints about governments determining tax and tariff levels without prior consideration of the views of private capital. Consultation processes can also build business confidence and thereby elicit the desired private investment responses. Greater state-business communication can therefore be mutually beneficial. Yet these emerging interactive relations are still in their infancy. Greater levels of consultation between governments and the private sector, particularly before policy changes are introduced, have so far not been achieved. State-business relations have also been subject to continuing political influence and control.

African political leaders have been unwilling to engage in regular dialogue with business leaders for a number of reasons. Partly because so many government economic decisions are actually determined by the international financial institutions, and also constitute important parts of the policy conditionality of the international donors, they are not considered subjects for local discussion.[91] Value-added tax provides an example of one such reform measure on which the business community has not been consulted concerning the merits of the tax as well as the details of its implementation. The Ugandan Ministry of Finance invited a number of business associations to 'briefing sessions' on VAT but the policy itself had already been determined by the ministry and the IMF, and was clearly not a matter for local review and consideration. In Ghana and Uganda, business resistance to VAT erupted shortly after its introduction, leading in Ghana to its withdrawal and in Uganda to various modifications. Governments are also averse to much participation in economic decision-making where business groups are associated with the political opposition, as was the case in Ghana in the 1990s. Because so many leading businesspeople were active on behalf of opposition parties in the 1992 elections, the following year the Ghanaian authorities sponsored a new umbrella business organization, the Confederation of Indigenous Business Associations (CIBA), composed of more politically acceptable partners, in an attempt to promote consultation with the business community which would be more acceptable to the government. Thus, where consultations have taken place in Africa, government representatives have interacted with particular entrepreneurs, usually ones they trust and support, on matters in which there is some local administrative discretion.

But the main reason for limited policy consultation between business and government lies in the continued failure of African political leaders to recognize the leadership of the private sector in development. President Museveni has arguably gone the farthest in conferring such recognition, at least in his public discourse. As he claims, government and private enterprise are 'partners in economic development and our roles are complementary ... It is, therefore, crucial that the private sector should have an input in the formulation of policies affecting the economy.' He even foresees a time when 'the private sector eventually overtakes the public sector' to become 'the dominant sector in our economy,' and, accordingly, 'assumes a higher profile in policy formation'.[92] Most African rulers, however, are highly reluctant to accept that governments have to create an enabling environment for private business to spearhead national economic expansion. And, by itself, the indigenous private sector is too weak economically to constitute the principal agent of economic transformation and needs the strong support of the state. Emphasis continues to be placed on the state for raising and sustaining economic growth, the more so because governments wish to retain their control over economic resources for patronage purposes as well as because the entire *raison d'être* of the state's developmental functions would be called into question by a vigorous private sector in a predominantly market-based economy.

In addition, in much of Africa foreign investors are often assigned much higher economic priority than local businesspeople, partly because they do not present an alternative centre of power to the incumbent political authorities, and partly because they contribute the most to state revenues. This soliciting of foreign operators, it is argued, shows the limited degree of official commitment to indigenous private capital becoming the driving force in the recovery of African economies. To the extent that the domestic private sector is not treated as an equal partner with the state (and foreign capital) in development, so its role in economic decisions will remain limited.

Private business associations are also weakly developed and generally unable to play important roles in economic policy matters. In the early 1990s, Ghanaian and Ugandan private sector organizations hardly possessed the staff and expertise nor the information and financial resources to undertake strong lobbying and negotiating activities with government. Equally important is that the leverage business can exercise over government is affected by the extent of its fragmentation. Internal divisions based on diverse economic interests hamper the private sector in its ability to unite in disputes over state economic decisions. Many have commented on the conflictual nature of inter-business relations in Nigeria.[93] Differences between manufacturers who favour tariff protection and traders who advocate trade liberalization constitute a common division within many African countries. Kenyan, Ghanaian, and Zimbabwean manufacturers have complained bitterly of the devastating impact imports were having on their industries, while commercial operators have called for even greater levels of trade liberalization. The different groups are often based in their own, separate business organizations.[94] For example, the Uganda Importers, Exporters and Traders Association (UIETA) has called for the lifting of excise duties introduced on imported products to protect local manufacturers from foreign competition, arguing that free trade is a global trend and that imports should not be restricted.[95] On the other side, the Uganda Manufacturers Association (UMA) has been opposed to lower levels of industrial protection which, it charges, would result in unfair import competition leading to local plant closures, higher unemployment, and lower tax revenues. In 1996, the strike initiated by the traders over VAT was not supported by the UMA even though both private sector associations shared common concerns about the tax. There are also differences within the agricultural sector. Skalnes writes of 'the division of the agricultural lobby in Zimbabwe'.[96] On the one hand were the interests of the commercial farmers who favoured liberalization of agricultural markets, and on the other the large number of small producers who wanted the system of administered prices and parastatal marketing to remain in place.

In Uganda, the 1990s have seen differences in the economic interests of foreign, mainly Asian, investors, and indigenous entrepreneurs. Local traders have complained bitterly about unfair and 'cut-throat competition that the Asians have introduced' driving them out of business. They also collided with the government when it increased excise duty on imported textile products and thus favoured Asian textile manufacturers at the expense of African traders, who argued that they were not only being over-taxed but were also contributing much more than Asian manufacturers to government tax revenues.[97] African resentment has increased as Asians have so evidently prospered in economically difficult times. If such differences blunt the political influence of private economic interests, private business is also politically weak where it is foreign-owned. The 'big foreign enterprises are seen as threatening in Zimbabwe. The mining companies, therefore, have to keep a very low profile.'[98] And similarly in East African countries, the dominant Asian business communities have to confront much African nationalist sentiment which obliges them to maintain a low political profile.

Only occasionally do different business groups co-operate and work together to resolve differences and provide coherent policy proposals. A central cohesive association may be required to mediate conflicting views or devise common positions. But in most African countries, an economic organization that speaks for the private sector as a whole barely exists. More typical are business associations competing with each other for supremacy and proximity to government. An effective umbrella organization of private capital is the Botswana Confederation of Commerce, Industry and Manpower (BOCCIM), but there are not many others. It has proved difficult to create a strong 'peak' association in situations where business is fragmented along various lines. Private sector interests remain disparate and are, at times, manipulated by politicians for their own ends. At times, also, they put forward conflicting demands on economic policy, thus limiting their political impact on government and the policy process.

Nevertheless, the political liberalization which is emerging in African countries in the 1990s has provided new opportunities for business organizations to play a greater role in advancing and defending their interests without the previous strong hindrance from government. Before the political opening in Kenya in late 1991, 'business leaders were often hesitant to voice their criticisms of public policy for fear of government retaliation. The government could deny access to import licences and foreign exchange or call in bank loans prematurely, causing great hardship or even sounding the death knell for some firms.'[99] In recent years, however, with a region-wide easing of political controls and restrictions, a number of private sector associations have become quite outspoken in their criticisms of state economic policy, especially on structural adjustment reforms that directly affect business operations. Manufacturers and commercial farmers, for instance, have challenged governments, publicly over trade liberalization reforms. Extensive lobbying by business groups has been permitted by many governments, but because of their agreements with the international financial institutions they have been obliged to implement economic reforms as determined by external agencies. However, special privileges have been conferred on individual firms, typically those whose owners have close links with the powers that be. Where business people have felt their grievances less well addressed and have engaged the authorities in direct political confrontation, as in the anti-VAT demonstrations and strikes led by commercial traders in several countries, then governments have had to resort to more repressive measures. But, for the most part, business organizations have been circumspect in their dealings with government. The state still retains control over many resources which can affect the economic fortunes of business operators. And, by lobbying for government intervention on their behalf, especially for state protection of local manufacturing, business interests have demonstrated their dependence on the state for the fulfillment of their economic needs. Certainly, business groups have become much more activist on economic policy issues. But business leaders continue to complain that their proposals are not given serious attention, that their actual influence on economic matters remains minimal, and that the state (together with the international financial institutions) remains dominant in economic policy.[100]

Moreover, business associations have continued to avoid involvement in overtly political issues. In the earlier post-independence decades, they were generally hesitant to criticize incumbent authoritarian regimes. Many business people collaborated with those in state power in order to benefit from governmental favours (such as lucrative state contracts) or to avoid government sanctions. In the early 1990s, it is asserted that 'an active business community played a leading part in the onset of regime transitions'.[101] Very probably private entrepreneurs who supported the pro-democracy movements were those such as 'many Bamileke businessmen [in Cameroon] whom [President] Biya had purposely excluded from profitable rent-seeking opportunities'[102], and who were no longer linked to ruling coalitions. They would have typically engaged in opposition roles, while the larger, well-connected businesspeople would have hardly seen many attractions in anti-government political dissent. Recent political liberalization has curbed somewhat the domineering ways of African governments, but many authoritarian tendencies continue to persist. Given the relatively undemocratic and unaccountable behaviour of top political leaders as well as the still ample patronage possibilities at their disposal, private sector interests have generally stayed out of the political process for fear of losing access to economic preferences and resources controlled by the state.

The politicization of private African capital

Ugandan, Zimbabwean, Ghanaian, Nigerian and other African examples
The political weaknesses of the private sector have not only meant that it is subordinate to government but also that the state is still virtually autonomous in economic decision-making. In fact, under the structural adjustment programmes the economic bureaucracy is being strengthened and this, in turn, enhances its autonomy and power vis-à-vis private business. Moreover, in spite of privatization and other market reforms, the state retains a controlling hand over many matters affecting private sector operations (licences, contracts, taxes, tariffs, special privileges), and therefore remains important for business entrepreneurs seeking government patronage. As in East Asia and elsewhere, African governments are using their discretionary powers to support those with close political and personal ties to the political leadership as well as to punish those allied with opposition groups and organizations.

In South Korea during the 1950s, Japanese-owned properties as well as state-owned enterprises were 'distributed, at extremely low prices, to individuals who had close political connections with the ruling elite'.[103] Moreover, select entrepreneurs with political connections were given loans, allowed to evade taxes, and provided with protective tariffs and preferential contracts for government projects. In exchange for these favours, the entrepreneurs had to make generous contributions to the government. Although some of the leading capitalists were arrested in the early 1960s, most were pardoned by the military regime that came to power in 1961. In return for political funds and economic co-operation in the implementation of development plans, they were granted many trade and tax privileges. It was this 'narrow development alliance between the military regime and select large capitalists that eventually shaped the capital accumulation process'.[104]

Collusion between political regimes and select capitalists has been very common in sub-Saharan Africa. Those in control of the state have used it partly to promote their own opportunities for profit and partly to consolidate their political support by apportioning benefits to politically favoured groups and interests. Considerations such as these have influenced the assistance provided to local private businesses. The available evidence suggests that governments aid those companies owned by the relatives and political associates of state personnel, while entrepreneurs linked to opposition politicians are regularly denied access to state patronage. As one experienced journalist wrote in regard to government-backed 'indigenization' schemes in Zimbabwe, 'The preferential treatment of black enterprises is open to abuse, particularly as preference appeared to be given to companies with good connections with the ZANU-PF party'. For example, 'the indigenisation of the construction industry meant that contracts had gone to firms with the best relations with the ruling party, not those that were best qualified'.[105] Following the award in 1997 of a highly lucrative mobile cellular telephone licence to a consortium in which President Robert Mugabe's nephew was a partner, and whose other directors included a former army commander and a batch of ruling party officials, many accusations were directed at top state officials and politicians for 'abusing government tenders to enrich themselves and their cronies'. Allegations were made that government tenders were being awarded mainly to relatives of the president (his nephew had won three multi-million dollar contracts in a row), some close political associates, and his fellow tribesmen.[106]

Generally, those with access to political influence have monopolized access to credit, contracts and concessions extended by state agencies and which are so essential for the development of domestic capital. In Côte d'Ivoire, for example, export marketing of the important cocoa and coffee crops has for a long been dominated by companies owned by the relatives of the country's two post-independence presidents. Under structural adjustment, exporting monopolies have been lifted by World Bank reforms, but the old export companies with their continuing political ties remain influential in the lucrative export business.[107] Moreover, public contracts have always been typically steered in favour of the politically well-connected. World Bank reforms have also begun to make the award of contracts more competitive, but much cronyism prevails, as in Côte d'Ivoire and Zimbabwe, in the big road projects and the building or rehabilitation of airports.

Furthermore, evidence abounds of recent economic reforms favouring private entrepreneurs associated with state rulers. For example, economic liberalization 'has given rise to a new group of Tanzanian business leaders, many with close connections to the ruling party'.[108] Evidence is also emerging, as indicated in the previous chapter, of payments being made from the proceeds of privatization to persons with family or political ties to the ruling elites. On the other hand, those businesses benefitting from state patronage reciprocate by providing political funds and other political and personal help to office-holders. An interesting example of such mutually beneficial associations occurred in Uganda in 1996 at a time when the National Resistance Movement (NRM) government was finding itself short of funds to finance its campaigns in the presidential and parliamentary elections. Elsewhere in Africa, for example in Ghana and Kenya in 1992, incumbent regimes in similar situations simply printed the desired amounts of money that they required for electoral purposes. In Ghana, the government increased the money supply by nearly 60 per cent to finance its election campaign. In Uganda, however, the ruling NRM 'set up its own trading company and gave it tax waivers to import items and sell them for windfall profits'. Five other privately owned companies – whose owners were closely associated with the NRM – were reported to have been given tax exemptions to import consumer commodities. 'The billions of shillings in profit ... left the Museveni campaign well-funded' as well as providing the private trading concerns with substantial monetary gains.[109]

Conversely, private enterprises owned by persons deemed to be politically unacceptable to those in power have invariably been denied state support. In Ghana, the 'political leanings' of local entrepreneurs interested in acquiring public companies 'are often subject to close government scrutiny. The privatization of a government-controlled enterprise may be stalled if an interested party is known to be sympathetic to the political opposition.'[110] In Nigeria, the military government in 1994 withdrew the oil prospecting licence of Summit Oil whose owner, Kola Abiola, is the son of the late Chief Moshood Abiola, the presumed winner of the aborted 1993 presidential elections. In Zimbabwe, the government has also withheld benefits from the businesses of individuals outside of ruling circles. In 1996, it even circumvented a Supreme Court ruling to prevent a local firm, ECONET, a subsidiary of T.S. Masiyiwa Holdings, from being licensed as the country's first private mobile cellular telephone service provider. A local academic noted that the governing elite was 'clearly not prepared to tolerate such attempts to develop autonomous power bases in the private sector'. It was 'opposed to the emergence of an African business class, autonomous of the state'. It 'feared that such a class would be less reliant on the politics of patronage and would therefore be less easy to control'.[111] Finally, virtually everywhere, anti-government entrepreneurs have been the victims of politically motivated harassment; many have had to face inquiries into their business activities, which have adversely affected the economic well-being of their enterprises.

In South Korea a shift took place from political allocation to economic performance as an important criterion of state allocation.

'But there was no question that it was political connection, not just a firm's capability, that determined who could participate in profitable projects doled out by the government.'[112] In sub-Saharan Africa, the relations between state and local business have invariably been influenced by patronage considerations. Governments are still continuing to use their remaining economic controls to allocate credit, licences, contracts, tax and tariff privileges to favoured clients, although some may also be pressing favoured capitalists to improve their economic performance.

Politically mediated access to government-controlled resources is the chief avenue to the emergence of a group of larger African capitalists in fields such as banking and manufacturing. This has been the case since independence: a class of wealthy individuals owes its wealth less to entrepreneurial enterprise in commerce and industry and more to political connections and favours. Also, nearly everywhere there are people who have made quick money through political favouritism. In Uganda, a handful of millionaires has arisen who only a few years ago were 'as poor as church mice'. Referring to President Museveni's brother, 'what is worrying everybody is how he got so much wealth in this short time'.[113] Allegations abound of political favouritism and suspicious business dealings,[114] which tend to confirm the public's views that a successful private sector is invariably tainted with corruption. Indeed, crony relationships between top state personnel and favoured business entrepreneurs commonly involve irregular dealings. Crony capitalist enterprise in sub-Saharan Africa is, in fact, marked by many corrupt practices such as tax evasion and illegal importation. Finally, it is apparent that the consolidation and long-term viability of such crony private entrepreneurs will be dependent on their patrons maintaining themselves in power. Business concerns which have been made profitable by virtue of connections to those in political power will find it difficult to survive the downfall of their political benefactors, especially if the new regimes wish to replace established entrepreneurs with their own politically acceptable ones. Where patron-client relationships have constituted the foundations of African regimes, new governments will want to realign previous 'reward structures' with ones more congruent with their own political support base.

NOTES

1. By the private sector we refer to the formal, profit-making segment of the overall private enterprise system in a country. A significant portion of Africa's private

sector comprises small-scale peasants, informal sector businesses and petty traders; these are excluded from consideration here. Although formal private sector enterprises constitute only a small part of the overall economy, their current importance lies in the role they are expected to play in leading national economic growth under structural adjustment.

2. Indigenization here denotes the sale by foreign firms of their equity to local citizens.

3. Robert Wade, *Governing the Market. Economic Theory and the Role of Government in East Asian Industrialisation* (Princeton, NJ, 1990); and Gordon White (ed.), *Developmental States in East Asia* (Basingstoke, 1988).

4. For a discussion of African entrepreneurship being impeded during the colonial period, see Paul Kennedy, *African Capitalism. The Struggle for Ascendancy* (Cambridge, 1988), Chaps.2–3.

5. *ibid.*, pp.42–5 for a detailed discussion.

6. For a discussion of the concerns of local entrepreneurs just before and after independence in Nigeria, see Thomas J. Biersteker, *Multinationals, the State, and Control of the Nigerian Economy* (Princeton, NJ, 1987), pp.52–69.

7. See Kennedy, *op. cit.*, pp.95, 96, 97. See also Chaps.4–5 for a more detailed discussion.

8. A Harare-based business magazine noted mockingly in 1994 that Zimbabwe's ruling ZANU-PF government, in power since 1980, had until recently had as 'one of its main preoccupations' the 'sniffing out of "capitalists" from among its ranks and ostracising them'. There 'was something very unpatriotic about aspiring to be rich, let alone becoming rich'. See the editorial in the *Southern African Economist* (Harare), April 1994. Indeed, in many parts of Africa, and not just the socialist-inclined ones, business people were treated as enemies of the state and subjected to anti-capitalist rhetoric and even physical repression.

9. Paul Kennedy, 'Indigenous Capitalism in Ghana', *Review of African Political Economy*, 8 (1977), p.32; See also, Kennedy, *African Capitalism, op. cit.*, p.68.

10. Carolyn Baylies, 'Zambia's Economic Reforms and their Aftermath: The State and the Growth of Indigenous Capital', *Journal of Commonwealth and Comparative Politics*, 20,3 (1982),p.251. However, Baylies also concludes that by virtue of parastatal inefficiencies private business activity was not stifled but, in fact, flourished (p.254)

11. Richard Sandbrook, *The Politics of Africa's Economic Stagnation* (Cambridge, 1985), p.133.

12. Biersteker, *op. cit.*, pp. 98, 145–6, 269.

13. David Himbara, *Kenyan Capitalists, the State, and Development* (Boulder, CO, 1994), p.6.

14. David Himbara, 'The Failed Africanization of Commerce and Industry in Kenya', *World Development*, 22,3 (1994), p.470.

15. Catherine Boone, 'The Paradox of Protection and Monopoly in Sub-Saharan Africa', in Rexford A. Ahene and Bernard S. Katz (eds.), *Privatization and Investment in Sub-Saharan Africa* (New York, 1992), pp.105, 106.

16. John Rapley, *Ivoirien Capitalism. African Entrepreneurs in Cote d'Ivoire* (Boulder, CO, 1992), p.48.

17. *ibid.*, p.130.

18. *ibid.*, p.79.

19. *ibid.*, p.104.

20. For this argument in regard to Kenya, see Nicola Swainson, *The Development of Corporate Capitalism in Kenya 1918–77* (London, 1980), Chap.5, and Colin Leys, 'Capital Accumulation, Class Formation and Dependency. The Significance of the Kenyan Case', in Ralph Milliband and John Saville (eds.), *The Socialist Register 1978* (London, 1978), 241–66. Swainson writes (p.182): 'The post- colonial state in Kenya has been dominated by the hegemonic fraction of indigenous capital and the apparatuses and functions of the state have been realigned since 1963 to foster the development of this class.' In Botswana, it was 'specifically the class of cattle accumulators (both black and white) which took control of the state at independence under Seretse Khama'. The 'post-colonial state has played a significant role in the transformation of Botswana's cattle accumulators into a dependent national cattle-based bourgeoisie' as well as helping this class in 'steadily diversifying into commerce, manufacturing and real estate'. See Balefi Tsie, 'The Political Context of Botswana's Development Performance', *Journal of Southern African Studies*, 22,4 (1996), pp.602, 611.

21. Biersteker, *op. cit.*, pp.155, 157–8, 161, 185.

22. Himbara, 'Failed Africanization', pp.476–8. For a similar argument see also Nelson Kasfir, 'State, Magendo, and Class Formation in Uganda', *Journal of Commonwealth and Comparative Politics*, 21,3 (1983), p.100. Also in Cameroon, the 'northern and Bamilike businessmen who had enjoyed a privileged position during Ahidjo's administration were' under the succeeding Biya regime 'increasingly replaced by Beti businessmen, the so-called Beti Mafia'. See Piet Konings, 'The Post-Colonial State and Economic and Political Reforms in Cameroon', in Alex E. Fernandez Jilberto and Andre Mommen (eds.), *Liberalization in the Developing World* (London, 1996), p.251.

23. Himbara, *Kenyan Capitalists, op. cit.*, p.69. The 'loss of state power following the demise of the Kenyatta regime in 1978 was apparently decisive in leading to the collapse of almost all the major Kikuyu enterprises...' (p.160)

24. Nicola Swainson, 'The Rise of a National Bourgeoisie in Kenya', *Review of African Political Economy*, 8 (1977), 39–55.

25. Himbara, *Kenyan Capitalists, op. cit.*, pp.6, 70.

26. Kennedy, *African Capitalism, op. cit.*, p.61.

27. K.D. Kaunda, 'Zambia's Economic Revolution'. An address to the National Council of the United National Independence Party, 19 April 1968, p.41. See also Roger Tangri, *Politics in Sub-Saharan Africa* (London, 1985), pp.59–63 for a discussion of the Zambian situation.

28. Catherine Boone, 'Commerce in Cote d'Ivoire: Ivoirianisation without Ivoirian Traders', *Journal of Modern African Studies*, 31,1 (1993), pp.68–9. Kwame Nkrumah feared that the emergence of a strong indigenous class of capital would undermine his own pre-eminence in Ghana. He once remarked to a cabinet minister: 'Any Ghanaian with a lot of money has a lot of influence; any Ghanaian with a lot of influence is a threat to me.' This is quoted in John D. Esseks, 'Political Independence and Economic Decolonization: The Case of Ghana under Nkrumah', *Western Political Quarterly*, 24,1 (1971), p.61.

29. The quote on Uganda is from Mahmood Mamdani, *Politics and Class Formation in Uganda* (London, 1976), p.281. See also Kennedy, *African Capitalism, op. cit.*, pp.70–71. For a similar argument in regard to Lebanese entrepreneurs in Senegal, see Rita Cruise O'Brien, 'Lebanese Entrepreneurs in Senegal: Economic Integration and the Politics of Protection', *Cahiers d'études africaines*, 15,57 (1975), p.112. For

Asian capitalists being used to undermine Kikuyu entrepreneurs in Kenya in the 1980s, see 'Kenya: The Asian Dilemma', *Africa Confidential*, 24 June 1987.

30. Catherine Boone, *Merchant Capital and the Roots of Power in Senegal 1930–1985* (Cambridge, 1992), p.12 .

31. Baylies, *op. cit.*, p.250. For a more detailed discussion of the Zambian case whereby 'the state becomes an important resource in the struggle to build private capital', see Carolyn L. Baylies and Morris Szeftel, 'The Rise of a Zambian Capitalist Class in the 1970s', *Journal of Southern African Studies*, 8,2 (1982): 195–201.

32. Elliot Berg, 'The Potentials of the Private Sector in Sub-Saharan Africa', in Tore Rose (ed.), *Crisis and Recovery in Sub-Saharan Africa* (Paris, 1985); and World Bank, *Private Sector Development in Low-Income Countries* (Washington, DC, 1995).

33. Keith Marsden and Therese Belot, *Private Enterprise in Africa. Creating a Better Environment* (World Bank Discussion Paper, No.17, Washington, DC, 1987), p.47.

34. *ibid.*

35. Ishrat Husain and Rashid Faruqee (eds.), *Adjustment in Africa. Lessons from Country Case Studies* (Washington, DC, 1994), p.6. See also World Bank, *A Continent in Transition: Sub-Saharan Africa in the mid-1990s* (Washington DC, 1995), pp.7–9.

36. A deputy trade minister in Ghana, Dan Abodakpi, countered business criticism of trade liberalization as follows: 'We are aware of the effects of over-liberalization of imports but instead of protection we provide assistance and support for local industry.' In Ghana's 1996 presidential election, the main opposition alliance promised protection for some manufacturing sectors. See IPS, 'Businessmen in Ghana split over candidates', 9 December 1996.

37. Husain and Faruquee, *op. cit.*, p.7. A leading article in the *Daily Nation*, 19 December 1994, p.6 stated: 'One of the reasons for Kenya's inability to attract investment capital – even chase it away – is the prevalent corruption.'

38. See *People's Daily Graphic* (Accra), 19 June 1993, p.1. For the response of the local businessmen, see *West Africa* (London), 9 August 1993, pp.1393–5. In Ghana in the 1990s, several of the large private entrepreneurs held leading positions in opposition political parties.

39. See the following articles on the Ghanaian situation, 'The missing ingredient', in *The Economist* (London), 22 August 1992, p.36, and Ruby Ofori, 'Ghana. Mixed Messages', *Africa Report*, September/October (1993), pp.70–71. It is also claimed that Ghana's private sector has been 'largely absent from the divestiture activity'. This may be an overstatement but perhaps by associating the business sector with the political opposition the 'government has not given enough incentives to encourage local entrepreneurs to take a leading role in buying up the shares on offer through the divestiture', which have, instead, often been acquired by foreign companies. See Kofi Marrah, 'Divestiture Progress', *Business in Africa* (London), (June 1997), p.45.

40. Michael Lofchie, 'Trading Places: Economic Policy in Kenya and Tanzania', in Thomas M. Callaghy and John Ravenhill, (eds.), *Hemmed In. Responses to Africa's Economic Decline* (New York, 1994), p.451.

41. *ibid.*, p.441.

42. For a detailed study of government actions in explaining East Asian economic success, see Wade, *op. cit.*

43. See *Daily Topic* (Kampala), 29 August 1994. In South Africa, the Minister of Public Enterprise has affirmed that the government will set up a national empowerment fund to encourage share ownerships by blacks in privatized companies.

44. Interview with the chairman of the Tanzania Chamber of Commerce, Industries and Agriculture, David Mwaibula, in *The East African* (Nairobi), 15 April 1996, p.11.

45. Crony capitalism denotes the use of one's position in the state to dispense favours to cronies in the business sphere.

46. For a discussion of government attempts to control and regulate business organizations in Senegal between 1968 and the early 1970s, see Boone, *Merchant Capital, op. cit.*, pp.172, 183–5.

47. See Note 44 above.

48. Chairman of the Importers and Exporters Association, protesting at the new tax rates introduced by the government on imported bicycles in Uganda. See *The New Vision*, 21 December 1995, p.31.

49. 'tax policy should be developed by a process of consultation and dialogue between Government and the private sector'. See Uganda Manufacturers Association, 'Effects of the 1993/94 Budget on Local Industries' (Kampala, 1993), p.9. Similarly, the president of the Confederation of Zimbabwe Industries, whilst demanding that the government act on the high annual inflation and punitive interest rates, declared in 1995: 'We want industry to be taken as a serious partner in the development programme of the state'.

50. 'Government's monopoly of power, electricity and telecommunication networks has led to inefficiency and misuse ... and eroded the competitiveness of local investors. This calls for the demonopolisation and, most important, privatisation of these utility companies.' See Uganda Manufacturers Association, *op. cit.*, p.6. See also World Bank, *A Continent in Transition, op. cit.*, pp.47–50, and World Bank, *Private Sector, op. cit.*, Chap.2.

51. Michael Holman, 'Still Trailing the Rest of the World', *The Financial Times* (London), 20 May 1996.

52. This case study was published originally in the *Journal of Modern African Studies*, 30,1 (1992): 97–111. The version presented here has been revised only slightly. In writing this section, I have also benefited from Elizabeth I. Hart, 'Liberal Reforms in the Balance: The Private Sector and the State in Ghana, 1983–1995' (Ph.D. thesis, Princeton University, 1996).

53. J.S. Addo, 'The Role of Private Investment in Ghana', Ghana Manufacturers' Association, Accra, 24 February 1984.

54. The National Commission for Democracy, 'Evolving a True Democracy', Accra, 25 March 1991, p.5.

55. Addo, *op. cit.*

56. P.V. Obeng (PNDC Member and Chairman of the Committee of Secretaries) to Chief Executive, Ghana Investments Centre, Accra, 14 March 1988.

57. 'ERP, Private Sector and the New Agenda', in *Business and Financial Times* (Accra), 5 December 1990, p.2.

58. William Adda, 'Role of the State Restructuring of Public Enterprises', World Bank Economic Development Institute/Ghana Institute of Public Administration Seminar, Accra, March 1991.

59. Obeng, *op. cit.*

60. Ghana Investments Centre, 'The Dialogue Between Government Members and the Private Business Community in Ghana on 21 February 1990' reprinted in *The Investor* (Accra), 1,1 (1990), p.23. World Bank figures differ slightly: private investment was estimated to be 3.3% of GDP in 1988, with public investment at 8.0%, according to members of the Bank's Resident Mission in Accra.

61. Ghana Investments Centre, 'Discussion Paper on Private Sector Development Issues, 1989/90', 1990, p.3.
62. Private interview, Accra, February 1990.
63. Ghana Investments Centre, report prepared for 'Think Tank on Private Sector Development Issues', March 1988.
64. Ghana Investments Centre, 'Discussion Paper', *op. cit.*
65. It is also alleged that PNDC leaders interfered in the affairs of the Association of Ghana Industries by influencing the removal of its president, A. Appiah- Menkah, an ex-government minister, from office in 1982.
66. *Africa Confidential* (London), 32,7 (1991), p.8.
67. Ghana Investments Centre, 'Discussion Paper', *op. cit.*
68. Speech by J.K. Richardson, president of the AGI, at the 29th Annual General Meeting held in Accra on 23 February 1989. See Hart, *op. cit.*, pp.127–41 for a discussion of the credit shortages facing Ghanaian private entrepreneurs in the early 1990s.
69. Statement issued by the Council of the AGI, reprinted in *Business Weekly* (Accra), 26 December 1988, p.8.
70. Speech by J.K. Richardson, president of the AGI, at the 30th AGM held in Accra on 23 May 1990. For subsequent discussions surrounding trade liberalization, see G.F. Asmah, 'Ghana. Industries Battle for Survival', *Africa Economic Digest* (London), 9 March 1992, pp.5–6, and E. Dentu, 'Ghana. Life Saver for Industries', *Africa Economic Digest*, 6 April 1992, pp.6,8. See also Hart, *op. cit.*, pp.115–27 for a general discussion of the impact of devaluation and trade liberalization on Ghana's private sector.
71. For one example of such criticism by Rawlings, see *People's Daily Graphic*, 3 May 1990.
72. *ibid.*, 12 January 1991.
73. Notably formulated in the PNDC's *Programme for Reconstruction and Development* (Accra, 1982).
74. Kwesi Botchwey, 'The Budget and Highlights of Economic Policy for 1990', 10 January 1990, Accra, pp.4–5.
75. See Thomas Siebold, *Ghana, 1957–1967. Entwicklung und Ruckentwicklung. Verschuldung und IWF-Intervention* (Hamburg, 1988), p.247.
76. *ibid.*
77. World Bank, *Ghana – Policies and Program for Adjustment* (Washington, DC, 1984), p.51.
78. Cited in Siebold, *op. cit.*, p.247.
79. See Ishan Kapur et al., *Ghana: Adjustment and Growth, 1983–91* (IMF Occasional Paper 86, Washington, DC, 1991), pp.10, 15.
80. World Bank Resident Mission, Accra.
81. *Ghanaian Times* (Accra), 18 May 1991.
82. See World Bank, *Sub-Saharan Africa. From Crisis to Sustainable Growth: a long-term perspective study* (Washington, DC, 1989), *passim.* We discuss further the subject of 'governance for development' in chapter 6 of this book.
83. Address by I.E. Yamson at the 31st Annual General Meeting of the Ghana Employers' Association held in Accra on 17 May 1991.
84. Chad Leechor, 'Ghana: Frontrunner in Adjustment', in Husain and Faruqee, *op. cit.*, p.178. For private sector-government relations in 1992, see Jon Offei-Ansah, 'Rawlings: The Tasks Ahead', *Africa Economic Digest*, 16 November 1992, 6–7.

85. Yamson address, *op. cit.*
86. Ajay Chhibber and Chad Leechor, 'Ghana: 2000 and Beyond', *Finance and Development*, (September 1993), p.26. Private investment in Ghana apparently fell to less than 4% of GDP in 1992.
87. World Bank, *Private Sector, op. cit.*
88. World Bank, *A Continent in Transition, op. cit.*, p.7.
89. *ibid.*, pp.47–50, and World Bank, *Private Sector, op. cit.*, Chap.2.
90. Antony Goldman, 'Ghana's Former Dictator Blazes Unlikely Trail to Democracy', *Christian Science Monitor*, 10 January 1997.
91. African governments appear to have included hardly any leading businesspeople on their IMF and World Bank negotiating teams.
92. Speech by President Y.K. Museveni at the second presidential forum on strategic management for investment promotion and export growth, 10 November 1994, Entebbe.
93. The 'relatively high degree of overt interassociational conflict' in Nigeria's business relations is considered in Mick Moore and Ladi Hamalai, 'Economic Liberalization, Political Pluralism and Business Associations in Developing Countries', *World Development*, 21,12 (1993): 1903–5.
94. 'The significant difference was that NACCIMA, which represents largely trading and financial sector interests, supported economic liberalization, especially the reduction of import controls and import tariff rates ... Conversely, MAN and the NTMA, representing manufacturing activities that had been nurtured under protection and various kinds of preference, were generally resistant to any substantial change in economic policy'. *ibid.*, p.1905.
95. *The New Vision*, 14 September 1996, pp.1–2.
96. Tor Skalnes, *The Politics of Economic Reform in Zimbabwe. Continuity and Change in Development* (Basingstoke, 1995). p.176.
97. See *The New Vision*, 1 November 1996, p.15, and *The Market Place* (Kampala), 18 July 1997, p.6.
98. Jeffrey Herbst, *State Politics in Zimbabwe* (Berkeley, CA, 1990), p.15.
99. Gary Hansen, *Constituencies for Reform. Strategic Approaches for Donor-Supported Civic Advocacy Programs* (USAID Programs and Operations Assessment Report, No.12, Washington, DC, 1996), p.34.
100. The World Bank notes African 'companies having little or no role in the state's decision-making process; indeed, they may not even be informed of important rule changes before they take place'. World Bank, *World Development Report 1997* (Washington, DC, 1997), p.34.
101. Michael Bratton and Nicolas van de Walle, *Democratic Experiments in Africa* (Cambridge, 1997), p.148.
102. *ibid.*, p.167.
103. Hagen Koo and Eun Mee Kim, 'The Developmental State and Capital Accumulation in South Korea', in Richard P. Applebaum and Jeffrey Henderson (eds.), *States and Development in the Asian Pacific Rim* (Newbury Park, 1992), p.124. See also Kyong Dong Kim, 'Political Factors in the Formation of the Entrepreneurial Elite in South Korea', *Asian Survey*, 16,5 (1976), 465–77.
104. *ibid.*, p.125. During the Asian financial crisis of 1997–8, Western newspapers carried articles showing the prevalence of crony capitalism in a number of Asian countries. In Indonesia, cronyism had allowed President Suharto's children and friends to get rich while would-be entrepreneurs without connections were stifled.

105. Andrew Meldrum, 'Zimbabwe. The Last Scandal', *Africa Report*, (January/February, 1995), p.30.
106. Reuter News Agency, 'Scandal hits Mugabe', 12 March 1997. In Senegal, 'relations between government and business were characterised by clientelism and cronyism, with access to loans, licenses, subsidies, and government contracts being greatly facilitated for persons claiming family or political ties to the ruling elite'. See Samba Ka and Nicolas van de Walle, 'Senegal: Stalled Reform in a Dominant Party System', in Stephan Haggard and Steven B. Webb, (eds.), *Voting for Reform. Democracy, Political Liberalization, and Economic Adjustment* (New York, 1994), p.304.
107. See 'Cote d'Ivoire. Stable but ...', *The Economist*, 12 December 1998, p.50. Similarly in Malawi it was shown in early 1998 that President Bakili Muluzi controlled some 60% of the country's sugar distribution trade which earned him huge profits. He was said to have awarded sugar quotas for distribution to retail outlets to companies owned by himself, his cabinet ministers, close friends and members of the ruling UDF. President Muluzi was said to be using his profits 'to build his political muscle' and promote the activities of the UDF. See *The Daily Times* (Blantyre), 20 April 1998.
108. Bruce Heilman and John Lucas, 'A Social Movement for African Capitalism? A Comparison of Business Associations in Two African Cities', *African Studies Review*, 40,2 (1997), p.155.
109. See comments by Charles Onyango-Obbo, in *The East African*, 6 January 1997.
110. 'The National Trade Estimates Report on Foreign Trade Barriers' (Office of the US Trade Representative, Washington DC, 1997).
111. Brian Raftopoulos, 'Fighting for Control: The Indigenisation Debate in Zimbabwe', *Southern Africa Report* (Toronto), 11,4 (1996), pp.3, 4. It is also alleged that Masiyiwa failed to get a licence to operate a mobile phone system 'because he would not bring the party leaders into his project'. See *The New African* (London), July/August 1997, p.31. For further details on how Strive Masiyiwa overcame officialdom and cronyism to prosper in his telephone business, see *The Economist*, 10 October 1998, p.76.
112. Koo and Kim, *op. cit.*, p.128.
113. See 'Salim Saleh Should Declare Wealth', *The New Vision*, 28 May 1997, p.15.
114. For a company owned by Salim Saleh being awarded a lucrative contract without proper tendering to remove water hyacinth from Lake Victoria, see *The New Vision*, 19 March 1997, p.32. Saleh himself resents 'this stupid persecution' of his business dealings. He is now offering to sell 50% of the shares in his multi-million dollar Caleb International holding company to the public so that, as he arrogantly puts it, Ugandans can 'benefit from my entrepreneurship'. See *The New Vision*, 31 May 1997, pp.1–2. For further questioning of how he has accumulated his wealth, and Saleh's new responses to sell all his businesses and create a rural development fund, see the articles in *The Sunday Vision* (Kampala), 18 October 1998, and *The Monitor*, 19 October 1998.

African Governments
& Foreign Business

Private foreign companies have had an important presence in sub-Saharan countries for a long time. In a few places, foreign firms controlled the early administration of colonial territories, as in the case of Zambia where the British South Africa Company ran that territory up to 1924. In Zambia as well foreign mining companies created entire townships which were almost completely under foreign company control. Throughout colonial Africa, colonial policy encouraged direct foreign investment and colonial governments assisted foreign concerns to become profitable. And substantial foreign capital was successful in achieving considerable control over leading economic sectors including export agriculture, mining, manufacturing and services.

Foreign penetration into African economies increased after independence,[1] although Africa's share of total foreign direct investment to developing countries remained small, amounting to about 17 per cent in 1960. Most of this investment – over half of the total – went into the resource-extraction sectors of African economies (mining and petroleum), but penetration of foreign enterprises into the manufacturing and service sectors also grew. Transnational oil and mining corporations increased their investments in those few resource-rich countries, while foreign manufacturing investment was spread more widely throughout the Africa region.[2] In agriculture, estate production by foreign firms remained important in export crops in a small number of countries, while all over Africa, banking and financial services were accounted for largely by foreign companies.

From the very early years of the colonial period, another form of non-African capital became prominent in a number of African countries. This was resident expatriate capital. Although viewed at times as a segment of domestic capital, it is considered here as another form of foreign capital, albeit, as Colin Leys puts it, 'a special category of foreign investors'.[3] In countries like Kenya and Zimbabwe, white settlers operated agricultural and commercial enterprises from early colonial times and later moved into services and manufacturing. In many East and West African countries, domestic commerce was for long in the hands of Asian and

Levantine entrepreneurs; from the 1950s, the larger traders also began investing in manufacturing and contracting. After independence, non-African resident capital became less strongly entrenched in the commercial and agricultural sectors, moving into manufacturing and services such as finance and banking and tourism. Many of the smaller, non-African entrepreneurs, unable to move from trade into manufacturing, or because of the political insecurities of investing locally, emigrated to other African countries (for example white settlers emigrating to South Africa) or to other continents (East African Asians emigrating to Britain and Canada).

Since independence, most of the non-African private investment has been accounted for by large foreign-owned companies. Non-African resident capital has become of lesser economic significance, although in some East and West African countries it is still of major importance as a source of investment. Moreover, the numbers and national origins of foreign firms have increased. No longer drawn predominantly from the European colonial powers, there has been a growth in American and Asian (Japanese, Indian, and Taiwanese and, very recently, Malaysian) foreign capital. The present chapter is concerned mainly with the larger foreign-owned companies, although some mention is also made of resident non-African entrepreneurs.

The early post-independence decades

At independence, African governments actively encouraged new, direct foreign investment. Private investment inflows were seen as indispensable for the provision of the capital, foreign exchange, technology, market access, employment, tax revenues, and management so essential for the growth of Africa's economies. All of these were scarce and in the 1960s were virtually only available from foreign companies. Foreign capital was economically critical and strongly wooed. Policies towards foreign enterprise were permissive. Various incentives were provided – tax holidays, repatriation of profits, restrictions on competing imports – and few limitations were placed on foreign investors. Multinational investment increased substantially in the early post-independence years, particularly in the larger African economies such as Kenya and Nigeria. Over 60 per cent of foreign investment was in estate agriculture, mining and petroleum production, much of the rest being in manufacturing and services.[4] Foreign-owned firms came to dominate Africa's modern economic sectors, accounting for large proportions of sales, employment and capital formation.

Although direct private foreign investment did promote economic growth (and in particular produced jobs for burgeoning local populations),

it soon began to be criticized for its adverse economic and social consequences.[5] Foreign companies were condemned for smaller than expected
impacts on employment, foreign exchange, balance of payments, technology transfer, etc. Foreign investors were widely perceived as seekers of
quick corporate profits which were also as quickly transferred abroad.
Indeed, net capital and income outflows were shown to be greater than
inflows in most African countries.[6] With the exception of a few oil-pro-
ducing countries, where net foreign investment offset outflows of income
(profits, dividends and remittances), most African countries were becoming net exporters of capital. The net benefits of foreign investment began
to be seen as limited, even negative, with concern being expressed at the
considerable surplus being withdrawn from Africa. In the 1980s, the repatriation of capital was also viewed as exacerbating Africa's debt problems.
As President Robert Mugabe of Zimbabwe argued: the more foreign
investment 'we have', 'the more the dividends we shall be remitting abroad
and the more the indebtedness'.[7]

Moreover, international capital was suspected of exploiting its organizational and economic strength for unfair profiteering. It was commonly accused of engaging in illegal transactions, particularly transfer
pricing (overpricing of imports and underpricing of exports to reduce
corporate tax liability). The behaviour of foreign firms provoked various dissatisfactions among African politicians and officials towards foreign investors, leading to a desire for greater national control of
especially strategic foreign-controlled economic activity. Where key
economic sectors were under private, foreign control, economically
powerful foreign companies could make important decisions affecting
local economies. This was precisely the concern of Nigeria's state elites
regarding the vital multinational oil corporations whose management
was external to Nigeria. As argued in Nigeria's second National
Development Plan (1970–74), 'a truly independent nation cannot allow
its objectives and priorities to be distorted or frustrated by the manipulations of powerful foreign investors'.[8] Only as a result of government
intervention could foreign capital be made to operate in ways consistent with national interests.

There was also a general resentment of the economic success of resident non-African capital, particularly that engaged in retail and wholesale trade. A government minister in Ghana commented in 1970 on a
government decree which prohibited much foreign enterprise from
venturing into small-scale economic activities:

> It is no secret that this legislation was directed against the Lebanese and
> Indians ... They were here doing things which Ghanaians can easily do, like
> buying and selling goods. They came with little capital. They do not train
> Ghanaians to succeed them ... They are a serious drain on our balance of

payments with their personal remittance quotas, and they have been deeply involved in illegal transfers and currency smuggling.[9]

In Zambia as well, local politicians in the late 1960s condemned the various illegal practices (over-invoicing and overcharging) being adopted by members of the European resident business community. To eliminate such practices as well as to satisfy local calls for indigenizing control of certain sectors of the economy, African governments everywhere moved to take over economic activities from non-African resident entrepreneurs. Such moves were directed particularly against the predominance of Asians in East African commerce. In the words of an official Ugandan document, 'the almost total absence of participation of African entrepreneurs' was seen as 'socially and economically unhealthy' as well as threatening future political stability.[10] Africanization of domestic retail and wholesale trade was to result in the substantial exodus of resident Asian communities such as that from Kenya in the late 1960s.

In addition, the 'neo-colonial' orientation of many African regimes came under severe criticism, especially in the late 1960s. In June 1968, Senegalese businesspeople attacked the role and privileges of French capital in the economy. They protested at the domination of commerce, industry, and banking by foreign economic interests 'while Senegalese vegetate in marginal sectors of the economy ... Nationals control only 5–10% of the economic activity in this country. After 10 years of independence, this situation is not acceptable.'[11] They called for economic 'Senegalization' with French firms being prohibited from certain economic sectors and indigenous participation being promoted in commerce and industry. But Senegalese opposition to foreign capital was more broad-based, with workers, students and the urban middle class joining local business to argue that foreign economic control had done little to raise living standards.

For such diverse reasons, a new critical attitude to foreign capital emerged from the late 1960s on. African governments began to revise the rules regarding the activities of foreign companies. The purpose was to ensure that a greater share of the economic benefits from foreign investment would be retained by the host country and that foreign investors would better serve host-country economic needs. A few African governments nationalized the assets of foreign investors, usually placing them under state ownership. Foreign assets were typically nationalized by governments of a more radical and socialist persuasion, such as those in Tanzania and Zambia. Elsewhere in Africa, nationalizations were less common but governments adopted policies that required specific percentages of the ownership of foreign concerns to be placed in indigenous hands. Many joint ventures were entered into between foreign firms and local partners, especially state enterprises, in manufacturing and services. Moreover, in many countries, specific economic sectors were reserved exclusively for national involvement. For example, in Nigeria as a result of the implementation of indigenization decrees in the 1970s, certain businesses, particularly in the commercial sector, were closed to resident foreign entrepreneurs. Other restrictions included limitations on the size of a foreign investor's stake in a local company, as well as regarding the repatriation of profits and capital earned in host countries. Employment of foreign nationals, technology transfer and access to local loan funds were also subjected to controls.

Generally, African governments adopted restrictive policies towards international investment. In Kenya, for example, the government exerted pressure on foreign-owned firms to reinvest a higher portion of their profits in the country. From 1974, firms with high rates of repatriation had their local borrowing rights curbed. Remittances of management and technical fees were also made liable to taxation. Moreover, foreign companies were urged to issue a portion of their share capital on the Nairobi Stock Exchange in order to promote a higher level of local ownership. And a government committee started evaluating proposed industrial projects by foreign investors to determine whether they were in the 'national interest' in terms of earning foreign exchange, increasing jobs, and promoting development in rural areas.

Indigenization of foreign businesses or restrictive government policies in regard to foreign capital also had other political origins, less concerned with national welfare. Nationalist pressures to control foreign business establishments were often evident at times when political elites were in need of popular support to maintain themselves in power. Appeals to nationalism as well as acquisition of assets of foreign concerns may have served, as Biersteker argued in the case of Nigeria in 1972, 'to legitimize the military regime's continued hold on power'.[12] By promulgating an indigenization decree, 'the military government gained popular support for its decisive nationalistic contribution to economic decolonization'.[13] In 1972 also, President Idi Amin's attack on the Asian community of Uganda was also designed to invoke collective support for the new military authorities in that country. The expulsion of Asians was greeted favourably by the African population and did much to consolidate Amin's political position. But there are further political reasons for governments pursuing economic nationalism. Just as African governments viewed the proliferation of state enterprises partly in terms of personal and political purposes, so they pursued indigenization programmes against foreign capital to promote domestic political objectives. Indigenization measures of various kinds (indigenization of equity and personnel) were pushed by state personnel seeking to further their own ends. State acquisition of, or dominant participation in, foreign enterprise could enhance opportunities for those in power to distribute resources (jobs, contracts, goods and services) in ways that could build up political support as well as personal wealth for themselves.

Arguments have also been made that initiatives towards economic nationalism were designed to serve the interests of local business. Colin Leys argued that in Kenya indigenous capital controlled the local state and promoted policies vis-à-vis foreign capital in furtherance of its own objectives.[14] And Thomas Biersteker showed the extent of local capital's dissatisfaction with foreign ownership and control of the Nigerian economy.[15] But he also argued that state personnel in Nigeria, unlike those in Kenya, were not beholden to local capital on indigenization. State elites had their own conception of Nigerian indigenization, and although they consulted local businessmen, they were able to act on their own convictions.

Yet, for all the controls and limitations, foreign capital was not easily subordinated by government interventions. International firms occupied a central position in most African economies. Their contribution to economic growth was also seen as indispensable. Where foreign firms could choose between alternative investment locations, they were able to bargain for very favourable conditions, especially with governments anxious for the benefits of external investment capital. Many foreign enterprises even retained control of their operations despite restrictions and prohibitions. As Biersteker argued regarding governmental indigenization measures in Nigeria, 'multinational firms had a broad array of means at their disposal to neutralise some of the state's objectives'.[16] Similarly, Okechukwu Iheduru showed how in Côte d'Ivoire the government's nationalist policies for the 'Ivoirianization' of the maritime industry were unable to prevent the continued domination of the sector by foreign shipping lines.[17]

Equally important has been the fact that African governments have not generally assumed 'an antagonistic stance to foreign capital'.[18] Given their dependence on external sources of capital, governments tended to posture against foreign investment, but usually adopted moderate and pragmatic positions. In many ways, a coincidence of interests has often existed between local state personnel and foreign business executives. Indeed, Steven Langdon refers to the 'symbiotic MNC-state relationship' in Africa.[19] State actions have been significant in maintaining economic penetration by overseas companies, as well as ensuring their profitability. African governments have granted multinationals extensive concessions and privileges, such as protection from imports, easy repatriation of profits, and tax benefits. They have also enabled foreign investors to by-pass approval and control mechanisms, and in various ways limited the impact of formal government constraints.[20] Indeed, many expatriate companies have been granted some degree of monopoly status, especially in manufacturing sub-sectors, which has ensured them high rates of profit. Protection from imports has been of particular concern to foreign firms in Africa's import-substituting economies. Langdon shows that, in 90 per cent of the cases he studied, the type and range of protection eventually agreed to by the Kenyan Government corresponded closely with the negotiating position of international manufacturing companies. And elsewhere in Africa, governments have also willingly accorded foreign manufacturers the tariff levels they desired to attract their investments in import-substituting industry.

On the other hand, foreign business has provided a variety of financial and political favours to leading politicians and bureaucrats which can help the latter to enhance their political and personal positions. Langdon observed, for example, that Firestone won a bid to establish a tyre factory in Kenya because it 'agreed to use African distributors exclusively for its tyres and to give the government some control over the appointment of those distributors',[21] who could be useful for mobilizing political support for the incumbent regime. Also, René Lemarchand described the 'close working relationships' between foreign business interests and Gabonese state personnel. The latter used the resulting 'material benefits' for private accumulation as well as to strengthen their political machine. 'For example, the substantial tax breaks accorded to Elf, the major French parastatal in charge of drilling, prospecting and commercializing Gabon's oil resources, are repaid in the form of a transfer of ten percent of petroleum sales to the Provision pour Investissements Diversifiés (PID), which in turn serves as a thinly disguised slush fund at the disposition of [President] Bongo and key members of his entourage.'[22] Some of the other benefits of foreign investment in which African state elites share, arise from foreign companies conferring on them coveted directorships, partnerships, and shareholdings, all of which can be used for political and personal purposes. Moreover, they also receive financial donations, especially from the more vulnerable Asian and Lebanese businessmen who make pay-offs to regime politicians to help secure their businesses. Nearly everywhere as well, foreign firms have made donations to finance the election campaign chests of ruling parties; Lemarchand notes the 'substantial campaign contributions made by Elf-Gabon to the Rassemblement pour la Republique (RPR) in 1980'.[23]

Close and co-operative contact has been no less common between resident non-African entrepreneurs and state elites. This has been especially the case in Kenya. A British magazine described the relationship between Kenyan President Arap Moi and Asian businessmen in the 1980s as 'close and mutually advantageous'. The president had 'consistently been a patron of the Asian business community'. For example, 'despite stringent currency controls, ... the Moi government has turned a blind eye to blatant infringements by an Asian community with which it enjoys close relations'. In turn, Moi sought 'to secure Asian financial weight as a political weapon against Kikuyu economic power'. Asian business was an important part of the President's strategy to undermine Kikuyu big business. It is true that a change in the government holding power could affect the fortunes of foreign private capital. A new regime could turn on foreign investments tied closely to those ousted from power. In Kenya, Asians are also acutely fearful of 'the possibility of a government less favourably disposed towards this privileged minority' coming to power. Yet, in reality, foreign firms have often survived changes in African governments. Foreign capital which was accommodating to the interests of state leaders was perceived as less of a political threat and more of a political and economic asset to incumbent authorities who reciprocated by granting economic privileges (such as import protection and tax benefits) and economic exemptions (such as foreign-exchange controls) to supportive foreign entrepreneurs.[24]

Nevertheless, many foreign companies found it difficult to overcome the constraints to their business operations ensuing from a state-organized system of monopolies, tariffs, contracts and concessions. In Zimbabwe in the mid-1980s, employment, wage and price regulations as well as limits on foreign-exchange allocations, high taxation and low income and profit repatriation were important factors inhibiting new direct foreign investment in the country. Official decisions on these matters were open to political discussion and bargaining but the authorities were not too amenable to accommodating the concerns of foreign investors. Jeffrey Herbst argues that the government was especially concerned that greater multinational investment in an economy already dominated by resident European capital had 'the potential to develop an alternative political power base' as well as that it would 'further decrease Zimbabwe's control over its resources'. The result was that between 1980 and 1986 new foreign investment amounted to less than US$50 million.[25] In many other countries as well, restrictive government policies and strategies led to a decline in flows of inward investment. These were also countries where state economic involvement was high and where the private sector's role confronted a myriad of restrictions and bureaucratic regulations. State corruption, in the sense of politicians and bureaucrats asking for illicit favours before making decisions on formal government regulations, was also emerging as a serious problem. When combined with the region's depressed economic conditions, macroeconomic instability and the emerging debt crisis, Africa's regulatory climate served as a serious deterrent to overseas investment. For resident non-African entrepreneurs, many of these same factors as well as pervasive political uncertainties resulted in very few of them entering into long-term investments. Asian and Lebanese resident capital tended to concentrate in light manufacturing and trading operations that could be relocated if local political conditions deteriorated.

During the 1970s, African countries came to be seen as unattractive investment sites, a fact reflected in Africa's investment rates being amongst the lowest in the world. In 1960, some 17 per cent of total foreign direct investment to developing countries went to Africa. Ten years later, the amount had declined to about 15 per cent. By 1986, Africa's share had plummeted to less than 5 per cent. New foreign investment in African economies fell to very low levels. In Kenya it dropped from $78 million in 1980 to $23 million in 1990.[26] Moreover, unremitted profits accounted for a large proportion of new foreign investment; in Kenya in 1986 they accounted for 45 per cent of it. In most African countries, no major new private foreign investment occurred in the 1970s; some even saw net disinvestment taking place.

Governments and foreign investors since the 1980s

Ugandan, Zimbabwean, Nigerian, Kenyan and other African experiences
From the late 1980s, an important reassessment of international investment began to take place among African governments. Less emphasis began to be placed on foreign investors being antithetical to economic expansion and national sovereignty and more on their constituting an important vehicle for growth and development. Major economic benefits were to be garnered from external investors and thus they had to be actively courted. The decline in direct foreign investment flows to African countries was having adverse economic consequences and had to be reversed as quickly as possible, especially at a time when other sources of foreign capital – particularly foreign aid – were decreasing. Sub-Saharan Africa had to be made more attractive to vitally needed foreign investment.

The shift to more pragmatic policies towards foreign investment was a consequence of a number of interrelated factors. Pressure emanated particularly from Western countries as well as the international financial institutions for improved access for the international capital regarded as essential for the promotion of Africa's economic recovery and growth. 'Given the dearth of long-term finance, modern technology, knowledge of foreign markets and management skills', argued the World Bank in the case of Uganda, direct foreign investment 'has a crucial role to play as the catalyst for the transformation of the economy.'[27] Direct foreign investment was also seen as vital to stimulate job-creating growth in countries confronting huge levels of unemployment. Local businesses – private as well as publicly-owned – could not generate enough jobs to absorb the sizeable number of new entrants into the labour market. Zimbabwe's President Robert Mugabe admitted that it had been wrong for his government to discourage private foreign investment which could have helped provide the capital to boost economic growth and reduce unemployment (officially estimated at more than 2 million in a population of 10 million).[28] Other African leaders realized the need to accelerate the pace of investment to tackle economic difficulties stemming from the fluctuating international climate for Africa's major export commodities. Ghana's President Jerry Rawlings bemoaned the deteriorating world prices for his country's cocoa exports and urged foreign business to engage in more local processing of cocoa and other products to raise value-added exports as well as promote domestic industry. Finally, nearly everywhere, African rulers wanted to attract foreign investors for the purposes of enhancing public revenues to help pay for state obligations. President Frederick Chiluba hoped to lure as much foreign capital as possible to buy the copper mines in Zambia so that 'the mines make money and contribute to the exchequer'.

The 1980s and particularly the 1990s have seen African governments adopting more receptive policies towards foreign investors. Nearly all governments have enacted new investment promotion legislation. New laws have removed restrictions placed on the entry and operations of foreign companies. Even governments which had been hostile to international capital – Ethiopia, Mozambique, Tanzania – have begun relaxing the restrictive policies of the past. Foreign participation has been allowed in various economic sectors including the operation of major utilities. For example, the Nigerian indigenization decrees of the 1970s have been modified to permit majority foreign participation in various economic enterprises. Investments with 100 per cent foreign ownership are also being permitted. Procedures for approving new investment proposals have been simplified and streamlined, and a range of incentives offered to foreign business. A growing number of investment agreements have been concluded especially with Western countries, designed to promote and protect foreign investment. Many countries have joined the Multilateral Investment Guarantee Agency (MIGA) set up by the World Bank to guarantee private investment. Controls of various sorts have also been eased, including repatriation of profit remittances and capital as well as the employment of foreigners in technical and management positions.

But sub-Saharan Africa still has very low levels of foreign investment inflow in comparison with other Third World regions, notably Asia and Latin America. In 1998, Africa's share in developing countries' total foreign investment was 4.7 per cent, a tiny fraction of that invested globally, or about $5 billion out of a total direct foreign investment in all developing countries of nearly $100 billion. Ghana, which introduced a package to attract foreign investors in 1985, had by the end of 1992 attracted only a total direct foreign investment of about $1 billion, most of it confined to the gold-mining sector. Foreign investors were also returning to Uganda, 'albeit cautiously'. Within three years of the promulgation of a new investment code in 1991, Uganda had managed to attract some $208 million in direct foreign investment. But this 'fell well short of the level required for Uganda's recovery to become self-sustaining'.[29] In both Ghana and Uganda, inflows of foreign direct investment represented only about 1 per cent of domestic capital formation in the late 1980s; and the figure for the mid-1990s was only slightly higher. In Nigeria in the late 1980s, and early 1990s, new direct foreign investment also remained at low levels in spite of the introduction of a new investment code. 'Much of the positive net flow of foreign investment' according to Tom Forrest 'was made up of the reinvestment of unremitted profits by existing companies.'[30]

Many reasons have been adduced as to why investment flows to Africa have remained weak compared with other developing regions. A long litany of economic factors has continued to make the climate for investment unattractive. These include the smallness of African domestic markets, the poor physical infrastructure, a poorly functioning financial services sector, the low level of skills and access to technology, a high level of indebtedness that leads to chronic foreign-exchange shortages that threaten repatriation of profits, and so on. Attracting region-wide investment is also strewn with infrastructural and administrative obstacles to cross-border economic activity. But political concerns have been particularly prominent in explaining why the Africa region has so far failed to attract much foreign direct investment. Political stability is usually cited as one such major concern. A number of economically important countries have been plagued by protracted civil conflicts (Angola, Liberia, Somalia, Sudan, Zaire(Congo)) while in some others just emerging after years of turmoil (Mozambique, Eritrea, Ethiopia, Uganda) foreign investment inflows will be a gradual and cautious process.

Just as serious have been the deep suspicions harboured by African political leaders about foreign investment. As Jerry Rawlings, chairman of Ghana's PNDC, stated at an investment promotion conference in 1990:

This is a sad but real fact. Our history and experience has taught us to look for the catch even when logic tells us that we need the partnership of foreign capital to develop our abundant resources to our mutual benefit.

He continued:

We, and other developing countries, can provide a catalogue of experiences which reveal what might be called the ugly face of international business.[31]

These apprehensions have been echoed by many of the region's political leaders. In August 1996, for example, the Nigerian Minister of Petroleum Resources accused Western oil companies of 'sharp practices', particularly 'tax evasion on a massive scale' but also, as journalists put it, 'spurious contracts, unfair treatment of Nigerian workers and contractors, lack of accountability and transparency in operations, and abuse of expatriate quotas'. To curb such irregular practices, the Minister stated that he would shortly introduce new rules governing oil sector operations.[32]

It is because governments have in the past found foreign investment to be less than desirable that they have either retained or imposed new regulatory structures governing the access and activities of foreign firms. As Rawlings declared: 'interventions to prevent injustice or serious damage' by foreign corporate capital are necessary. The consequences of unregulated foreign investment are feared. The behaviour of foreign companies cannot be left unchecked. To ensure that they act in the interests of the local people, foreign investors have been faced with various obligations and controls: export and/or domestic content requirements; conditions to mitigate harmful environmental impacts; requirements that specific investments take the form of joint ventures with a parastatal or with local (usually politically well-connected) entrepreneurs; and the reservation of certain economic sectors exclusively for local ownership. Ethiopia's 1996 Investment Proclamation, for example, prohibits foreign firms from participating in financial services (such as domestic banking and insurance), telecommunications, large-scale electricity production, and small services (such as barber shops).[33] In the telecommunications sector, Kenya has since 1997 been enforcing a requirement that any firm licensed to provide services should have at least 70 per cent of its equity owned by Kenyans. Moreover, various government organizations such as ministries and revenue-collecting authorities see themselves as custodians of the national interest and therefore insist on examining investment applications with regard to their benefit to the national economy. All these government-imposed conditions and controls (even if less restrictive than in previous decades) inconvenience and discourage foreign capital.

Similarly, anti-foreign sentiments expressing concern at the perceived 'Asianization' of the economy in Tanzania, as Asian-owned concerns take over many state-owned enterprises, and the outspoken attacks on Zimbabwe's resident white minority of farmers and businessmen as well as multinationals for their local economic dominance, have deterred foreign investors in those countries. In late 1996, Kenya's Minister for Commerce and Industry announced that the government would enforce a nearly thirty year-old law, the Trade Licensing Act of 1967, which had sought to provide indigenous Kenyans with exclusive rights to deal in certain products as well as to engage in business in designated urban areas. 'In the long term' the minister stated, 'the Ministry's intention is to see an increasing share of trade and industry in indigenous control.' Affirmative action was needed to ensure 'indigenous people control a major part of our economy, especially the retail and wholesale sector'. Although the minister also remarked that the 'policy will not involve taking away anything from foreign control, but by increasing the indigenous share of the expanding economy', a Kenyan journalist noted that 'the minister's statement last week was expected to cause anxiety among business people of Asian and European extraction'.[34]

In addition, in much of the Africa region, privatization has yielded only meagre inflows of direct foreign investment compared with other regions such as East Asia and Latin America. 'Only a few (usually smaller) enterprises have been privatized so far, in many cases without significant participation by foreign investors. Of 80 enterprises sold in Sub-Saharan Africa during 1988–92, only 21 had foreign participation ...' Divesting public assets to foreigners has always been politically controversial. Even in Uganda, where foreign business has been permitted much unrestricted economic participation, strong sentiments of economic nationalism have not been uncommon. Parliamentarians have on a number of occasions warned the government not to sell the 'family silver' to non-indigenous groups. As elsewhere in Africa, favouring indigenous Ugandan buyers of state companies rather than foreign concerns offering higher prices – as in the sale in 1997 of the Uganda Grain Milling Corporation – serves to deter foreign investors.[35]

Nevertheless, Uganda is one of the very few African countries providing foreign capital with an officially warm welcome. Since the late 1980s, its investment policy has been oriented towards promoting rather than controlling foreign capital. Direct foreign investment is strongly courted as a critical source of funds to finance economic recovery, the more so as the local capacity to generate resources is very limited. Uganda's savings and investment rates are so low that little economic growth can take place without a strong inflow of foreign capital. Moreover, the NRM Government has been emphasizing the significant tax revenues generated by foreign investors. Given the government's desire to increase social welfare expenditures as well as to improve road infrastructure, foreign companies can help provide the necessary state revenues. For these reasons, few restrictions are imposed on foreign investors, unlike in other African countries where they are only allowed to enter specific sectors and projects. Emphasis is placed especially on ex-Ugandan Asians (tens of thousands of whom had been expelled from Uganda in 1972) returning to repossess their expropriated properties as well as to initiate new investments. Little official notice is given to views – increasingly being voiced – that the economic benefits of external investment may be outweighed by its costs. Nor does the government pay much heed to nationalist sentiments that Asians, because of their resources and business competitiveness, are dominating the industrial and commercial economy and preventing African commercial competition as well as purchasing most of the larger state concerns in the government's privatization programme. Such criticisms are dismissed because well over half of the new actual external investment – perceived officially as providing the essential financial impetus to economic transformation in Uganda – has come from Asians whose many companies are also contributing substantially to state revenues.

The political benefits to be gained from investment provide another reason for welcoming it and pushing aside any negative comments. Not only can foreign capital contribute to economic and social progress and enhance the regime's political legitimacy but it can also – and particularly the Asian investors – provide funds for the government's political purposes (such as financial contributions during the 1996 election campaigns). In addition, through profitable joint-venture investments foreign investors can promote the business interests of a number of high-ranking politicians and government officials as well as their relatives. For example, the President's brother, Salim Saleh, has entered into various ventures with foreign investors such as those in gold-prospecting, cargo-handling, and manufacturing. Such economic and political co-operation is also beneficial to foreign capitalists. Asian investors have been able to get the Ugandan Government to adopt favourable tariff protection for their products as well as lower taxation rates. Not surprisingly, such co-operation has led to increases in new foreign corporate capital which have proved greater than in most neighbouring countries. Nearly 8000 Asians are said to be resident in Uganda and their investments in the past decade are estimated to total over $600 million.[36]

Some African political leaders, including President Rawlings, who showed suspicion and even hostility to foreign business have begun to temper their mistrust as they realize that foreign investors can be of importance to both their economic and their political objectives. With their large investment resources, their modern technology, and their ability to create employment and tax revenues, they are a potentially vital economic asset. And, as we have seen, African rulers have found foreign firms useful for consolidating their power and enhancing their personal fortunes. Yet suspicion of the desirability of foreign capital, although gradually diminishing, remains a deterrent to foreign investment in many African ruling circles. In addition, there are many other domestic political obstacles which impede international investment. The absence of good governance – in particular the demand for bribes by public servants – has dampened the interest of foreigners. In the 1980s, corruption was one of the main reasons why so many American companies were reported to have disinvested from Kenya. And, similarly, in the 1990s, new foreign investment has been constrained by Kenya's highly discretionary approval process which has involved various corrupt practices. In Nigeria rampant bureaucratic corruption has virtually destroyed investor confidence outside the oil industry. A 1996 survey of British firms revealed that three-quarters of them would not do business in Nigeria because of its reputation for fraud. Only a few investors able to operate in corrupt business environments will not be frightened by the endemic bureaucratic and political corruption found throughout Africa. In Tanzania, 'the Asian-dominated business sector, finding its way blocked by bureaucracy, used its financial clout to sidestep the system'.[37] To be sure, it is only a small number of Asian businessmen who have been linked with top state personnel in various financial scandals (such as the Goldenberg affair which cost Kenya over $400 million in state funds) but, nevertheless, the Asian business community has learned to 'cut corners' to function effectively in corrupt East African business systems.[38] For foreigners disinclined to engage in business under such conditions, a predictable legal system, free from corruption and undue influence, and which demonstrates respect for contracts and the rule of law, is of crucial importance to attract their investments. Such an environment has been distinctly lacking in much of Africa.

In some countries such as South Africa, labour militancy has meant that the torrent of direct foreign investment hoped for since April 1994 has remained a trickle. In Lesotho, serious industrial unrest in mid-1991 not only led to declining investment inflows but also resulted in a number of investors pulling out of the country.[39] And, in Senegal, government incentives for attracting foreign investment have achieved little in recent years, partly, it is claimed, because of high labour costs, inflexible labour laws (especially as regards removing employees), and various labour disputes. Moreover, the high levels of crime in South Africa, especially in Johannesburg and Gauteng province, as well as the ethnic clashes in Kenya, have also frightened potential foreign investors. Finally, foreign capital is also unlikely to be encouraged without a country first creating an environment in which its own citizens, including those of non-African origin, are willing to invest. Low levels of domestic private investment discourage foreign investors since government policies are viewed as not conducive to private investment.

Conclusion

Only a few African countries are attracting important new inflows of foreign private investment. Many of these are the ones which have already acquired substantial foreign capital as well as those which are rich in resources. 'Six of the seven countries where foreign direct investment exceeds 1 percent of GDP rely primarily on oil or minerals for their export revenues.'[40] Foreign corporations are also likely to be attracted to infrastructure such as telecommunications in some of the larger African countries. For example, France Telecom has acquired a 51 per cent stake in Côte d'Ivoire's state telephone company and promises investments of more than $450 million over five years. It is also possible that in these few countries an unfavourable enabling environment may not constitute too serious an impediment to investments by foreign-owned concerns. Given the huge profits to be made, Western mining companies have frequently concluded investment pacts with the political leaders of undemocratic and corrupt regimes such as those that have existed in Cameroon, Gabon, Nigeria, Sierra Leone, and Zaire (Congo-Kinshasa).[41] More recently, the privatization in Côte d'Ivoire, Ghana, and Zimbabwe of state telephone companies as well as public electric power utilities to foreign investors has also been surrounded by much controversy and allegations of political favouritism and corruption. For instance, the electricity company in Côte d'Ivoire was privatized 'to a French firm with close ties to people in the prime minister's inner circle',[42] while in the country's largest privatization in 1997, France Telecom won the bid to take over the telephone parastatal by teaming up with a local private company owned partly by President Konan Bedié. In Ghana in 1997 Ghana Telecom was sold to a Malaysian company which was in partnership with a group of politically well-connected businessmen.

For most African countries, however, economic and political conditions will mean that sub-Saharan Africa is unlikely to capture a significant amount of international investment. Between 1993 and 1996 foreign direct investment flows to sub-Saharan Africa as a share of GDP amounted to only 0.9 per cent compared to 1.1 per cent in Latin

America and over 3 per cent in East Asia. Some evidence also suggests that foreign corporate capital may actually be disinvesting from many African economies, especially those not favoured by the petroleum and mining sectors. British and French companies with investments in West Africa have been withdrawing in recent years, given the poor local economic and political circumstances.[43] In the case of Kenya in East Africa, the stock of foreign direct investment declined from US$670 million in 1980 to less than US$400 million in 1990.

Foreign direct investment will therefore not be the panacea for the economic problems of African countries. It is generally too limited to generate much economic growth. In a few countries, foreign capital may make an important contribution to economic recovery. But even where foreign capital inflows take place and foreign entrepreneurs provide technical and managerial training, they may contribute little to national development. Although important for overall economic activity (average contribution of foreign investment to GDP was perhaps 20 per cent), the impact of non-oil foreign corporate enterprises on the balance of payments in most African countries has been less positive ('the outflow of investment income – at least since the mid-1970s – has generally been higher than the inflow of new investment').[44] Moreover, foreign business has not done as much to provide additional financial resources, management skills, technologies and access to markets as was expected of it. The evidence from the first three post-independence decades is that foreign companies have been more oriented towards maximizing profits and repatriating surpluses than seeking to meet Africa's developmental needs (bearing out President Rawlings' and others' mistrust). Although they can help to relieve resource and other constraints, there are major limits to the economic, financial, technological, managerial and entrepreneurial benefits that can be acquired from external investment.[45]

One oft-cited example of this is the garment industry which has been a foreign-dominated export enclave in a number of African countries. In Lesotho, the Chinese-owned textile firms have exhibited few domestic inputs other than a large number of unskilled (and low-paid) female workers. Spin-offs such as technological advances and local entrepreneurial development have been virtually absent. Even in the case of joint ventures which have been proposed as a means of increasing local capabilities, the evidence suggests that little has been achieved in the transfer of technology and management skills to local entrepreneurs. For example, the Nigerian Government has complained about Western oil companies taking on expatriates 'in defiance of government's indigenization policy and in some cases at the expense of capable Nigerians' as well as that 'transfer of technological know-how is ineffective'.[46]

The view that foreign capital can make a significant contribution to the expansion of African economies has been strongly propounded. Domestic resources are insufficient to sustain economic development and need to be complemented by foreign inflows. On the other hand, the view has been advanced that expatriate capital adds little to domestic resources and, in fact, displaces domestic savings through the flow of royalties, dividends, fees and profits out of the host country. Certainly it would seem that disproportionate emphasis has been placed on foreign entrepreneurs and foreign-owned companies in economic growth and that much greater attention has to be given to promoting domestic enterprises in Africa's total private investment. However, in view of the reservations about the local private sector's ability to play a leading role as well as the limited domestic private investment activity, governments will have to continue to rely more on direct foreign investment as well as resident non-African capital to provide jobs, exports, tax revenues, etc. Their dilemma will continue to be that, although they need to attract greater multinational investment, they also need to regulate it to minimize detrimental and maximize positive effects without deterring potential investors. But, in addition, African governments have learned that there are important political benefits to be derived from foreign business. The evidence suggests that political interactions between state and foreign concerns in the post-independence period have been mutually advantageous. They have permitted foreign capital considerable autonomy and advantages in conducting its operations while, oftentimes, conferring huge private fortunes and political support on many of Africa's political leaders.

NOTES

1. For further details, see Colin Kirkpatrick and Frederick Nixson, 'Transnational Corporations and Economic Development', *Journal of Modern African Studies*, 19,3 (1981), pp.374–9.
2. See Leslie L. Rood, 'Foreign Investment in African Manufacturing', *Journal of Modern African Studies*, 13,1 (1975), 19–34.
3. Colin Leys, *Underdevelopment in Kenya. The Political Economy of Neo-Colonialism 1964–1971* (London, 1975), p.120. David Himbara regards non-African resident capital (particularly Asian capital in Kenya) as the most important segment of domestic capital. See his *Kenyan Capitalists, the State, and Development* (Boulder, CO, 1994), pp.22–5. Although his argument is persuasive, it is important not only to distinguish between Asian and European resident capital, on the one hand, and black African capital on the other, but also to treat the former as a segment of foreign capital. Himbara acknowledges that Kenyan Asians 'are still regarded as foreigners' (p.162). Lebanese entrepreneurs in Senegal and other West African countries are also seen locally as foreigners.

4. For sectoral distribution of direct foreign investment in East Africa in 1964, see Table 1 in J.F. Rweyemamu, 'The Political Economy of Foreign Private Investment in the Underdeveloped Countries', *The African Review*, 1,1 (1971), p.114.

5. See Lawrence Cockroft, 'The Past Record and Future Potential of Foreign Investment', in Frances Stewart et al. (eds.), *Alternative Development Strategies in Sub-Saharan Africa* (Basingstoke, 1992), pp.341–7 for a brief general discussion. In the 1990s, foreign companies in Africa also began to be criticized for the adverse environmental impacts of their operations, as, for example, oil companies in Ogoniland, Nigeria.

6. See Table 2 in Rweyemamu, *op. cit.*, p.115 for details on East Africa.

7. Quoted in Howard P. Lehman, 'The Paradox of State Power in Africa: Debt Management Policies in Kenya and Zimbabwe', *African Studies Review*, 35,2 (1992), p.30.

8. Quoted in Thomas J. Biersteker, *Multinationals, the State, and Control of the Nigerian Economy* (Princeton, NJ, 1987), p.74. Similarly in the 1980s, shortly after the attainment of independence, Zimbabwe's political leadership advocated state takeovers in view of the 'unacceptably high' level of foreign ownership. In regard to illicit outflows, overinvoicing in Nigeria was 'estimated to have amounted to as much as 12 per cent of total imports from 1970 to 1988, while from 1977 to 1983 it is estimated to have exceeded the total outflow of investment and fee income'. See Stewart et al., *op. cit.*, p.20.

9. Quoted in J.D. Esseks, 'Economic Policies', in Dennis Austin and Robin Luckham (eds), *Politicians and Soldiers in Ghana, 1966–1972* (London, 1975), p.48.

10. Quoted in David Himbara, 'The 'Asian' Question in East Africa', *African Studies*, 56,1 (1997), p.3.

11. Quoted in Catherine Boone, *Merchant Capital and the Roots of State Power in Senegal 1930–1985* (Cambridge, 1992), p.168.

12. Biersteker, *op. cit.*, p.80.

13. *ibid.*, p.94. See also similar arguments as regards the second indigenization decree of 1977, pp.159–60, 170, 174.

14. Colin Leys, 'Capital Accumulation, Class Formation and Dependency. The Significance of the Kenyan Case', in Ralph Milliband and John Saville (eds.), *The Socialist Register 1978* (London, 1978), p.251.

15. Biersteker, *op. cit.*, pp.57–69.

16. *ibid.*, p.242.

17. Okechukwu C. Iheduru, 'The State and Maritime Nationalism in Côte d'Ivoire', *Journal of Modern African Studies*, 32,2 (1994), 215–45.

18. Raphael Kaplinsky, 'Capitalist Accumulation in the Periphery: Kenya', in Martin Fransman (ed.), *Industry and Accumulation in Africa* (London, 1982), p.212.

19. Steven Langdon, 'Multinational Corporations and the State in Africa', in Jose J. Villamil (ed.), *Transnational Capitalism and National Development. New Perspectives on Dependence* (Hassocks, 1979), p.229. For a discussion of how the Senegalese Government underwrote the profitability of private French manufacturers during the 1960s and 1970s, see Boone, *op. cit.*, pp.113–22.

20. See, for example, Paul Collins, 'Public Policy and the Development of Indigenous Capitalism: The Nigerian Experience', *Journal of Commonwealth and Comparative Politics*, 15,2 (1977), 127–50.

21. Steven W. Langdon, *Multinational Corporations in the Political Economy of Kenya* (New York, 1985), pp.172–3. See also Robert H. Bates, *Markets and States in Tropical Africa* (Berkeley, CA, 1981), pp.103–4.

22. René Lemarchand, 'The State, the Parallel Economy, and the Changing Structure of Patronage Systems', in Donald Rothchild and Naomi Chazan (eds.), *The Precarious Balance. State and Society in Africa* (Boulder, CO, 1988), p.159.

23. *ibid.*, p.159. See also Rita Cruise O'Brien, 'Lebanese Entrepreneurs in Senegal: Economic Integration and the Politics of Protection', *Cahiers d'études africaines*, 15,5 (1975), p.112.

24. For a discussion of MNC-Government relations in Kenya in the mid-1970s, see Steven Langdon, 'The Multinational Corporation in the Kenyan Political Economy', in Raphael Kaplinsky (ed.), *Readings On the Multinational Corporation in Kenya* (Nairobi, 1978), pp.161–200. For President Moi's relations with Asian businessmen, see *Africa Confidential*, 'Kenya: The Asian Dilemma', 24 June 1987, pp.5–7.

25. Jeffrey Herbst, *State Politics in Zimbabwe* (Berkeley, CA, 1990), pp.126, 127. For a more detailed discussion, see Roger C. Riddell, 'Zimbabwe's Experience of Foreign Investment Policy' in Vincent Cable and Bishnodat Persaud (eds.), *Developing With Foreign Investment* (London, 1987).

26. Figures cited by the Executive Director of the Federation of Kenya Employers in *The Daily Nation* (Nairobi), 14 October 1994, p.16.

27. World Bank, *Uganda. Growing Out of Poverty* (Washington, DC, 1993), p.140.

28. 'Mugabe Accepts Blame for a Damaged Economy', *Business Day* (Johannesburg), 27 October 1993, p.6.

29. *The Financial Times* (London), 'Survey on Uganda', 10 June 1994, p.1.

30. Tom Forrest, *Politics and Economic Development in Nigeria* (Boulder, CO, 1995), p.216.

31. *People's Daily Graphic* (Accra), 1 March 1990, p.5.

32. 'Nigeria gets tough with oil firms', Reuter News Agency report dated 26 August 1996 as well as other press reports.

33. In 1998 the Ethiopian government announced that foreign investment would soon be allowed in energy and telecommunications as well as the defence industry.

34. Mbatau wa Ngai, 'Doubts Emerge Over Kenya's Stand on Liberalisation', *The East African* (Nairobi), 2–8 December 1996, pp.1,2. Similar sentiments were expressed by President Robert Mugabe in regard to the economic empowerment of the indigenous people in Zimbabwe. 'We do not want to disempower the whites. We want them to help create room for black participation.' See interview in *The Financial Times*, 'Survey on Zimbabwe', 24 October 1996, p.2. See also 'Black Empowerment Lobby Frightens Off Investors', *Africa Analysis* (London), 3 May 1996, p.6. In Tanzania, of the 90 public enterprises privatized by the end of 1995, only 15 were said to have been acquired by indigenous buyers.

35. The quotation is from *African Social and Economic Trends* (1995 Annual Report of the Global Coalition for Africa, Washington, DC, 1996), p.28. For Uganda, see Patrick Kiggundu, 'Family Silver Is Going for Peanuts', *The New Vision*, 16 May 1997, p.4; and John Kakande, 'Privatisation Should Be Discriminative', *The New Vision*, 10 October 1997, p.22: 'it will be tragic and reckless for government to allow foreigners to take over strategic sectors of the economy ... like banking, telecommunications, energy, aviation and agriculture ...'

36. 'Museveni Brushes Aside Resentment', *Africa Analysis*, 23 August 1996, p.4. Dr Tom Forrest informs me that foreign capital is coming into Uganda but a high proportion of it is based on quick returns rather than the long term (such as investment in coffee plantations), as the latter involves greater risks.

37. Michela Wrong, 'Tanzania's Egalitarian Dream Now Nightmare of Corruption', *The Financial Times*, 4 October 1996.

38. See Michela Wrong, 'Kenya Asians feel ground shifting under their feet,' *The Financial Times*, 13 August 1997, p.4.

39. Roger Tangri, 'Foreign Business and Political Unrest in Lesotho', *African Affairs*, 92,36 (1993), 223–38. Labour unrest was affecting investment in the textile sector in 1997 and 1998.

40. World Bank, *Adjustment in Africa. Reforms, Results, and the Road Ahead* (Washington DC, 1994), p.156. 'In spite of the strong possibility that the rebel Alliance of Democratic Forces will soon seize the southern province of Shaba, foreign companies are queuing up to sign joint ventures with Gecamines, the state-owned copper and cobalt mining company.' Michela Wrong, 'Foreign Investors Eye Kasombo Mine', *The Financial Times*, 26 March 1997.

41. See the article by Howard W. French, 'Sure, Africa's Troubled, But There Is Good News', *New York Times* (New York), 15 June 1997. Despite political risks in Nigeria, Shell and other oil companies have expanded their investments there in recent years primarily because of its high profit potential.

42. Ernest J. Wilson III, 'A Mesolevel Comparative Approach to Maxi and Mini Strategies of Public Enterprise Reform', *Studies in Comparative International Development*, 28,2 (1993), p.53.

43. See, for example, Paul Bennell, 'British Industrial Investment in Sub-Saharan Africa: Corporate Responses to Economic Crisis in the 1980s', *Development Policy Review*, 8,2 (1990): 155–77; and 'British Manufacturing Investment in Sub-Saharan Africa: Corporate Responses During Structural Adjustment', *Journal of Development Studies*, 32,2 (1995), 195–217.

44. See Cockroft, *op. cit.*, p.364 and pp.341–9 for an assessment that direct foreign investment in Africa is 'making a positive and significant contribution to GDP, but a negative contribution to the balance of payments'.(pp.345–6)

45. See Stewart et al., *op. cit.*, pp.20–22, 25 for such arguments.

46. See Note 32. Some specialists on Nigeria would argue that it is the weaknesses and incapacity of Nigerian governments which are primarily responsible for the failure to promote skills and technology.

Conclusion: The Politics of African State Economic Governance

Sub-Saharan Africa's economic crisis of the early 1980s forced increasing attention on the economic role of the state in a region where the economic arm of the state had been so extensive. Particular attention came to be focused on the state-owned enterprises undertaking important shares of production and investment in African countries. In a context of serious economic decline, the almost universally sub-standard performance of the public enterprise sector was placed under close scrutiny. State-run enterprises were held responsible for many of the economic ills confronting sub-Saharan countries. Not only had they contributed little to national economic growth but they also constituted a serious economic cost to domestic public finances. The budgetary burdens of African public enterprise deficits averaged some 4 per cent of GDP in the early 1980s. Much of the region's external debt had also resulted from borrowing by the parastatals. It was clear that public corporation debts and deficits had to be reduced,[1] and this was only possible through a major reappraisal of the role of state-owned concerns.

Calls for a major reassessment of the state enterprise sector were more the result of prompting from the international financial institutions[2] than from domestic pressures, although by the late 1980s, at a time of generally intense fiscal crisis, African governments were exhibiting growing concern regarding the economic performance of their publicly-owned firms. International donors pushed strongly for the transfer of assets and control of public enterprises to private ownership. African governments came under pressure to divest the state of its economic holdings. Calls for some form of privatization of state companies became louder over the years. Although at first interested primarily in public enterprise reform – retaining ownership of public firms but attempting to improve their performance – most African governments gradually affirmed their support for greater state enterprise divestiture. Indeed, much effort and resources have been devoted to the promotion of privatization. But everywhere domestic-based political constraints have obliged governments to be cautious and slow in its

129

implementation. In hardly any African country has privatization proceeded far enough to lead to an important disengagement of the state from direct participation in economic activities. By the late 1990s, however, under renewed pressure from external agencies, privatization appeared to be gaining some momentum, although it was also becoming evident that many divestiture transactions were subject to the political and personal interests of those in state power. Many state-owned enterprises were being taken over by those who were closely associated with leading politicians and bureaucrats.

Calls for state enterprise divestiture were accompanied by a growing emphasis on the need to develop a strong private sector and for a greater private enterprise role in African economies. International lending agencies pressed strongly for more encouragement and assistance to private domestic business as well as direct foreign investment. Most African governments acknowledged the need to support private enterprise development but, apart from encouraging foreign capital, they have done little to promote the expansion of local entrepreneurial groups. Political impediments have been among the diverse constraints limiting the increase in domestic and foreign private investment; private investment levels have remained low. Africa's private sector is still at an embryonic stage. However, new efforts are being made to promote its development, although the initiatives are strongly influenced by political considerations. State assistance to private capital has tended to go primarily to those with political and bureaucratic connections. As in the case of the beneficiaries of privatization transactions, the business entrepreneurs – both local and foreign – being favoured are those with ties to top politicians and senior state officials.

Patronage politics has been the pervasive form of rule in sub-Saharan Africa since independence. African political leaders have relied on the economic prerogatives of the state to create and sustain their regimes in power as well as to enhance their personal wealth. As we have argued in the preceding chapters, patronage politics has influenced the operations of Africa's public enterprise sector, determined the pace and beneficiaries of its privatization process, and also mediated access to government-controlled resources to select business entrepreneurs. Patronage politics has subverted the performance of parastatals, particularly since those in control of the state have used state-owned enterprises to consolidate their ruling coalitions as well as to enrich themselves personally. It has also impeded the reform and divestiture of public companies, especially as top state personnel have not wanted to lose their opportunities to mobilize and distribute public resources. In addition, the actual implementation of privatization has been affected by diverse political and personal considerations. Moreover, because a strong private sector represented a threat to the ruling group, little was done to promote the advance of indigenous private capital. Foreign capital was often promoted instead, and where the few larger African entrepreneurs have emerged, especially in recent years of economic reform, they have done so usually on a patronage basis, being linked to and dependent upon those in state power.

The crisis of African post-colonial economies is attributable, in part, to the adverse economic consequences of patronage politics on local public and private enterprise sectors. International donors now contend that if the region's economic revival is to be initiated, then a reorientation of state economic functions has to take place as well as a significant improvement in state economic performance. As advocated by the international financial institutions, rearranging the economic role of the state, and also ensuring that its remaining economic responsibilities are competently carried out, is critical for Africa's economic recovery and economic growth. But largely state-run economies have been essential for enabling African rulers to acquire the political support of various societal interests as well as to further their private wealth accumulation. A market-run economy, as envisaged by external lending agencies, would deprive African political leaders of their economic opportunities and pose a threat to the patronage basis of their regimes. This concluding chapter examines these issues by focusing, first, on the moves to reorient the economic role of African states; secondly, on the political economy of African state economic governance; and, finally, on the limitations of international donors to check the patrimonial proclivities of African rulers.

The economic role of the state

Governments have always been important to economic success. Even those who favour a minimalist state acknowledge that governments have their uses as agents of economic transformation. The evidence from the most economically successful countries in the past fifty years – the newly industrializing countries (NICs) of East Asia – supports extensive state intervention as being beneficial to economic growth. But only in a few Third World countries have effective developmental states emerged. Political factors were important in the creation of successful developmental states in East Asia, particularly in South Korea and Taiwan.[3] A distinctive colonial heritage, development-oriented political leaderships, competent public bureaucracies, and a favourable geopolitical situation constituted some of the political conditions requisite for the East Asian developmental 'miracle'.[4] Developmental states are unlikely to be easily established in sub-Saharan Africa. Neither domestic leaderships for whom development is an overriding priority, nor strong economic bureaucracies, nor a conducive international economic and political environment are present as they were in the East Asian countries.[5] Hardly any African government can implement a strong state-led approach to development.

Yet it is evident that some state involvement will be needed in Africa's development process, although the appropriate extent and type of state activity is a matter of disagreement. The main reason for government intervention is the presence of market failure. Markets may not provide certain goods and services or may do so in ways which fall below an optimum level. This is particularly the case in monopoly or non-competitive economic sectors in which African markets may not operate optimally (such as utilities – electricity generation, telecommunications, gas and water supply – as well as areas such as commercial banking and agricultural marketing). Because of market distortions (such as where agricultural trade is in the hands of a few private monopolists), government intervention may be needed to stimulate competition as well as to prevent abuse and mitigate the harsher effects of private business.

State intervention can take the form of public regulation and government monitoring of the operations of private firms. The state engages in a range of regulatory activities to check the consequences of unrestrained private sector economic activities. Government regulatory authority is usually also needed in arbitrating in commercial disputes, maintaining quality standards, protecting consumers, monitoring direct foreign investment as well as limiting monopolies and cartels. International donors have wanted to reduce the scope of public regulation in African economies, especially financial regulation (covering interest rates and foreign exchange rates) which, they argue, has proved economically stultifying for private business and investment. Many countries have been implementing regulatory reforms and much financial and economic regulation has been eliminated. However, some types of public regulation have been maintained, even increased, to promote either a more competitive private sector or to restrain the abuses of economic power in non-competitive markets.[6]

But state intervention may also be through the medium of state-owned companies. For example, public marketing firms could be set up to foster competition and reduce private agricultural trading monopsonies. In Uganda, the proposed privatization of the Uganda Commercial Bank elicited fears that the new private owners would close down most of the rural 'up-country' branches and confine banking services to the urban centres. Or as a parliamentarian commented about the proposed break-up and sale of the Uganda Posts and Telecommunications Corporation, 'whoever buys the corporation will primarily be interested in maximising profits' rather than 'providing essential services to the public'.[7] Thus, to cope with such potential market imperfections, African governments will be called upon to provide goods and services in key economic areas. Although direct government economic provision may no longer be viewed with the favour it was in previous decades, in certain circumstances (where the enterprise provides vital services) state-owned enterprise may be essential if competitive and efficient markets are to emerge.[8] On the other hand, little economic and social justification exists for the retention in government ownership of more commercially oriented public enterprises which operate in potentially competitive markets. Unless there are compelling security reasons, state companies in manufacturing, hotels, insurance, trade and farming can be sold off. And in much of the Africa region, these are the types of public firms being disposed of in the national privatization programmes.

Unlike the state firms of the post-independence decades, however, public enterprises in the 1990s are obliged to operate in a more competitive environment. In many areas, they are being exposed to competition from private sector agents, both domestic and foreign. A mix of public and private provision is emerging, and the dominance of state enterprises in key markets is being ended. Public companies also have to function as market-oriented concerns, operating on the basis of commercial principles. Everywhere in Africa, reform programmes are attempting to strengthen the management of public enterprises, especially those expected to remain for years in government ownership. Moreover, state enterprises can be managed by private management. Governments are beginning to use management contracts and leases to private firms if this is more likely to enhance commercial efficiency and profitability in publicly-owned companies.[9]

The African state will also be called upon to play an important role in developing a strong private sector, local and foreign. It is the state that will have to be primarily responsible for creating an enabling environment for private sector investment and growth. Of central importance for private entrepreneurs is that the law and property rights are respected. Governments have to ensure that property rights are secured in a region where official anti-business sentiments and arbitrary state actions have led to many instances of private business assets being seized or destroyed. If greater investment is to be forthcoming, private investors have to be assured of the security of their property rights (irrespective of race, religion, or ethnicity). In Uganda, the return in recent years of properties expropriated by previous regimes to their former Asian owners is viewed by investors as evidence of the government attempting to protect and respect private property rights. Moreover, the existence of a legal system that is seen as adjudicating contract and business disputes impartially and speedily is also essential for potential investors. Africa's legal systems have hardly provided a reliable framework for economic activities. Corruption has been prevalent (too many police and judicial officers are believed to be 'for sale') and political considerations influential in determining the outcome of business cases. Too often the due process of justice has been replaced by a due process of politics. Everywhere, the African state's role in improving the system for dispensing justice will be crucial for private business development.

Furthermore, public investment will be required to evoke greater private sector activity. Government spending in education, health, roads, railways, and research and development (R&D) is vital for stimulating confidence and investment in the private sector. According to one writer, 'it is clear that private sector growth is being constrained by Ghana's weak infrastructure', and his call for greater public sector investment spending is one that could be echoed throughout the Africa region.[10] But nowadays state involvement in certain public goods and services need not mean either direct provision by government or that government should be the sole provider. Especially in the large infrastructure projects, governments will be obliged, for financial and technical reasons, to enter into ventures with private investors.

Governments may, as did the East Asian NICs, also follow active interventionist policies in facilitating economic development and, in a world of economic competition, create national competitive advantage through a range of economic measures such as indirect subsidies, tax concessions, and tariff protection. At times, African governments may, as in the case of East Asian ones, be involved in credit provision. Affordable credit may not be readily available from privately-owned financial institutions. Government interventions are very likely needed as well to enhance the capabilities of small and medium-sized private enterprises. In particular, support may be important not only in the financial but also in the technical and marketing spheres of private sector activity. When confronted with cases of serious business failure – as in the banking sector – the state may have to step in to save failing enterprises. Even foreign-owned mining companies turned to and received government aid in Zimbabwe in 1982 to keep their ailing mines operating.[11]

Thus the private sector will not by itself get African economies moving. African states have potentially important developmental roles to play. But since independence, the African state has exhibited only limited capabilities, and its economic interventions have also been heavily politicized. State economic involvement has proved developmentally disastrous. Economic statism has been characterized by state economic failure. As the newly-elected Zambian leader, Fredrick Chiluba, put it in 1991: 'In this present crisis, government alone is not the solution to our problems. For too long, government was the problem.'[12] Or as the Ugandan President declared in 1994: 'government has been extremely inept in the conduct of business'. In contrast to the extensive state tutelage manifested by the developmental states of East Asia, sub-Saharan African governments are being strongly discouraged from active participation in the management of their economies. The international financial institutions emphasize the limitations and the poor record of African state economic activism. Arguments for reforming state systems are no longer given much credence by international donors, as they were in the early 1980s. Instead, they are insisting on a redefinition of the state's economic responsibilities, to get governments to focus predominantly on the core public activities regarded as essential to development and private sector advance.

African countries are said to have 'too much government', being involved in too many inappropriate activities – especially industrial and commercial ones for many of which alternative provision exists. Public enterprises are the prime target of external agencies aiming to reduce the size of the public sector. But also a diminution of state involvement in general is being sought through the dismantling of extensive state regulation as well as reductions in government spending. At the same time, however, it is argued that there is 'too little government' in some areas. Greater state involvement and an increasing share of public expenditure are needed in priority areas (such as protection of the public interest through environmental regulations or provision of public goods, as in the limited investment in roads). To this end, governments should facilitate the expansion of the market and the private sector as well as protect property rights, provide legal and regulatory frameworks, invest in infrastructure, utilities, education and health care, and become more involved in environmental and consumer protection.

As a recent World Bank report concluded, 'reforms over the last decade or so have tried to trim back the state's role in some areas of the economy and refocus the released resources on core functions'.[13] Nearly everywhere a gradual reorienting of state activities is beginning to take place. Unlike Western countries where quite intense debate took place over the public sector in the 1980s, in African countries the international financial institutions have largely determined the conception of the economic role of the state. International donors have been insistent that direct government ownership and production of goods and services should be reduced while the state concentrates on facilitating the market, perhaps only being involved in economic activity as a last resort to ameliorate certain problems arising from the operation of the market. Many of the selective state interventions found in East Asia are also not viewed as appropriate for African governments. The likelihood of successful state promotion of specific industries, especially those in export markets, is considered beyond the reach of African bureaucracies, given their limited capabilities. The domain of government economic involvement should be accordingly restricted as far as possible.

Resistance to this diminution of state economic roles and deregulation has not been absent, as indicated in our discussion on privatization and as seen in the slow and limited extent of restructuring of the state apparatus that has taken place in African countries. A 1993 World Bank report on Ghana declared public sector employment to be 'excessive' and the scope of government functions to be 'overextended' in a country where state reordering had received some priority since the mid-1980s. 'State control of economic activities', it concluded, 'remained pervasive.'[14] To be sure, some belief in the virtues of state economic management still prevails among African leaders. But, evidently, it is the ability of governments to maintain their call on public resources for the purposes of rewarding their political support bases that constitutes a more important consideration for seeking to contain state sector reforms.

Nevertheless, opposition to a reduction in state economic roles has been limited in its occurrence. Partly this is because of a growing recognition that state economic failings have discredited pervasive African state ownership and state economic interventionism. This recognition is reflected, for instance, in African leaders such as Presidents Chiluba and Museveni accepting the need for some privatization. Partly, too, it is because the reordering of state economic roles has been a gradual process and has so far not diminished substantially opportunities to mobilize and distribute patronage. This can be seen in the share of public spending in GDP remaining the same, with only the composition of government expenditures having altered slightly. And, partly, it is because state leaders have, as in the case of privatization and private sector assistance discussed in previous chapters, been able to manipulate changes in ways that do not undermine their personal and political interests.[15] The ideas of the World Bank about the economic role of the state are gaining ground. But the state's role in various areas of the economy has not changed substantially and, together with the new promotional, enabling, and regulatory functions that state personnel have to perform, they are still enabled to control and allocate public resources to consolidate their regimes and promote their private accumulation.

The political realities of economic statism

If the African state is to play its diverse (and redefined) developmental roles effectively, then it is essential that its capacity and management be strengthened. Given the deep malaise of African public institutions – inefficiency, mismanagement, low morale, corruption, arbitrariness, nepotism – improving the administrative and technical quality of public sector management is crucial.[16] In East Asia, highly competent and technocratic economic bureaucracies were important in shaping and implementing development policies. By contrast, through World Bank-initiated civil service reform programmes, attempts are being made to enhance the technical competence of African government personnel, especially those concerned with economic and financial management. Similarly, World Bank-inspired public enterprise reform programmes seek to bring about major improvements in the management and financial administration of public firms remaining in government ownership. But creating more efficient and effective government administrations is intrinsically a gradual (and politically difficult) process. Public sector reforms in Africa have in the few years of implementation been mainly concerned with reducing the numbers of overstaffed civil services and closing or selling inefficient state enterprises in line with what the World Bank describes as 'the redimensioning of the state'.[17] Some reductions in staffing have been achieved, although after several years of retrenchment the size of African public services remain large. Reform efforts have hardly focused on revamping internal personnel, financial, and performance management. Most important, however, is the fact that little consideration has been given to insulating public institutions from the partisan and patronage politics which in much of Africa have sustained corruption and favouritism in public bureaucracies.[18]

As emphasized throughout this study, African governments have been built around patronage networks whereby followers are rewarded for their support in the form of public jobs and resources. Politicians and bureaucrats have used the public sector to generate the benefits and patronage needed to fashion patron-client linkages of support. Top state personnel have enjoyed wide latitude in decision-making, especially economic discretion, and have rarely been accountable for their actions, such as in their disposition of public funds. The relative insulation of state elites from societal pressures as well as the weaknesses of civil society have enhanced both the power and the autonomy of African rulers. To be sure, they have been susceptible to quite forceful international and domestic pressures for policy changes in recent times, but in the actual exercise of power state personnel have been relatively unrestrained in their actions.[19] In this respect, state power in Africa has not been very different from that in East Asia. It is the uses to which it has predominantly been put which are different. In sub-Saharan Africa, it has been used partly to secure and enrich those in control of government and partly to the advantage of favoured groups and interests. Political and personal goals have informed the actions and decisions of state leaders, and African public administration has been marked by ubiquitous political intrusion resulting in abuse of authority, serious state corruption, arbitrariness and political favouritism. Even countries with reputations for efficient and prudent administration like Botswana have been shown to be no different from elsewhere in Africa: ministers and senior civil servants have manipulated circumstances for their personal and partisan advantage.[20]

To be sure, partisan and patronage politics as well as corruption and political favouritism have been manifestly evident in East Asian governments in the past forty years. For example, in South Korea in the 1960s, government policies to restructure the economy 'did not depoliticize the economy, nor did they eliminate either corruption or the importance of political connections'.[21] Yet political considerations appear to have been much less pervasive in economic decision-making, while developmental factors were of greater prominence in the economic transformations achieved by East Asian regimes. On the other hand, predominantly patrimonial political leaderships in sub-Saharan Africa have been strongly characterized by authoritarianism, lack of accountability, corruption, and political manipulation.

African public administrations have invariably been patrimonial administrations. For example, patronage politics has inspired top-level personnel decisions in African public services. Top administrators have been appointed frequently on the basis of personal and political ties to those in power. Everywhere, top bureaucratic officials (especially those in key positions) have been drawn overwhelmingly from a chief executive's ethnic group. In Cameroon, President Paul Biya's higher civil servants were drawn until recently, almost exclusively from his southern Beti ethnic group.[22] Moreover, throughout the Africa region, senior public officials have been purged, especially when the politicians with whom they have been allied have fallen from political power. This has occurred in recent years with changes of government in Ethiopia, Lesotho, Malawi and Zambia. In Uganda, within a few years of the National Resistance Movement coming to power in 1986, senior administrators lacking in sufficient political loyalty to the new leadership were removed from office, as in the case of at least five permanent secretaries (the highest officials in government ministries) including the Secretary to the Treasury. Ten years later, in 1996, the head of the Ugandan Civil Service was retired, mainly on political grounds.[23]

State economic management in post-colonial Africa has rarely been developmentally oriented; it has been largely patrimonially oriented. Public economic administration has clearly been an arm of politicians and senior bureaucrats. John Cohen has described how Kenya's public sector has been used for political and personal purposes. Especially from the mid-1980s, senior public servants 'were selected for their political or ethnic connections rather than their technical competence' to help influential ministers stay in power. Moreover, the public bureaucracy was used to enhance the enrichment of politicians. Powerful 'political "godfathers" ... were more concerned about private deals than the stewardship of Kenya's economic future'.[24] Not only the civil service but also public enterprise management as well as processes promoting privatization and private enterprise development have been heavily politicized. Cohen argues that in Kenya positions in 'ministries, national financial institutions, and parastatals' have been used 'to advance the business/economic interests of the President and his supporters'. President Arap Moi also 'encouraged his supporters in the ministries and parastatals to hamper businessmen ... who criticised his administration'.[25] Not surprisingly, a public service that has served the interests of the Moi regime so well has proved strongly resistant to the major administrative reforms proposed in recent years by international donors, even though such reforms, as elsewhere on the continent, have hardly addressed the profound effects that patrimonial tendencies have had on African public sector organizations.

The successful developmental states in East Asia have been highly authoritarian for much of the past forty years. In sub-Saharan Africa, however, authoritarian regimes have been anti-developmental. In particular, domestic political factors (such as corruption and patronage politics) are viewed as having undermined the rational economic use of state resources. Since the late 1980s, the international financial institutions have contended that in Africa democratic systems are essential for improved economic performance. Multilateral organizations have concentrated mainly – as we do here – on government operations. Under its policy of promoting 'good' governance especially in the economic sphere in Africa,[26] the World Bank has advocated greater openness and transparency in bureaucratic procedures, processes, appointments, contracts, procurements and investment decisions as well as seeking to strengthen accountability measures, including scrutiny by the legislature and prosecution by the courts. International donors are realizing that African state economic decisions are driven pre-eminently by political and personal rather than by economic and technical considerations. Designated governance mechanisms (accountability, transparency, and participation), together with an elected legislature, an independent judiciary, a free press, and a proliferation of independent civic associations, are what are needed to develop effective oversight of government economic actions and transactions as well as to ensure that official operations follow the notions of 'good' economic governance so essential, for instance, for business entrepreneurs investing in productive activities.

But most African leaders stand in a fairly tenuous relationship to democratic and 'good' government. Although many countries now have multi-party systems, governing parties still seek by various means to hold on to political office. Tor Skalnes writes of 'the manipulation of electoral arrangements and undisguised intimidation of opposition politicians and their supporters' in Zimbabwe, while Michela Wrong declares that in Kenya 'as in so many African countries, a corrupt elite subverted the [multi-party] system, remaining in power by buying votes, outwitting an egotistical opposition and exploiting tribal tensions'.[27] Achieving transparent and accountable government in Africa will be a difficult process. Incumbent political leaderships still possess and want to preserve virtually uncontrollable power. Few African rulers are willing to accept limits to their discretion over decision-making. The World Bank reported that in Ghana there is much 'resistance to change from a traditionally highly centralized process of decision making'.[28] And many of the institutions and mechanisms of democratic governance are too weak to control the executive power, partly because they are not well-developed and partly because they are not independent of government influences.

For example, the situation in most sub-Saharan countries is one of a dominant executive and a weak legislature. The following brief illustrations from Kenya show the problems that parliamentary committees have had, even under the new multi-party system, in holding high-ranking state personnel responsible for their actions. Opposition members of the Public Accounts Committee – the parliamentary watchdog on public funds – alleged in 1996 that attempts to get certain people to testify or to make available vital documents regarding irregular official expenditures totalling $627 million had failed.[29] The PAC had also been denied access to crucial sites such as military bases to verify facilities on which the government had spent over $10 million. Also in 1996, the Public Investments Committee named former (and some current) parastatal chief executives allegedly involved in irregular deals and demanded that they be prosecuted and surcharged. The government ignored the report.[30] 'Parliament is being effectively bypassed', concluded the *East African*. 'It is not being allowed to work as it should.'[31]

In similar ways, in Kenya as elsewhere in sub-Saharan Africa, legislative (as well as judicial) oversight of the conduct of government is limited. To be sure, legislators in many countries are seeking to play a more active role, as in the appointment of government ministers and in determining the budget. But nearly everywhere there is an atmosphere of some executive intimidation, most acutely, for example, in Zimbabwe as a result of President Mugabe's attacks on disloyal parliamentarians and his criticisms of the Speaker in early 1998. Also important, as Bratton and van de Walle observe, is that the political executive is 'able to coopt the legislature within the context of clientelistic relations to prevent it from playing an effective independent oversight role', as happened recently in Zambia where President Chiluba bestowed 'lucrative favours on backbenchers to keep them quiet'.[32] Moreover, oversight is commonly in the hands of persons chosen for their loyalty to the political leadership. Thus in Uganda, the 'anti-corruption institutions, because they are often doled out as part of the government's patronage, have turned into bodies for managing a few extreme cases, not combating graft'.[33] As a result of such constraints on the institutions of governance, state economic decision-making in Africa remains largely embedded in patrimonial politics and personal interests, phenomena so evident in our discussion of privatization and private sector development as well as in many other areas involving financial transactions, the provision of goods and services, and the investment of resources. Much of what happens at the top of the state apparatus in regard to economic matters occurs in disregard of legal rules and procedures and in conformity with political and personal factors. The manifestations of relatively unrestrained and unaccountable state power – corruption, cronyism, favouritism – continue to characterize many government economic actions.

To be sure, Africa's media are beginning to speak up on 'the misdeeds of an increasingly corrupt executive' in Uganda as well as in the far worse cases of Zambia and Zimbabwe.[34] But incumbent leaders 'chafe against the limits on their personal power which these [political parties and the mass media] (and other) restraining structures' represent, and seek to weaken them 'by means of intimidation, cooptation, and the distribution of patronage'.[35] And despite the reintroduction of democratic structures and the more regular occurrence of elections, African regimes continue to depict a wide range of traits associated with authoritarian rule. Political power remains personalized in the hands of a single ruler or a small oligarchy who exercise considerable unencumbered discretion over access to public resources as well as employing various coercive measures to maintain their hold on state power.[36]

As important as measures to improve the economic managerial capacity as well as the quality of governance in the building of developmental states, may be a reduction in the economic role of the state. An economically minimalist state could lessen the struggle for state power which is so intense everywhere in Africa. A less activist state would no longer be so central to the control of scarce resources and economic opportunities as the economically interventionist state of the early post-independence decades. It would not constitute the predominant means of access to resources and benefits (jobs, contracts, loans, etc.) in society. The private sector would also be involved in resource allocation and accumulation. Moreover, not only would state power not be so highly valued but also the state would not be penetrated so much by societal interests clamouring for favours and benefits. If African governments were less economically valuable, then they would be more insulated from domestic demands for the distribution of valued resources, and more able to pursue necessary development policies. Reducing the centrality of state economic management could therefore weaken patrimonial politics and strengthen the emergence of state leaderships more oriented to development.

Already commentators are noting that economic liberalization 'is changing the nature of politics in Uganda'. As privatization proceeds and as state economic management is reduced, so will patronage politics be undermined.

> It is difficult for politicians to get rich quick when contracts are awarded in the private sector, the value of forex is decided by the open market, and banks award loans on a commercial basis.

> As a result we should start to see a new brand of politicians emerging who are guided more by principle and policy concerns than by the opportunity to make financial gains through political patronage ...[37]

This may go too far in its claims as regards actual developments in Uganda. Because more market-run economies and less state-managed ones are likely to threaten the patronage base of African ruling groups, they will evolve only gradually. Those in control of the state will seek to retain their ability to distribute benefits and patronage (and also influence divestiture decisions and the emergence of a specific class of local entrepreneurs) in order to maintain their hold on state power. Nevertheless, a reduction in the availability of resources to political leaders may undermine their ability to reward supporters and maintain patronage networks. It may also undermine endemic African state corruption.

The extensive economic and interventionist roles of African states have for long provided copious opportunities for those controlling the economic apparatus to enhance their material wealth. Heavy statist economic management and authoritarian polities provided plenty of fertile ground for abuse of office and for the personal enrichment of state personnel. Everywhere the opportunities for rent-seeking and corruption through public institutions proliferated. 'Officeholding in Nigeria', wrote Larry Diamond, 'has come to mean the opportunity for phenomenal illicit gain.'[38] In Kenya the Attorney-General admitted in 1995 that the level of corruption in public office was reaching 'dangerous levels', while an editorial in the *Financial Times* of London in 1997 stated that a 'series of financial scandals over the years' had shown that in Kenya 'graft is endemic'.[39] High-level corruption was not absent in Taiwan and was quite serious in South Korea. In sub-Saharan Africa, the extent of state corruption may not be any greater, although the economic costs may be higher. Government corruption has to be reduced, and this is possible 'if opportunities for corrupt gain shrink while its risk rises'. World Bank-sponsored structural adjustment programmes aim 'to reduce rent-seeking in state office by cutting back on the state's role in the economy'.[40] Ugandan President, Yoweri Museveni, concurs in such thinking: 'Privatisation is the strategic answer to corruption. The long-time answer to corruption is the reduction of public servants in money making activities.'[41] The 'only sure way of dealing with corruption in Uganda is through selling the "plates" [government parastatals] from which these corrupt officials are eating'.[42] On the other hand, Tanzanian judge, Joseph Warioba, while acknowledging 'that monopolistic institutions created after nationalisation ... contributed significantly to the corruption problem in Tanzania', is forceful in arguing that in 'the war against corruption' there is 'need to have a system which ensures transparency and accountability in government and other institutions....'[43] But so long as African political leaders rely on public resources to maintain themselves in power and to build their own and their close supporters' wealth, then they will only slowly privatise, only gradually give up some of their control over economic decisions, and only do the minimum to promote accountable and transparent state economic governance. Where they do privatize, they will ensure that ownership of public companies is transferred to loyal elements; and where they do promote 'good' governance, they will ensure that designated governance mechanisms are in the hands of loyal supporters and limited in their independence.[44]

For a variety of historical and geopolitical reasons, East Asian political elites have been deeply committed to rapid economic growth. Economic development has been taken as the sacred mission of the state.[45] Until recently, and with the possible exceptions of Botswana and Côte d'Ivoire,[46] economic growth has not been accorded top political priority in sub-Saharan Africa. The pursuit of political and personal goals has been all-important. But, confronted with an unprecedented economic crisis, political leaders are being obliged to assign higher priority to national economic recovery. For economic and political reasons, Africa's grim economic conditions have to be reversed. The motivations of those in state power are changing. For President Museveni the top goal is economic 'modernization', and his priorities are publicly specified as more roads, poverty elimination, proper land use, universal primary education, and a living income for peasants. President Museveni is also said to be 'one of those rare figures on the continent – Rwanda's Paul Kagame is another – whose ambition extends beyond self-enrichment and self-adulation'.[47] Economically oriented state elites are appearing in several other African countries, most recently in Eritrea. They acknowledge that the state approaches of earlier decades will not induce attainment of their diverse 'modernizing' objectives and are attempting to achieve them by following market-based policies. But Africa's rulers also have compelling political concerns which affect state economic governance in important ways.

To be sure, Africa's modernizing rulers are very different from the authoritarian and avaricious leaders many sub-Saharan countries have had in the recent past. But the critics of the new rulers argue, nevertheless, that although they may be giving greater emphasis to economic development, economic decisions continue to be made within the framework of personal rule, patron-client politics and state corruption. Politically, Africa's new rulers, like their predecessors, are the single most powerful figures in their countries, a fact reflected in a country still being equated with its particular leader. The domination of a ruler has continued the post-independence pattern of personal and patrimonial rule. For instance, international donors have criticized the cost of maintaining large government executives in a number of African countries, including Côte d'Ivoire, Uganda and Zimbabwe. In Uganda in 1996, President Museveni increased the number of executive-level positions in his new government from 42 to 61, thus abandoning the ministerial mergers that the World Bank had initiated in 1992. 'I had to have enough cake to pass around', he argued, referring at a swearing-in ceremony of the cabinet and state ministers to the need for regional balance in his government. President Museveni is also criticized for tolerating corrupt practices by senior politicians and public officials. Many anti-corruption measures exist in Uganda but, according to some international observers, 'the population seems to be unconvinced of the determination of the leadership to effectively combat corruption'.[48] For example, although the interim Parliament passed the Leadership Code of Conduct in April 1992 – intended to check on the behaviour of persons holding public office with regard to the accumulation of wealth – it remained unimplemented till early 1997. As elsewhere in Africa, in Uganda 'a lot of corrupt acts are done by people believed to be the president's men or connected to him through family'. That is why 'Museveni will be condemned by posterity for his lukewarm approach against corruption'. But that is how 'the NRM government sustains itself in power by allowing the law to be broken as the pork passes around ...'[49] Moreover, political concerns in Uganda further reflect themselves 'in the government's sectarian expenditure of development funds only in a few parts of the country'. Mounting allegations that President Museveni's government has been favouring his south-western region in terms of senior public sector appointments and development projects only serve to strengthen public perceptions of the persistence of patrimonial governance working to the advantage of the 'big and the connected', the elite of the currently dominant ethnic groups.[50] The commitment of top African leaders to economic growth as well as the principles of good governance is developing; but the imperatives of patronage politics still take precedence.

Arguments have been made that structural adjustment programmes will curtail the opportunities of state leaders to promote their patronage systems. Jeffrey Herbst writes that the 'ability to distribute patronage will be threatened to some degree by structural adjustment'.[51] Restrictions on public sector employment and on state spending including the elimination of government subsidies are reducing the public resources political leaders can offer to acquire political support. Privatization and deregulation will result in many economic decisions being removed from government organizations, thus reducing the ability to use the state to provide resources to favoured constituencies. Especially 'politically painful' is when 'a government must get out of commodity marketing', thus 'removing the hand of politicians from the most lucrative game in the land'.[52]

To be sure, there will be some closing off of the possibilities for governments to offer public resources. But this is far from a total or even substantial elimination of opportunities to provide patronage. In spite of market reforms, the state still overshadows the private sector in African economies. The government remains the largest single spender in all African countries. In Zimbabwe, public expenditure accounted in 1997 for a huge 38 per cent of GDP.[53] African regimes have also benefitted from the inflow of external resources and loans provided by the international financial institutions. The IMF and the World Bank lend primarily to governments and have provided high levels of resources to existing regimes. For a country such as Ghana this has meant the receipt of over $800 million a year for each of the past ten years. This outside support has also meant that the share of public spending in GDP has remained much the same as before structural adjustment, although the composition of government expenditures may have changed slightly.[54] Moreover, African rulers will still control a significant number of economic decisions (taxes, jobs, tariffs, contracts, licences) as well as influencing government spending.

Top state personnel in government ministries, remaining parastatals, and the many new statutory authorities that have been established in recent years will still have projects and patronage to distribute. They will continue to influence resource allocations and economic decisions to build a political support base for themselves as well as to reap personal benefits. Public resources will become more limited but the fund of patronage will remain sufficiently large to maintain governments in power.[55] For all the economic and political liberalization taking place, the patrimonial foundations of government remain secure. And the requirements of patronage politics will continue to subvert accountability and probity in state economic governance.

Historically, an economically viable and politically well-organized capitalist class is viewed as essential in the building of developmentally oriented states. Not only in Western Europe but also in East Asia, capitalist growth and capitalist power enabled private entrepreneurs to play roles as important as those of the state in resource allocation. Capitalism generated countervailing sources of wealth and power, independent of those controlled by the state. Also, by means of political organization a capitalist class was able to undermine patrimonial politics as well as to advance the emergence of a developmental state. Similarly, it is argued, a strong African private sector could ensure that the private sphere provides many of the benefits and resources that have for long been monopolized by governments. In addition, powerful capitalist interests could, as in other regions, organize to hold governments to account as well as to undermine state patronage politics.

But African capitalist sectors are still economically weak; they account for only a small proportion of domestic economic output. Foreign and resident non-African investors are often more important in overall economic activity but, nevertheless, it is the state that remains the largest employer and investor in African countries. Economic resources are predominantly in the hands of top state personnel. Also, so important and dominant is the state that business entrepreneurs – local as well as foreign – depend on the political patronage of government for their economic advancement, thereby affecting the possibilities for private capital to play much of a role in confronting and limiting state power. Moreover, economic weaknesses are compounded by the various divisions of interest within business communities as well as the organizational and political shortcomings of indigenous capitalists. John Rapley demonstrates the limited political impact of local business: 'At the time of independence, indigenous bourgeoisies in much of sub-Saharan Africa were politically weak ... The new ruling elites, unconstrained by bourgeois civil societies, were left with surprising latitude to use – and abuse – the state',[56] thus precluding developmental states – as opposed to patrimonial ones – from emerging in African countries. Only when the private sector has economic power independent of the state will business people emerge who are capable of countering the influence of the state and its attendant patronage-based economic policy processes. At the moment, however, a private sector (as well as a civil society) which can delimit state power is far from being in existence

Concluding remarks

Over the past decade, African economic reform programmes have been initiating public enterprise reforms and privatization, although progress has, until the mid-1990s, tended to be slow. Changes in the political economy of African countries are also producing a business environment more propitious for private investment, although the changes have been slow and uneven. Both privatization and private sector development have been subject to the political interests of those in state power. Moreover, elected legislatures, an independent judiciary, and a free press are developing to check government corruption and abuse of authority, albeit in a limited way. And reductions in state economic roles are slowly eroding the opportunities and resources for political allocations. Yet patronage politics persists and is currently the defining political pattern in African countries. So long as the driving motivations of those in control of the state – maintaining state power as well as enhancing personal accumulation – continue as overriding goals, they will influence significantly the performance of African economies, the quality of public administration and state economic governance, and the nature of privatization and private sector development.

Since the early 1980s, external agencies – chiefly the international financial institutions and bilateral Western donors – have been important in pushing structural adjustment programmes in sub-Saharan countries. Faced with an acute economic and fiscal crisis, the need for foreign finance and other assistance has sufficed for heavily indebted African governments to agree to external prescriptions for broad-based structural adjustment and economic liberalization. Policy reform packages – seeking essentially to reduce the role of the state as well as to enlarge the scope of the private sector – have been similar throughout Africa, demonstrating that they have been largely initiated by external actors, especially the IMF and the World Bank. Notwithstanding claims that adjustment programmes are 'homegrown' and possess strong African 'ownership', in reality they have involved limited local participation in their actual formulation. Public enterprise reform and private sector development programmes nearly everywhere in the region have been designed by the World Bank, though there has been some consultation with high-level national officials. Such programmes have also been subjected to little local debate and have usually not required legislative consent.

But the international lending agencies have had far less influence on the way policy changes are carried out.[57] Those who occupy positions of state power have determined the actual outcomes of reform programmes. External actors have hardly influenced the actual implementation of policy reforms. Domestic state elites have exercised most influence in how privatization and private sector development programmes are put into action. To be sure, external donors have expressed concern about the restructuring of parastatals, the pace of their privatization, and the levels of private investment. Generally, IMF/World Bank missions assess overall progress in meeting specified targets. For example, in Kenya in 1996 the international financial institutions wanted to ascertain progress in splitting the Kenya Posts and Telecommunications Corporation into three entities, as well as the divestiture from various parastatals, thus meeting the annual target of twenty privatizations. But little concern exists regarding to whom a state company is divested and on what terms, or who the beneficiaries of private enterprise development measures are. In Kenya the external financial agencies have come under mounting criticism from opposition politicians for turning a blind eye to irregularities in the operations of state companies as well as their privatization. IMF and World Bank lending has gone ahead to many African governments where there has been ample evidence of a lack of openness in decision-making, and of corruption and cronyism. Very recently, however, lending has been held up in several countries such as Cameroon, Côte d'Ivoire, and Kenya, mostly by governance-related issues such as customs scandals, secret presidential accounts, and high-level government sleaze.

Although aware of the influence of patronage politics, external actors possess only a limited understanding of its continuing significance in the economic actions and transactions of African states. Nor do they have the capacity to monitor state management closely. The assertion that 'external monitoring of economic reform … attacked the prebendal state' exaggerates the leverage exercised by international agencies.[58] The World Bank may posit a relationship between 'good' governance and development, but the structures of domestic governmental decision-making remain largely impervious to its influence. In Ghana in 1993, the World Bank noted that in 'several important areas, donors' support for reform made little difference'.[59] Although strongly behind the recent processes of building developmental states and productive private capitalism, international donors have proved incapable of doing much to prevent their deep permeation by the political and personal logics of African rulers.

In the World Bank's 1997 *World Development Report* 'rampant patronage' is referred to several times as the root cause of Africa's economic and social ills. But little is said of its causes (such as the premium placed on attaining and maintaining political power, especially as alternative routes to wealth are still limited) and consequences (such as the development of crony capitalism). Much of the World Bank's hopes for improved state economic management rest on a reduction in the scope of state economic intervention and of government largesse which would make it difficult to retain the support of important political constituencies. And, to be sure, governments are finding it difficult to muster the patronage resources needed to uphold political support. Yet 'the privatisation process in many countries reinforced patterns of patron-client relations which the exercise itself was supposed to eliminate'.[60] African governments, too, retain considerable ability to reward their political support base. Patronage resources to reward or co-opt key individuals and groups have only partially been depleted by reform measures. It is possible that donor efforts to reform African public sectors, to promote transparency and accountability, and to strengthen civil society groups will lead gradually to desired improvements in state economic governance. But where state office and public resources remain crucial to political leaders remaining in power then achieving 'good' governance will be a highly contested process with African rulers taking little more than token steps to attain it. For the moment, sub-Saharan states are still fundamentally patrimonial systems, and patronage politics is not easily undermined.

NOTES

1. See World Bank, *World Development Report 1988* (New York, 1988), Chap. 8 on improving public finances through state-owned enterprise reforms.
2. See World Bank, *World Development Report 1983* (New York, 1983), p.74.
3. Alice Amsden, *Asia's Next Giant. South Korea and Late Industrialization* (New York, 1989), and Robert Wade, *Governing the Market. Economic Theory and the Role of Government in East Asian Industrialization* (Princeton, NJ, 1991) provide detailed studies of developmental states in East Asia.
4. See Ziya Onis, 'The Logic of the Developmental State', *Comparative Politics*, 24,1 (1991), 109–26, and Adrian Leftwich, 'Bringing Politics Back In: Towards a Model of the Developmental State', *Journal of Development Studies*, 31,3 (1995), 400–27 for discussions of the politics and character of developmental states.
5. See E. Gyimah-Boadi and Nicolas van de Walle, 'The Politics of Economic Renewal in Africa', in Benno Ndulu, Nicolas van de Walle, and contributors, *Agenda for Africa's Economic Renewal* (New Brunswick, 1996), for a discussion of the absence of such factors in sub-Saharan Africa.

6. In sub-Saharan Africa, a supervisory and regulatory framework has to be established because privatization, for various reasons, 'tended to lead to uncompetitive monopolistic markets'. See Thandika Mkandawire, 'The Political Economy of Privatisation in Africa', in Giovanni Andrea Cornia and Gerald K. Helleiner (eds.), *From Adjustment to Development in Africa* (Basingstoke, 1994), p.200. Many economists would dispute this statement. It is cited here as an indication of the need for an adequate regulatory capacity.

7. Chairman of the Sessional Committee on Transport, Communications, Work and Housing quoted in Sam Mukalazi, 'Slow Down on Sale of Firms, State to be Told', *The East African* (Nairobi), 23 September 1996, p.2. See also Manza Tumubweine, 'Selling Off UCB Is Playing with Fire', *The Monitor* (Kampala), 4 April 1997, p.3.

8. For a discussion of the role of state marketing boards in encouraging the growth of competitive markets as well as performing other important functions, see John Rapley, *Understanding Development. Theory and Practice in the Third World* (Boulder, CO, 1996), pp.94–96.

9. In Mozambique, the parastatals that have remained in government ownership – ports, shipping, customs – have been restructured and their management contracted to private enterprise. For a brief discussion on the changing role of state-owned enterprises, see Jeffrey Herbst, *The Politics of Reform in Ghana, 1982–1991* (Berkeley, CA, 1993),pp.109–113. For improving their performance, see World Bank, *World Development Report 1988, op. cit.*, Chap.8.

10. Tony Hawkins, 'Back in the Intensive Care Ward', *The Financial Times* (London), 9 July 1996. The author argues the same in regard to Zambia: 'More than anything else, the infrastructure – in the very broadest sense of the word, encompassing education, training and health facilities as well as roads, railways, electricity and telecommunications, threatens to hold back Zambia in the 21st century.' See Tony Hawkins, 'Welcome Global Trend', *The Financial Times*, 4 March 1997.

11. See Jeffrey Herbst, *State Politics in Zimbabwe* (Berkeley, CA, 1990), p.158. Many of these state roles in support of private sector growth are not considered appropriate by the World Bank for developing countries. But in the successful Asian industrializing countries, interventionist policies were practised by governments. See Sanjaya Lall, 'Industrial Policy: The Role of Government in Promoting Industrial and Technological Development', *UNCTAD Review*, (1992), 65–89. In sub-Saharan Africa, it is argued that more limited government intervention will be necessary.

12. Inauguration speech by President Frederick Chiluba on 2 November 1991.

13. See World Bank, *World Development Report 1997. The State in a Changing World* (Washington, DC, 1997), p.158. This report as well as World Bank, *World Development Report 1991. The Challenge of Development* (New York, 1991) provide overviews of the World Bank's conception of the changing economic role of the state.

14. Quoted in Eboe Hutchful, 'Why Regimes Adjust: The World Bank Ponders Its "Star Pupil"', *Canadian Journal of African Studies*, 29,2 (1995), p.304. See also the discussion on pp.306–10.

15. Moreover, the regulatory regime to which privatized firms are subjected may be one where private enterprise autonomy is limited and political interventions continue to occur. Robert Shaw argues in the case of Kenya that 'a number of companies that were in the public sector and now have at least one foot in the private sector have problems which are ... caused by the Government and its officers treating them as

if they are still Government departments'. He continues: 'they can often be subjected to the negative hand of bureaucracy, political pressure and even possible extortion. Banks such as Kenya Commercial Bank and National Bank of Kenya are obviously vulnerable to these sorts of pressures. Another is Kenya Airways.' See *Sunday Nation* (Nairobi), 15 June 1997, p.7.

16. In explaining Côte d'Ivoire's economic success in the first three decades of independence, Richard C. Crook argues that state capacity was 'clearly a crucial element in its economic record'. See 'Patrimonialism, Administrative Effectiveness and Economic Development in Côte d'Ivoire', *African Affairs*, 88,351 (1989), p.207. For some specific examples of the lack of effective state capacity in economic management in African countries, see World Bank, *World Development Report 1997, op. cit.*, pp. 83–4.

17. World Bank, *The Reform of Public Sector Management: Lessons of Experience* (Washington, DC, 1991), p.1.

18. For discussions on African bureaucracies and public service reform, see Goran Hyden, *No Shortcuts to Progress. African Development Management in Perspective* (London, 1983); David Leonard, 'The Political Realities of African Management', *World Development*, 15,7 (1987), 899–910; and Richard Sandbrook, *The Politics of Africa's Economic Recovery* (Cambridge, 1993), pp.56–86. Crook, *op. cit.*, argues that the patronage system in Cote d'Ivoire in the 1970s and 1980s did not necessarily undermine state capacity.

19. In most African countries, decision-making power has been centralized in the cabinet and in the top echelons of the bureaucracy. However, in the case of Zimbabwe, Tor Skalnes documents the significant role played by economic interests (especially the European settler-dominated organizations) in economic policy. See his *The Politics of Economic Reform in Zimbabwe. Continuity and Change in Development* (Basingstoke, 1995).

20. See Kenneth Good, 'Corruption and Mismanagement in Botswana: A Best-Case Example?', *Journal of Modern African Studies*, 32,3 (1994), 499–521 for a discussion of how Botswana's 'high reputation for good government has crumbled since 1991'. (p.500).

21. D. Michael Shafer, 'Sectors, States, and Social Forces. Korea and Zambia Confront Economic Restructuring', *Comparative Politics*, 22,2 (1990), p.131.

22. For some figures on the preponderance of Beti in pivotal administrative positions in 1991, see Joseph Takougang, 'The Demise of Biya's New Deal in Cameroon, 1982–1992', *Africa Insight*, 23,2 (1993), pp.95–6.

23. In another example of patrimonial administration, President Robert Mugabe has 'disarmed potential opponents and secured the continuing loyalty of adherents by spending about 54 per cent of Zimbabwe's gross national product on a public sector riddled with patronage appointments. The public service has grown from 40,000 in 1979 to 189,000 in 1992.' Michael Hartnack, 'Mugabe Faces Revolt over Patronage System', *Business Day* (Johannesburg), 17 September 1992, p.4. Nearly seven years later, and in the midst of serious economic and political trouble, a journalist posed the question of whether Mugabe could be ousted from power. 'His system of political and economic patronage has long held the presidential edifice together – and it is seemingly still holding fast. The recent gestures over war veterans allowances and farmland reallocation, while apparently short-sighted and economically disastrous, could well bolster his position with the rural electorate'. See Dianna Games, 'Mugabe plays Santa at end of annus horribilis,' *Business Day*, 5 January 1999.

24. John M. Cohen, 'Importance of Public Service Reform: the Case of Kenya', *Journal of Modern African Studies*, 31,3 (1993), pp.467, 466. The World Bank also notes that in Kenya's patronage-based bureaucracy 'political appointments run quite deep'. See World Bank, *World Development Report 1997*, *op. cit.*, p.9.

25. Cohen, *op.cit.*, pp.472, 473.

26. World Bank, *Sub-Saharan Africa. From Crisis to Sustainable Growth: a Long-term Perspective Study* (Washington, DC, 1989), pp.55–6; World Bank, *Governance and Development* (Washington, DC, 1992); and World Bank, *Governance. The World Bank's Experience* (Washington, DC, 1994). It would appear that international donors have too readily accepted that East Asian countries possessed the attributes of 'good' governance in their public sectors. In fact, evidence is emerging that they, too, featured weak accountability, low levels of transparency, and substantial corruption.

27. Skalnes, *op. cit.*, p.74, and Michela Wrong, 'Moi Faces Challenges Within and Without', *The Financial Times*, 9 January 1997.

28. Quoted in Hutchful, *op. cit.*, p.305.

29. See *The Nation* (Nairobi), 24 and 25 May 1996. A large portion of this amount related to the so-called Goldenberg affair in which the Central Bank and the Treasury lost over $400 million in a massive financial scandal in the early 1990s.

30. See Mbatau wa Ngai, 'We Are Paying a High Price for Corruption', *Sunday Nation*, 26 May 1996, p.7.

31. Editorial in *The East African*, 27 May 1996, p.8. In December 1997, Kenya's parliamentary standing orders were amended to give control of the PAC and the PIC to the party with a majority in the legislature. However, the chairperson of these committees was still to be drawn from the opposition parties, unlike in Uganda where under the new 1995 Constitution the chairpersons are drawn from the ruling movement.

32. See Michael Bratton and Nicolas van de Walle, *Democratic Experiments in Africa* (Cambridge, 1997), p.247.

33. Charles Onyango-Obbo, 'The NRM Factor in Uganda's Corruption', *The East African*, 26 November 1997, p.9. President Museveni comes from the south-western region of Uganda. A prominent opposition leader and parliamentarian, Ms Cecilia Ogwal, 'lashed at the Government, accusing it of gross nepotism. "How can you investigate and catch Salim Saleh [the president's brother accused by a parliamentary committee of alleged corruption] when the IGG [the main anti-corruption authority], the Attorney-General, the Solicitor-General, the Director of Public Prosecutions, the Public Accounts Committee chairman, the head of internal security, the Auditor-General, the CID chief and many others in-charge of Government are from western Uganda" she asked?' See *The New Vision*, 11 December 1998.

34. *The Monitor*, 31 October 1997, p.3. In an editorial, *The Post* (Lusaka), 16 June 1997 described the ruling MMD government as 'this conglomeration of drug traffickers, thieves, liars and certificate forgers'. On Zimbabwean and African political leaders, see the editorial in *Zimbabwe Independent* (Harare), 26 September 1997.

35. Richard Sandbrook, 'Transitions Without Consolidation: Democratisation in Six African Countries', *Third World Quarterly*, 17,1 (1996), p.85. In regard to the media, a number of countries such as Uganda (up to 1996) and Malawi (in 1998) ban state advertisements in independent newspapers.

36. For a similar argument as regards executive non- accountability, state corruption, and a new authoritarianism in South Africa since 1994, see Kenneth Good, 'Accountable to Themselves: Predominance in Southern Africa', *Journal of Modern African Studies*, 35,4 (1997), 547–73.

37. Editorial in *The New Vision*, 26 January 1996, p.4.

38. Larry Diamond, 'Political Corruption. Nigeria's Perennial Struggle', *Journal of Democracy*, 2,4 (1991), p.78.

39. *The Financial Times*, editorial, 30 July 1997. Kenyan members of parliament belonging to a newly-established select committee on anti-corruption described the situation in the country as entailing 'massive looting, outright theft and embezzlement of billions of Kenya shillings from public coffers'. See *Business Africa* (Nairobi), 18 September 1998, p.1.

40. Diamond, *op.cit.*, p.81.

41. Quoted in *The Monitor*, 24–27 March 1995, p.7.

42. Quoted in *The Monitor*, 19 January 1996, p.8. In Uganda as well as other sub-Saharan countries, anecdotal evidence suggests that corruption has increased at the highest levels of government under structural adjustment. If true, this may be a temporary phenomenon as state personnel seek to acquire as much as possible before policy changes limit the patronage available to them.

43. See interview with Judge Warioba in *The East African*, 1 February 1997. In February 1996, Judge Warioba led a Presidential Commission on Corruption in Tanzania, and the interview comprised some comments on the Commission's published report.

44. It is also clear that senior incumbents of state office are rarely prosecuted for alleged corrupt activities. Even after the 1996 Wairoba report exposed many instances of high-level corruption in Tanzania (and after the president was provided with a confidential list charging a number of top officials with gross corruption), only one senior government official, who had also fallen out of political grace, was sued for wrongdoing. In Nigeria where the years of military government under Babangida and Abacha were marked by unprecedented heights of corruption and outright theft by military rulers and their inner circles, not one of them faced any criminal charges, even after the regimes no longer held state power. In Cameroon, Côte d'Ivoire, Kenya, and Zambia – indeed all across Africa – civilian and military leaders have seldom been called to account before the courts for alleged abuse of public office.

45. Ziya Onis states that economic development 'constitutes the foremost and single-minded priority of state action'. See Onis, *op. cit.*, p. 111.

46. 'The government is led by a cohesive group of elites who see themselves as modernizing agents'. Louis A. Picard, *The Politics of Development in Botswana. A Model for Success?* (Boulder, CO, 1987), p.271. See also Crook, *op. cit.*, p.225: 'The elite has pursued since independence a set of policies aimed at maximizing economic growth at all costs.' By the early 1990s, however, in Botswana the 'governing elite's manifest ethos' was being described as that of 'individual self-enrichment'. See Good, 'Corruption', *op. cit.*, p.512.

47. Joshua Hammer, 'Goodbye Mr. Moi', *Newsweek*, 11 November 1996, p.4.

48. EDIRP GPSM and Transparency International, 'Ethics, Accountability and Transparency in Uganda' (Paper presented to the Integrity Workshop in Uganda 11, Mukono, Uganda, November 1995).

49. Odoobo C. Bichachi, 'Has Museveni Hung his Gloves on Corruption?', *The Monitor*, 21 October 1996, p.9. See also editorial in *The Crusader* (Kampala), 1 October 1996.

One of Uganda's leading and highly respected journalists wrote that people 'are disgusted at the corruption in government, and the protection and comfort that the Museveni regime seems to be giving to thieves ...' See Charles Onyango-Obbo's column in *The Monitor*, 22 April 1998 as well as the one of 7 January 1999. For the views of a strong supporter and leading member of the ruling organization in Uganda, see Augustine Ruzindana, 'The Importance of Leadership in Fighting Corruption in Uganda', in Kimberly Ann Elliott (ed.), *Corruption and the Global Economy* (Washington, DC, 1997). A report prepared for the World Bank estimated that Uganda suffered an economic loss of $250–350 million a year as a result of corrupt tendencies by its civilian and military officials. Western donors were also critical of the actions of the top Ugandan leadership in dealing with corrupt state officials. See Isabirye Musoke, 'Corruption costs Uganda 350 bn/= in '98', *The Monitor*, 28 December 1998, p.1.

50. Editorial in *The Monitor*, 16 October 1996, p.3. Senior government positions concerned with economic affairs (including Permanent Secretary, Ministry of Finance; Minister of Trade; and heads of the Uganda Commercial Bank, the Uganda Revenue Authority, the Uganda Investment Authority, and the Uganda Development Bank) were during the 1990s all in the hands of persons from the south-western region of Uganda. Worth noting here is that members of the Parliamentary Standing Committee on Appointments complained to President Museveni that nominees sent to them for approval 'seem to be a roll-call of political associates, friends and relatives'. See *The Crusader* (Kampala), 10 July 1997, p.2. See also Note 33 above.

51. Jeffrey Herbst, 'The Structural Adjustment of Politics in Africa', *World Development*, 18,7 (1990), p.952. A top Kenyan businessman, Chris Kirubi, also put forward this argument. He argued that 'the need for political patronage in business has been voided by economic reforms', and that there was no longer much need to turn to government for 'business favours'. See *Sunday Nation*, 15 December 1996, p.2.

52. Howard W. French, 'Africa Resentful as Asia Rakes in Aid', *New York Times* (New York), 8 March 1998. French's remarks refer to the privatization of CAISTAB in Côte d'Ivoire, but all over sub-Saharan Africa official agricultural marketing boards concerned with export crops have for long provided considerable sums for politicians to use as they wish.

53. One journalist claimed in Zimbabwe 'high government spending on a political patronage system aimed at sustaining it in office'. See Chris Chinaka, 'Calls Mount for Zimbabwe's Embattled Mugabe to Quit' (Reuters News Agency, 25 February 1998).

54   Public expenditure as a share of GDP has averaged between 26 and 29% in sub-Saharan countries during the 1980s and 1990s.

55. See the brief discussion in Peter Lewis, 'From Prebendalism to Predation: the Political Economy of Decline in Nigeria', *Journal of Modern African Studies*, 34,1 (1996), 79–103 for new outlets for state patronage under structural adjustment.

56. Rapley, *op. cit.*, p.149. See also pages 145–9 for an interesting discussion of the importance of a well organized indigenous capitalist class for the creation of developmental states.

57. For a discussion of external agencies not possessing the capacity to monitor closely the economic management of African states as well as the manipulation of structural adjustment reforms to serve the political and economic interests of African

governing elites, see Christopher Clapham, *Africa and the International System. The Politics of State Survival* (Cambridge, 1996), pp.173–81.

58. Crawford Young, 'Democratization in Africa' in Jennifer A. Widner (ed.), *Economic Change and Political Liberalization in Sub-Saharan Africa* (Baltimore, 1994), p.239. Similarly, his following assertion seems to me to be exaggerated: 'so reduced' have been 'the resource flows available for patrimonial distribution that the prebendal underpinning of power management was fatally weakened'. See 'Democracy and the Ethnic Question in Africa', *Africa Insight*, 27,1 (1997), p.9.

59. Quoted in Hutchful, *op. cit.*, p.304.

60. Adebayo Olukoshi, 'The Impact of Recent Reform Efforts on the African State', in Kjell Havnevik and Brian Van Arkadie, (eds.), *Domination or Dialogue. Experiences and Prospects* (Uppsala, 1996), p.62.

Selected Bibliography

Christopher Adam, William Cavendish, and Percy S. Mistry, eds. *Adjusting Privatization. Case Studies from Developing Countries* (London, 1992).

Adebayo Adedeji, ed., *Indigenization of African Economies* (London, 1981).

Claude Ake, 'How Politics Underdevelops Africa', in Adebayo Adedeji et al eds., *The Challenge of African Economic Recovery and Development* (London, 1991), 316–29.

David E. Apter and Carl G. Rosberg, eds., *Political Development and the New Realism in Sub-Saharan Africa* (Charlottesville, 1994).

Kwame Arhin, Paul Hesp, and Laurens van der Laan, eds., *Marketing Boards in Tropical Africa* (London, 1985).

Robert H. Bates, *Markets and States in Tropical Africa. The Political Basis of Agricultural Policies* (Berkeley, 1981).

Robert H. Bates and Anne O. Krueger, eds., *Political and Economic Interactions in Economic Policy Reform* (Oxford, 1993).

Carolyn Baylies, 'Zambia's Economic Reforms and their Aftermath: The State and the Growth of Indigenous Capital', *Journal of Commonwealth and Comparative Politics*, 20,3 (1982), 235–63.

Jean-Francois Bayart, *The State in Africa: The Politics of the Belly* (London, 1993).

Paul Bennell, 'Privatization in Sub-Saharan Africa: Progress and Prospects during the 1990s', *World Development*, 25,11 (1997), 1785–1803.

——, 'Foreign Direct investment in Africa: Rhetoric and Reality', *SAIS Review*, 17,2 (1997), 127–39.

Elliot Berg and Mary M. Shirley, 'Divestiture in Developing Countries' (World Bank Discussion Paper, No.11, 1987).

Elliot Berg, 'Privatization in Sub-Saharan Africa: Results, Prospects, and New Approaches' (paper prepared for the World Bank, February 1994).

Robert J. Berg and Jennifer Seymour Whitaker, eds., *Strategies for African Development* (Berkeley, 1986).

157

Bruce J. Berman and Colin Leys, eds., *African Capitalists in African Development* (Boulder, 1994).

Henry Bienen and John Waterbury, 'The Political Economy of Privatization in Developing Countries', *World Development*, 17,5 (1989), 617–32.

Thomas J. Biersteker, *Multinationals, the State, and Control of the Nigerian Economy* (Princeton, NJ, 1987).

Catherine Boone, *Merchant Capital and the Roots of Power in Senegal 1930–1985* (Cambridge, 1992).

———, 'Commerce in Côte d'Ivoire: Ivoirianization without Ivoirian Traders', *Journal of Modern African Studies*, 31,1 (1993), 67–92.

Michael Bratton and Nicolas Van de Walle, *Democratic Experiments in Africa. Regime Transitions in Comparative Perspective* (Cambridge, 1997).

Vincent Cable and Bishnodat Persaud, eds., *Developing with Foreign Investment* (London, 1987).

Thomas M. Callaghy and John Ravenhill, eds., *Hemmed In. Responses to Africa's Economic Decline* (New York, 1993).

Michael Chege, 'Introducing Race as a Variable into the Political Economy of Kenya Debate: An Incendiary Idea', *African Affairs*, 97 (1998), 209–30.

Christopher Clapham, *Third World Politics. An Introduction* (London, 1985).

———, *Africa and the International System. The politics of state survival* (Cambridge, 1996).

John M. Cohen, 'Importance of Public Sector Reform: the Case of Kenya', *Journal of Modern African Studies*, 31,3 (1993), 449–76.

Paul Cook and Colin Kirkpatrick, eds., *Privatization in Less-Developed Countries* (Hemel Hempstead, 1988).

———, *Privatization Policy and Performance. International Perspectives* (New York, 1995).

Giovanni Andrea Cornia and Gerald K. Helleiner, eds., *From Adjustment to Development in Africa* (London, 1994).

Richard C. Crook, 'Patrimonialism, Administrative Effectiveness and Economic Development in Cote d'Ivoire', *African Affairs*, 88,351 (1989), 205–28.

Rita Cruise O'Brien, 'Lebanese Entrepreneurs in Senegal: Economic Integration and the Politics of Protection', *Cahiers d'etudes africaines*, 15,57 (1975), 95–115.

Larry Diamond, 'Class Formation in the Swollen African State', *Journal of Modern African Studies*, 25,4 (1987), 567–96.

———, 'Political Corruption. Nigeria's Perennial Struggle', *Journal of Democracy*, 2,4 (1991).

Poul Engberg-Pedersen et al eds., *Limits of Adjustment in Africa* (Oxford, 1996).

Tom Forrest, *Politics and Economic Development in Nigeria* (Boulder, 1995).
———, *The Advance of African Capital. The Growth of Nigerian Private Enterprise* (Edinburgh, 1994).
Martin Fransman, ed., *Industry and Accumulation in Africa* (London, 1982).
Kenneth Good, 'Debt and the One-Party State in Zambia', *Journal of Modern African Studies*, 27,2 (1989), 297–313.
———, 'Corruption and Mismanagement in Botswana: a Best-Case Example?', *Journal of Modern African Studies*, 32,3 (1994), 499–521.
———, 'Accountable to Themselves: Predominance in Southern Africa', *Journal of Modern African Studies*, 35,4 (1997), 547–73.
Barbara Grosh, *Public Enterprise in Kenya. What Works, What Doesn't, and Why?* (Boulder, 1991).
Barbara Grosh and Rwekaza S. Mukandala, eds., *State-Owned Enterprises in Africa* (Boulder, 1994).
Stephan Haggard and Robert R. Kaufman, eds., *The Politics of Economic Adjustment* (Princeton, 1992).
Kjell Havnevik and Brian Van Arkadie, eds., *Domination or Dialogue. Experiences and Prospects* (Stockholm, 1996).
John Heath, ed., *Public Enterprise at the Crossroads* (London, 1990).
Jeffrey Herbst, *State Politics in Zimbabwe* (Berkeley, 1990).
———, 'Political Impediments to Economic Rationality: Explaining Zimbabwe's Failure to Reform its Public Sector', *Journal of Modern African Studies*, 27,1 (1989), 67–84.
———, 'The Structural Adjustment of Politics in Africa', *World Development*, 18,7 (1990), 949–58.
———, *The Politics of Reform in Ghana, 1982–91* (Berkeley, 1993).
David Himbara, 'The Failed Africanization of Commerce and Industry in Kenya', *World Development*, 22,3 (1994), 469–82.
———, *Kenyan Capitalists, the State, and Development* (Boulder, 1994).
Ishrat Husain and Rashid Faruqee, eds., *Adjustment in Africa. Lessons from Country Case Studies* (Washington, DC, 1994).
Eboe Hutchful, 'Why Regimes Adjust: The World Bank Ponders Its "Star Pupil"', *Canadian Journal of African Studies*, 29,2 (1995), 303–17.
Goran Hyden, *No Shortcuts to Progress. African Development Management in Perspective* (London, 1983).
Robert H. Jackson and Carl G. Rosberg, *Personal Rule in Black Africa* (Berkeley, 1982).
Richard Jeffries, 'Rawlings and the Political Economy of Underdevelopment in Ghana', *African Affairs*, 81,324 (1982), 307–17.
Alex E. Fernandez Jilberto and Andre Mommen, eds., *Liberalization in the Developing World* (London, 1996).

Richard Joseph, *Democracy and Prebendal Politics in Nigeria. The Rise and Fall of the Second Republic* (Cambridge, 1987).

——, 'Africa, 1990–1997: From Abertura to Closure', *Journal of Democracy*, 9,2 (1998), 3–17.

Raphael Kaplinsky, ed., *Readings On the Multinational Corporation in Kenya* (Nairobi, 1978).

Nelson Kasfir, ed., *Civil Society and Democracy in Africa. Critical Perspectives* (London, 1998).

Paul Kennedy, *African Capitalism. The Struggle for ascendancy* (Cambridge, 1988).

Sunita Kikeri, John Nellis, and Mary Shirley, *Privatization. The Lessons of Experience* (Washington, DC, 1992).

Tony Killick, *Development Economics in Action: A Study of Economic Policies in Ghana* (London, 1978).

——, *Policy Economics* (London, 1981).

——, 'The role of the public sector in the industrialization of African developing countries', *Industry and Development*, No.7 (1983), 57–87.

Anthony Kirk-Greene and Daniel Bach, eds., *State and Society in Francophone Africa since Independence* (New York, 1995).

Steven W. Langdon, *Multinational Corporations in the Political Economy of Kenya* (New York, 1985).

——, 'Multinational Corporations and the State in Africa', in Jose J. Vilamil, ed.,*Transnational Capitalism and National Development. New Perspectives on Dependence* (Hassocks, 1979), 223–40.

Adrian Leftwich, 'Bringing Politics Back In: Towards a Model of the Developmental State', *Journal of Development Studies*, 31,3 (1995), 400–27.

Peter M. Lewis, 'From Prebendalism to Predation: the Political Economy of Decline in Nigeria', *Journal of Modern African Studies*, 34,1 (1996), 79–103.

Michael F. Lofchie, *The Policy Factor. Agricultural Performance in Kenya and Tanzania* (Boulder, 1989).

Paul M. Lubeck, ed., *The African Bourgeoisie. Capitalist Development in Nigeria, Kenya and the Ivory Coast* (Boulder, 1987).

Mahmood Mamdani, *Politics and Class Formation in Uganda* (London, 1976).

Luigi Manzetti, 'The Political Economy of Privatization through Divestiture in Lesser Developed Economies', *Comparative Politics*, 25,4 (1993), 429–53.

Mick Moore and Ladi Hamalai, 'Economic Liberalization, Political Pluralism and Business Associations in Developing Countries', *World Development*, 21,12 (1993), 1895–1912.

Benno Ndulu et al eds., *Agenda for Africa's Economic Renewal* (New Brunswick, 1996).

John Nellis, 'Public Enterprises in Sub-Saharan Africa' (World Bank Discussion Paper, No.1, 1986).

John Nellis and Sunita Kikeri, 'Public Enterprise Reform: Privatization and the World Bank', *World Development*, 17,5 (1989), 659–72.

Joan M. Nelson, ed., *Economic Crisis and Policy Choice. The Politics of Economic Adjustment in the Developing Countries* (Princeton, NJ, 1990).

Walter O. Oyugi, ed., *Politics and Administration in East Africa* (Nairobi, 1992).

Robert M. Price, 'Neocolonialism and Ghana's Economic Decline: A Critical Assessment', *Canadian Journal of African Studies*, 18,1 (1984), 163–93.

V. V. Ramanadham, ed., *Privatization in Developing Countries* (London, 1989).

John Rapley, *Ivoirien Capitalism. African Entrepreneurs in Cote d'Ivoire* (Boulder, 1992).

———, *Understanding Development. Theory and Practice in the Third World* (Boulder, 1996).

John Ravenhill, ed., *Africa in Economic Crisis* (London, 1986).

Donald Rothchild, ed., *Ghana: The Political Economy of Recovery* (Boulder, 1991).

Donald Rothchild and Naomi Chazan, eds., *The Precarious Balance. State and Society in Africa* (Boulder, 1988).

Douglas Rimmer, *The Economies of West Africa* (London, 1984).

Richard Sandbrook, *The Politics of Africa's Economic Stagnation* (Cambridge, 1985).

———, *The Politics of Africa's Economic Recovery* (Cambridge, 1993).

Sayre Schatz, *Nigerian Capitalism* (Berkeley, 1977).

Tor Skalnes, *The Politics of Economic Reform in Zimbabwe. Continuity and Change in Development* (New York, 1995).

Richard L. Sklar, *Corporate Power in an African State* (Berkeley, 1975).

———, 'The Nature of Class Domination in Africa', *Journal of Modern African Studies*, 17 (1979), 531–52.

Frances Stewart, Sanjaya Lall, and Samuel Wangwe, eds., *Alternative Development Strategies in SubSaharan Africa* (London, 1992).

Ezra N. Suleiman and John Waterbury, eds., *The Political Economy of Public Sector Reform and Privatization* (Boulder, 1990).

Nicola Swainson, *The Development of Corporate Capitalism in Kenya 1918–77* (London, 1980).

Daniel Swanson and Teffera Wolde-Semait, 'Africa's Public Enterprise Sector and Evidence of Reforms' (World Bank Technical Paper, No.95, 1989).

Roger Tangri, 'Foreign Business and Political Unrest in Lesotho', *African Affairs*, 92,36 (1993), 223–38.

Balefi Tsie, 'The Political Context of Botswana's Development Performance', *Journal of Southern African Studies*, 22,4 (1996) 599–616.

Robin Theobald, *Corruption, Development and Underdevelopment* (New York, 1990).

Raymond Vernon, ed., *The Promise of Privatization: a Challenge for U.S. Policy* (New York, 1988).

Nicolas van de Walle, 'Privatization in Developing Countries: A Review', *World Development*, 17,5 (1989), 601–15.

John Waterbury, *Exposed to Innumerable Delusions. Public Enterprise and State Power in Egypt, India, Mexico and Turkey* (Cambridge, 1993).

Jennifer A. Widner, ed., *Economic Change and Political Liberalization in Sub-Saharan Africa* (Baltimore, 1994).

Ernest J. Wilson III, 'Strategies of State Control of the Economy: Nationalization and Indigenization in Africa', *Comparative Politics*, 22 (1990), 401–19.

The World Bank, *Accelerated Development in Sub-Saharan Africa. An Agenda for Action* (Washington, DC, 1981).

———, *World Development Report 1983* (Washington, DC, 1983).

———, *World Development Report 1988* (Washington, DC, 1988).

———, *Sub-Saharan Africa. From Crisis to Sustainable Growth* (Washington, DC, 1989).

———, *The Reform of Public Sector Management: Lessons of Experience* (Washington DC, 1991).

———, *World Development Report 1991* (Washington, DC, 1991).

———, *Governance and Development* (Washington, DC, 1992).

———, *Adjustment in Africa. Reforms, Results and the Road Ahead* (Washington, DC, 1994).

———, *Governance. The World Bank's Experience* (Washington, DC, 1994).

———, *A Continent in Transition: Sub-Saharan Africa in the mid-1990s* (Washington, DC, 1995).

———, *Private Sector Development in Low-Income Countries* (Washington, DC, 1995).

———, *Bureaucrats in Business: The Economics and Politics of Government Ownership* (Washington, DC, 1996).

———, *World Development Report 1997* (Washington, DC, 1997).

Crawford Young, *Ideology and Development in Africa* (New Haven, 1982).

Ralph Young, "Privatization in Africa", *Review of African Political Economy*, No.51 (1991), 50–62.

Index